PADDLING
TO
JERUSALEM

PADDLING
TO
JERUSALEM

David Aaronovitch

FOURTH ESTATE • *London*

First published in Great Britain in 2000
by Fourth Estate Limited
6 Salem Road
London W2 4BU
www.4thestate.co.uk

Copyright © David Aaronovitch 2000

1 3 5 7 9 10 8 6 4 2

The right of David Aaronovitch to be identified as the author of this work
has been asserted by him in accordance with the Copyright, Designs and
Patents Act 1988.

A catalogue record for this book is available from the British Library.

ISBN 1-84115-101-7

Typeset by Palimpsest Book Production Limited,
Polmont, Stirlingshire
Printed in Great Britain by
Clays Ltd, St Ives plc

Contents

Acknowledgements

I am indebted to several companies for the use of their equipment. In particular to Pyranha who made *The Subtle Knife* – a jewel of a boat. Lendal supplied the elegant black-and-white state-of-the-art paddles, Wildwater some excellent gear to keep a chap dry in the wettest of circumstances, and Field and Trek saved my life with a fleece and the sleeping bag coveted by Goitre.

So many books were bought in preparation for the journey that Waterstones should dedicate their Hampstead branch to me, but I do want to recognise two debts of honour. One is to David Matless, whose recent *Landscape and Englishness* is a classic, from which I borrowed the story of the CPRE and the fascists; and the other is the late Raphael Samuel, a historian of rare humanity whose way of remembering was unique.

My thanks to my agent Georgia Garrett. Many writers are a bit in love with their agents, but with Georgia that's spectacularly easy. And she brought me together with my editor, Andy Miller, who has improved every page of this book – in particular those never printed.

I would never actually have gone had it not been for Jane Taylor, who is a remarkable woman and an absolutely wonderful friend. Her sceptical encouragement was as vital as her practical assistance was generous. I thank my mother for her life story – and for mine. And Sarah and the girls – Rosa, Lily and Eve – for not complaining about my absence as I would surely have complained about theirs. Every time there has been a test, my family has come through it. I don't deserve them.

To those who gave great and small succour to the traveller, from PS of Buckby Wharf to the Cardy family from Enfield who shouted something nice at me near Stourport, I shall not forget your kindness. And, finally, a message to the crew of the

Duxbury, as she passed over the Pennines in the last week of June 1999, and especially to the man with the moustache and red-check shirt. You mean sods. I might have been Jesus, and then you'd have been in trouble.

Prologue

The Bedfordshire Ouse, Easter 1966

The world was inverted. A moment earlier the water had been below me, and the sky above. Now I looked upwards at the river, as at the ceiling, and only beyond the clear brownish water did the shiny grey of the heavens move in choppy waves. It was perplexing. My clothes, unexpectedly heavy, exerted a downward pull on my limbs. At the same time, fighting the drag, the air in my lungs made my body buoyant, sending me back to the surface. How odd this was, this immersion! How strange that my trousers and shoes should want to drown me! I broke surface, spluttering, with the strange taste of unprocessed water in my mouth and nose.

Easter was early that year, and cold, and snow waited to fall. I swam, encumbered, past the upturned canoe, towards the green, rain-glistening bank. In the ten seconds between red-haired Steve capsizing the boat with a clumsy push of his foot, and my coming up for air, only a couple of my fellow young canoeists had noticed that I was in the water. We had been straggling behind the others, the last canoe to disembark at the spot where the meadow sloped obligingly down to the waterside. The adult leaders were already in the field, putting up tents and lighting fires. So there were just two or three twelve-year-old girls, and Steve himself, to witness my struggle against the river.

They stood and watched me, mouths open. Were they seeing something mundane and everyday – an eleven-year-old boy swimming a few yards in a friendly river – or present at the early, strangely calm moments of a tragedy, which would end in police divers, whey-faced parents and them being driven abruptly back to hushed homes?

I'd always been a good swimmer, taught in the freezing spring water of the open-air Lido on Hampstead Heath by an old man called Mr Millichap. One by one I had hunted the distances – a length, a hundred yards, a quarter mile, a mile – and mounted them on my walls like the heads of wildebeest or antelope. So I made it to the bank easily enough, and Steve – apologetic and relieved – pulled me out.

By now the adults were arriving at the gallop, their heads full of scenarios involving hypothermia and investigations. No one was still in the water, no one had been drowned and their relief was palpable; they were very pleased with me for having survived: everyone was my friend.

They made me undress in the open field. With my body temperature dropping this was no time for pubescent modesty, so, skinny and hairless as a shorn poodle, I stood and shivered while the whole group – including the girls – gathered around me and (as I thought) took careful note of my stick-insect limbs and supremely unintimidating organs of generation. Brandy was given to me in a flask and, after what seemed an age, a large blanket was produced which enfolded me entirely.

I can see that field now, feel the cold and that first chilly appraisal from female eyes. Immediately afterwards I had wanted to go home, hugely embarrassed by being among people who had seen me shaking and exposed that afternoon. As my wet clothes steamed by the wood fire, my toes ached with the cold of the damp grass. There wasn't much to be said for canoeing at that moment.

As time passed, though, my idea of what the scene represented changed. The fact of the accident was not an argument against adventure – quite the reverse. Falling in cold rivers was something that one survived, that I had survived. The moment, for all its attendant embarrassments and discomforts, was mentally filed under 'Triumphs'.

And so, for years, I tasted the brandy and forgot the smell of the water.

CHAPTER I

Thirty Years Later, London

One night, not long after my fortieth birthday, Death visited me as I slept. 'You are going to die,' he told me, in a voice that sounded like my own. 'You personally. Not someone else, not President Kennedy, not the victims of some road crash that happened in Derbyshire an hour ago, not poor old Auntie Olive aged ninety-one – but you. It's already half over, this life of yours, and you're not having another.'

I found myself suddenly awake, sitting bolt upright in bed, shouting, 'No!' at the top of my voice. Panic – that was what I felt. The panic of someone with an exam in an hour's time, three years' worth of undone work to make up, and no chance of getting through it before the Great Invigilator invited me to turn over my final paper.

So that was it, then. I would now never hitch-hike across America from California to the New York Island. Nor would I become lead singer in a folk-rock band. I had left it too late to become Prime Minister. Most of the places I hadn't gone I would now never go; virtually all the things I had not become, I would never be; and just about every rumple-sheeted night of passion with every woman (and the occasional boy) that I had never enjoyed, I would now never-ever know. I wasn't young any more. Not in any way. I was too scared even to weep.

The next morning I realised that I was, of course, at the beginning of my mid-life crisis. And I could deal with this, essentially, in one of three ways.

The first strategy involved capitulating and meekly accepting that the interesting bit of my life was over. We would go on holiday to Crete or Cyprus every year, where Costas would reserve our usual rooms. At work I would eventually be kicked upstairs, become head of strategic evaluation and then get a good redundancy package at forty-nine years and eleven months. At home there would be ushered in two decades of baggy pullovers, elasticated slacks and gentle jibes about my ballooning figure. But who would really care that I was getting very pudgy, inside and out? Maybe I'd take up golf and complaining. At seventy or seventy-five or eighty I'd die.

Strategy two would be to make an old fool of myself. I would buy a motor-bike, take flying lessons, have my nipples pierced, pull my hair back in a ponytail and stop eating. The *Independent* would be thrown away, and instead I'd scan the pages of men's magazines for clothes ideas. I'd start dressing myself in the DKNY and Issey Miyake togs that look sexy only on a seventeen-year-old heroin addict. In the office by day I would prowl the corridors looking for young women to make suggestive remarks to. One night I would finally get my leg over a youthful employee with whom I'd been having an email dalliance, and then carry on a preposterous relationship which would end with my getting caught, shamed and possibly divorced. At which point I could revert to strategy one, or repeat strategy two for as long as my health and money held out.

And then there was strategy three: make the best of it. Every now and then you meet someone tanned and bright-eyed, laughter lines creasing their upper faces, good white teeth, fond wives and daughters, and they tell you that they're sixty-seven and off to the Galway fiddle festival to meet up with old friends. And you think, that'll do for me.

But, to stand a chance of eventually becoming one of these gorgeous pensioners, my life had to change. Specifically, I had to do two things: first, get out of my terrible, mind-fucking job, and, second, have an adventure. Within months I had accomplished the former. I had handed in my notice to general amazement, and departed. Did I feel better for it? Yes, I did. And the adventure? The adventure came a bit later.

On the last day of May 1998, at the age of seventy-eight, my father died. Despite a decade of various cancers, he'd managed to have a very good last twenty years. Until a large tumour was found attaching itself to one side of his liver, he'd dashed around Europe with his insane partner, Annie, driving hundreds of miles to see a loved painting in a German art gallery, before heading for the Dolomites, where he would happily scramble across glaciers. Dad had managed to postpone his retirement until his mid-seventies, and, till the last week, still worked a good ten hours a day on the projects that interested him, commissioned from the academic consultancy that he had set up at one of the new London universities. I'd grown very fond of him in the final few years.

During the quiet, tearful period after his death, we took the kids off to Center Parcs, where families ride bikes between shady chalets and tropical swimming domes and eat pancakes made of Play-doh. We'd needed to get away from sympathy and phonecalls.

My five-year-old daughter and I were paddling a large green plastic canoe across the artificial boating lake, when a very good idea came into my head. I knew, at last, what my adventure would be. I would propel a kayak across England. Of course! Using canals and rivers I'd construct a journey that would take me through cities and countryside. The moment I had this idea, there was never really any doubt that I would actually do it. Why hadn't I thought of it before? Just for emphasis I did an extra lap of the lake, overtaking a dinghy and shooting past a surprised pedalo.

As the week went on, I conducted a secret internal dialogue about this journey. After furtively consulting the atlas in the car, I could see a number of routes that would take me through places I wanted to visit and then back again, by water. These varied between one thousand and twelve hundred miles in length, depending upon diversions. It was unlikely that my bosses at the newspaper where I now worked, though a generous lot, would allow me to abscond for more than two months, so that was the length of time I fixed within which to complete the trip.

But where was I going to stay? Everywhere and anywhere. At hotels, in small waterside inns, at isolated bed and breakfasts, wherever there were encounters with my fellow country-persons to be had. Hell, I would take a tent and camp by the river, just as I had all those years before. This would be a proper journey.

The trouble, I told myself, was that just about every trip one could possibly imagine had already been done, and mostly within the last year or so. The comedian Michael Palin on his own had – selfishly, in my opinion – used up the Pole to Pole trip, the Pacific rim voyage, and even now was embarked on following in the footsteps of Ernest Hemingway across four continents.

In addition to the prolific funnyman, at any one time, dozens of my compatriots were hang-gliding across the Central African rain-forests, rafting the iceberg strewn Sea of Okhotsk, or rolling down Antipodean mountainsides in large plastic globes. You could not walk across anything remotely resembling a wilderness these days, without being trampled by someone writing a book about it. Most viewers of BBC2 knew how to make a flint spear, set a bird trap, or how to gut a moose. Thirty ordinary Britons, chosen by psychologists, were about to be marooned on a Hebridean island for a television programme. Spending a month in conditions of zero hospitality, with only a knife and a satellite phone to help you was, to Millennium Man, a cliché.

But no one, as far as I knew, had canoed across England. They were for ever walking across it, of course. Even Janet Street-Porter had just done it. From south to north, around the coast, up the middle, round the sides, in wheelchairs, on one leg, carrying heavy electrical goods, with no money, with a dog, with a horse, in the company of Ian Botham, each walk slightly more improbable than the last. Walking, though, usually meant sticking to tracks and paths, thus avoiding towns and conurbations, the places where things actually happen. The pace was right – England is far too small to be seen by car, or even by bicycle. It is a micro-country, where everything is in the detail, and any speed of more than 5 mph means that most of what England has to offer must be missed. We have no great open vistas, no arid, dusty wastelands, so walking speed was appropriate. It was the mode that was wrong.

Water, I reasoned to myself, was better. The rivers were England's first highways. All those tedious goods that the Phoenicians traded with the early Britons (tin and pots and stuff like that) were carried into the interior by the waterways that nature had carved through the landscape. For the 1300 years between the collapse of the Roman empire and the early stages of the Industrial Revolution, no effort was made to maintain England's roads. When Daniel Defoe rode the kingdom in the 1720s, the best highways were still those laid down by the legions over a millennium earlier, the rest was potholes and footpads. Water was the way to get about. The great castles commanded the heights above the rivers, and the fords across them. The Thames was navigable for 150 miles, the Severn for 150, the Trent for 180.

And the engineering! The canals, created to carry coal, porcelain, gravel, anything, crossed rivers via great iron aqueducts; they climbed hills using flights of locks; they dived through hills in tunnels several miles long. And after half a century of neglect and desuetude, the English canals were being revived, one by one. They would be a great way, I reassured my doubting alter ego, to come at England from behind, to sneak up and listen to local conversations I wasn't supposed to be hearing. Canals and rivers enter our cities almost unobserved, meandering by our back doors.

However, invisible interlocutors – friends, colleagues, potential publishers – questioned my sanity. Why England? If it was adventure I was after, wouldn't it be better to go somewhere wild and dangerous? Like an arid waste, for instance. There aren't really any arid wastes in England, except perhaps for South London. I ought to be enduring places that were very hot, or very cold. Or at least, voyaging to some undiscovered bourne from which no traveller ever returns. Otherwise, what was the point?

Well, I wanted to treat England fairly.

In the late 1990s a whole slew of books had been published dealing with the country as though it were a disease. Mostly these were enthusiastic and loving evocations of the underclass by journalists called Nick. The Nicks travelled into the heart of darkness that are our housing estates and inner cities, and discovered conditions there that should shame us all; indictments that chill or sear (according to how you like your indictments done). One Nick had found a 'land full of trouble, violent and dispossessed, in some places close to anarchy'. Another Nick had spent a fruitful six months among the child prostitutes of the East Midlands. Their England was all broken glass, meaningless violence, sex for money, crack houses and brothels.

It wasn't that I doubted that such things existed. But they also existed in Scotland, and yet no one was suggesting that Scotland was a land on the edge. Nicks weren't crawling all over Glenwhatsit searching for eight-year-old rentboys who spent their leisure hours pushing alcoholics off railway platforms. No, Scotland was a new and confident country, flexing its autonomous muscles. Scottish culture was great, Scottish youth were great. Scottish authors basked gaily in their Scottishness.

Our own languid English writers, meanwhile, lamented that, as a nation, we were little better than a theme park; a country dominated by nostalgia, by Princess Diana, racism, the Blitz and Ealing comedies. They harked back to George Orwell who, in 1941, talked of a culture bound up with 'solid breakfasts and gloomy Sundays, smoky towns and winding roads, green fields and red pillar boxes'. And he was trying to be complimentary.

Now it had all been put in a blender with the worst imports from America: Jerry Springer, *Natural Born Killers* and Barney the purple dinosaur. In 1999 the boring old English weren't even authentically boring. Scots like Tom Nairn wrote books lecturing us on our lack of identity.

I didn't feel it myself, but I was aware of a long intellectual tradition that mistrusted the English suburban impulse, from Forster and T.S. Eliot through to today. Politically, many in the metropolitan class pessimistically despaired of the phenomenon of Middle England; the voters who inhabit those vast areas of terra incognita, marked 'here be carriage lamps'. English inertia had been combined with American selfishness to create a politics that they found uniquely disgusting. Middle Englanders despoiled the countryside by going to live on the edge of it, they deprived our cities by not wanting to stay in them, they drove increasing numbers of four-wheel drive monsters between school and vast hypermarkets, and they refused to pay large amounts of extra taxes to subsidise the arts or to help turn eight-year-old rentboys into useful members of society.

At their most rampant, it was believed, they had maintained the Thatcher regime for nearly two decades, and even when benign they insisted on being represented by that archetypal suburbanite, Tony Blair. Given half a chance they would take all the money away from single parents, and spend it on retiling the patio area.

Because I had the notion that this pessimism about the English was misplaced, this year in which the Scots got their own parliament and the Welsh their own assembly, seemed like a good time to find out. In my little canoe I would paddle into the heart of Middle England, away from the city, observe its customs and rhythms, and talk to the people in it. Then I'd come back and write the truth about it.

I also hoped that I'd come back a better person. Mr Sunny goes to work, banters with the secretaries, wouldn't say boo to a goose, has never been known to raise his voice. His desk is decorated with pictures of smiling toddlers and a soft-focus wife. Everybody likes working with Sunny. But at 7 p.m. it's Mr Storm who arrives home, full of anger, looking to be slighted.

I'm Storm. There should be an organisation called Angries Anonymous. 'My name is David,' I'd tell my group in the draughty church hall, 'and I'm always angry. I've been angry ever since I can remember. Sometimes I can go without being angry for days, but I know it's always there, waiting to make my face to go red and ugly, and my chest to feel as though it's a pressure cooker. Now I want to stop, be far more patient with my kids, to be kinder to my partner, to be calm.'

It's true. Within me was a vast pool of magma, dormant in the company of strangers, but looking to be vented as soon as there was an excuse. I should be a really good father; I have the imagination for it. But the least excuse and up well those bad, ancient emotions. What sort of dad is it that chucks the reading book across the room if his children aren't listening properly? They'd watch me, and then – in their own ways – begin repeating my behaviour.

Was that perhaps what I had been doing? I'd always had a difficult, rather dangerous relationship with my mother, and for many years a rather distant one with my father. As a teenager I'd cut myself off from my family as much as I could, and far more than my sister and my brothers. I knew there must be something about my parents that helped explain some of my deficiencies. They had had, in different ways, difficult lives. But in what way had those lives shaped mine?

The country I'd travel through was very much their country. I thought that, maybe, two months alone, passing though places associated with them, could help me. On those waterways I'd wrestle with that ferocious savage and his history. First I'd understand what had given rise to him, and then I'd paddle him to death. Sunny would return alone from the journey, leaving Storm floating face down in an isolated stretch of the Leeds to Liverpool canal.

This was a whole lot of agenda for one journey. Sort out your country, find yourself and paddle a thousand miles. It was, on any proper reflection, a silly thing to do. Quite unlike me.

So I went out and bought the maps.

CHAPTER 2

Getting Ready

Once we returned from Center Parcs, the waterway guidebooks, Ordnance Survey 1.25 inches to the mile maps and canoe equipment catalogues soon began to spill out of my study and down the stairs. It now occurred to my partner, Sarah, that I might be serious about this journey. She was alarmed. She tried to make me see sense.

'Are you sure,' she asked me one afternoon in the garden, 'that this is the adventure for you?'

'Of course,' I replied.

'But you won't survive,' she said. 'You're too fastidious. You can't face the morning without a power-shower. You change your knickers twice a day. You feel undressed unless you're wearing a slap of Xcess or Paco Rabanne.'

I grunted. She had a point.

'You even had a facial once,' she continued. 'Why not do a guide to great bathrooms of the world instead?'

I was stung.

'Before I met you,' I reminded her, 'I was a very active outdoors sort of guy. I went camping in the woods. I could light a fire with damp moss and one match. Wet? I've been wet. I've woken up in the morning to find snow two feet thick around my tent. When I was twenty-one, in the Brecon Beacons, I wore the same underpants for a week, and had to cut them off with a clasp-knife. I used to adore shouldering a heavy rucksack and then walking in misty bogs. Ah, the sound of the squelching between my toes! But then you came along with your Siena, your Duccios, your duplex apartments with shared use of a swimming pool, and I became effete and aesthetic. But the mountain-man is still there inside me, don't you worry.'

Sarah persisted. 'Anyway,' she asked, 'when was the last time you actually went canoeing? I've never heard you talk about your years in a kayak.'

No, I admitted, I had last canoed at the age of eleven. But I'd liked it. I'd loved it. It had been great. Besides, canoeing was not, I told my sceptical spouse, quantum physics. Essentially, you slipped into this little low boat, and paddled it forwards. Not much could go wrong. There were no complicated gizmos, no levers, no winking lights — just you, the boat and the paddle. Just in case I fell in — and that was pretty unlikely — I promised to wear a life-jacket (or, to be more accurate, a buoyancy aid) at all times, I'd be careful and, of course, I would get myself trained before setting out. I'd join a canoe club and spend the early spring evenings doing Eskimo rolls, whatever they were. The great brotherhood of canoeists would lend me their advice and assistance.

'All right,' said Sarah. 'Even if you don't drown, there's still more than one way to die.' She ran a sceptical eye along me. 'You probably weigh about three times as much as you did when you were eleven. Men like you are a heart attack waiting to happen.'

She leant back against the ivy-clad wall, arms crossed.

I had to admit her thinking was sound. At sixteen and three-quarter stone I was near my record bodyweight high. When I was eighteen my waist had been 28 inches. Now I was straining miserably at 38 inches. These days I would sit down to the accompaniment of two great groans: one from the air being forced out of me, and one from the air being forced out of the chair or sofa I had landed on. Over the years I had accumulated over three stones of excess fat. Three stones is 42 pounds. Imagine 42 pounds of tripe or lard sitting in the butcher's window. If, for some peculiar culinary reason, you wanted to buy all that glistening fat, you wouldn't even attempt to take it home by hand for fear of a hernia. You'd go and get the car and you and the man from the shop would carry it all to the boot, bag by awful bag. And I was toting it everywhere; upstairs and downstairs, each time I ran for the train or bus. It had become a tiring business. Unless I did something to lose it, then I would indeed get about five miles up the canal, my arms would give out, and I would sink among the dead dogs and the supermarket trolleys.

The next Monday, at 9 a.m., I was down the gym, holding one of those silly cards that marks out the virgin gym-attender, and reminds them that the groin-press should be set at 7, with 12 repetitions.

The majority of gyms are dominated by one of two types of gym-goer: groaners or preeners. Groaners are the ugly ones that wear leather belts, lift vast weights, and walk bandy-legged around the gym looking at their upper thighs in the mirror. Preeners are beautiful, lift minute weights, drink energy-giving concoctions out of tubes, listen to portable CDs, wear leotards, and sit for ages on bits of equipment looking at their upper thighs in the mirror.

My gym, however, was specially chosen because it was a third type: a gym dominated by fat people who want to be svelte, by old people who want to live a bit longer, by lumpy thirtyish women on the hunt for men; by people, in short, who ask for the mirrors to be taken down.

In only one area was an excessive vanity visible: the men's shorts. Below thirty-five the younger men wear quite long ones, down to the mid-thigh. Above fifty, the greybeards (many referred by the physiotherapy departments of the local hospital) all tend to do their slow circuits in voluminous tracksuit bottoms. But for ten terrible years, many of my fellow male gymsters scamper about in teeny shorts of a satiny fabric, slit at the thigh, and revealing their unappetizing haunches. It's as though they are trying to tell the lumpy young women in the step classes that, yes, for one last, limited season only, they are still sexually available. Nice. I swore on that first day never, ever to wear teeny, satiny shorts.

Unfortunately, after my first few hours at the gym, I found myself getting bored. There was no dialogue, no goals in view save those I set myself. Auto-athleticism was not enough. I needed help. I needed encouragement. I needed to be brutal-ised. Personal trainers are bullies employed by the comfortable to make them feel less comfortable. I sought one who wouldn't take 'Can't we just stop for a moment, I've broken my leg,' for an answer. So, one Friday, Lynn – recommended by a friend of a friend of my friend Jane's trainer – appeared at my door.

Lynn could run ten miles before breakfast, then skip breakfast and do a thousand press-ups. She could fit in two hours of aerobics before lunch, forget about lunch, kick-box for ninety minutes, take a step-class for advanced athletes, lift weights and skip for another hour. As suppertime approached she might get on the Nordic skier and do the equivalent of Oslo to Trondheim, throw in an hour's yogic stretching before, finally, forgetting about supper.

I didn't know all this when I first met her. What I saw was a thin, muscular, dark-haired woman with a large bag of mysterious implements and a sceptical expression. The implements turned out to be a plastic adjustable step, two bars, two elasticated manacles, two mats and a sound system. The sceptical expression turned out to be entirely justified.

We set up the equipment in the living-room, and faced each other over the step, thin Lynn and Big Dave. The music pulsed. 'March it out!' she commanded, performing an exaggerated walk in which the elbows pumped and the knees bent. I marched it out. It wasn't so difficult.

'Come up to your step!'

I came up to it.

'Step up with your left!'

I stepped up with my left, and stood there, that one foot on the step. There was a pause. 'You can actually put the right foot up now,' Lynn said, adding, 'and then you can step down again.'

Soon I had the hang of this too. Then she went and complicated things. 'Tap and change feet!' she commanded. Tap what, I wondered. Change which foot? The one I was leading with, or the one I was following with? Thinking hard about it, and possibly too anxious to oblige, I sort of led with both feet, and fell over the step.

Lynn laughed – not a cruel laugh, but a 'we've got our work cut out here, haven't we?' kind of a laugh. 'Even my Jewish women can do better than that,' she told me. I discovered later that her Jewish women were a class of highly Orthodox matrons, who wore large, heavy wigs and modestly exercised in their overcoats. So great was the weight of their clothing that they could barely lift their legs.

That day, after we had done the 'step' we spent an hour on fairly mild exercises, including something called 'squats', in which I had to lower my bottom towards the floor and then raise it again, thus exercising the muscles of leg and buttock. When we had finished I thanked Lynn, expressed my belief that we could push my body even further next time, and said goodbye until the next week. That hadn't been too bad.

The next day I was stiff and the day after that I couldn't walk. In the night someone had shoved two metal rods in my bum, one through each buttock, and connected them with my knees. Unable to use my legs except to stand on, I pulled myself upstairs by my arms and then found that there was no way of getting back down again, short of rolling. I felt a little discouraged.

We stuck at it, though, Lynn and I. I went to the gym twice a week and power-walked for forty minutes, and on Fridays I stepped higher and more often, squatted with increasing dexterity, lifted weights and skipped lunch. Whenever I felt a bit tired I would feign exhaustion and Lynn would allow me to ease off. After a couple of months the vague outlines of muscles began to appear through the flesh, like an Egyptian edifice through the desert sand. I felt physically prepared for the arduous journey ahead. Now all I had to do was to get in a boat.

I had posted various queries on the Internet seeking advice and help with my route. The results were not encouraging. Some correspondents on the various relevant newsgroups then began to converse with each other about me, as though I wasn't there. They'd caught one or other of my recent intermittent appearances on television, and wondered aloud whether I'd actually fit in a kayak. Did they make them that big? Narrow boaters wrote to say that they'd never seen anyone quite as large as they thought I was, paddling on the Cut (that's what they call canals).

However, an Albertan called Claude emailed me from the Rockies to say that he weighed 22 stone, yes of course they made kayaks that big, but that it would be wise to try out a few first. And, by the way, did I actually have any experience in river kayaking?

I had all the handbooks and manuals, with pictures of cartoon men deftly handling their craft, but Claude was right, it was all theory. It was time to get out there and paddle a bit.

At a friend's suggestion I phoned up a man called Trevor, who was the secretary of a canoe club on the Thames. I explained to Trevor about my great journey, and anticipated his enthusiastic co-operation. He sounded moderately uninterested, but nevertheless agreed to let me come along that Tuesday evening, and he undertook to find somebody well qualified to take me out and show me the ropes. He had, he said, a person in mind.

At 5 p.m. on a windy Tuesday in April I arrived by the Thames at Richmond. Situated next to a fire-gutted hotel, the canoe club was a large building on the river bank, in front of which an iron pontoon floated at the end of a wooden walkway. The house itself consisted of a large warehouse-sized room below, each wall decorated with three rows, two deep, of different canoes. There were long ones with pointy ends, short ones with snub ends, Canadian open canoes like Pocahontas paddled, doubles, singles, elegant varnished wooden ones, and scuffed ugly plastic ones. Paddles were leaned against the walls, from which were strung buoyancy aids, like orange garlic in a psychedelic delicatessen. All of it smelled sourly of river.

Down a dank corridor were the showers and changing-rooms. The men's was almost third world. Ill-lit, the floor was awash with a liquid that one hoped was water. In the shadows burly young South Africans and Frenchmen, with shoulder muscles the size of camel's humps, were slipping into and out of undergarments and waterproofs, and holding incomprehensible conversations about training regimes and kilometres covered. I felt a little intimidated.

'Are you David?' asked a high, reedy voice behind me. I had imagined that the person whom Trevor had had 'in mind' to train me would be a former SAS man, an Olympic canoeist, who himself had just returned from circumnavigating the globe in a rowing boat. But maybe it would be one of these muscle-bound South Africans. Instead, turning, I found myself peering down on the wiry frame of an elderly man, with a wispy white beard and thick glasses from the centre of whose lenses two sharp little eyes blinked. The beard parted slightly for a querulous half-smile. 'Hello,' he said, 'I'm Dick.'

Canoeists are not as chic as skiers or as vain as rollerbladers. Even so, Dick's outfit was peculiarly unprepossessing. He looked like a very ill, very dishevelled Leghorn chicken.

On top was a baseball cap of considerable antiquity. His glasses were held in place by a head-strap, to the back of which was attached a small float made out of polystyrene. A mouldy and stained red sweatshirt came next, from the bottom of which two skinny legs stuck out, encased in black tights. The ensemble was completed with a pair of peeling wet-shoes.

Dick was a talker. He was one of those men who holds animated conversations with himself about what you should all do next. We would, said Dick, go and get the boats out now and we two would go on the river. Or, he added, we would wait until his friend Robert arrived and we three would go on the river. We two would go on the river and wait by the bank until Robert arrived. Robert and I would go out on the river and wait till Dick arrived with Wo Chung. But Wo Chung wasn't yet here, mused Dick, so maybe it would be better if Robert went on ahead and then we two could go on the river and wait. Or Robert could go out with Wo Chung and we'd just go on the river alone.

I tried to take part in this deliberation, but eventually realised that my views merely complicated things, and made an already long process interminable. Besides, I didn't know Robert and I didn't know Wo Chung. So I said that perhaps I should go and change into my canoeing togs, and maybe by the time I was ready the ideal combination of myself, Dick, Robert and Wo Chung would have suggested itself to Dick.

I was just climbing out of my trousers and wondering just how Dick, Robert and Wo Chung were all going to train me simultaneously, when the door of the changing-room banged open and Dick came staggering in.

At first I thought he'd been shot in the head. From under the shapeless lime-green baseball cap, four or five crimson rivulets were running down over his pale features, including one over each lens of his spectacles. The gore was matting his beard, dripping on the mouldy sweatshirt, speckling his black tights and plinking into the shallow pool at his feet. He looked like the old woman in *The Battleship Potemkin*.

There is nothing quite as alarming as an emergency in a place where you've never been before and in which you do not belong. You don't know where anything or anybody is; you don't know anyone's name. Fathers-to-be feel like this in hospital delivery rooms. Except that here there was only me, and a blunt-featured bloke called Norman, paddling about in the pinkening water on the floor.

Norman took the initiative. 'You stop the blood,' he told me, after – aghast – we'd contemplated Dick for a minute or two, 'while I get the first-aid kit.' Discarding the idea of tying a tourniquet round Dick's neck, I seized a handful of toilet paper from the loo next to the shower, and – stark naked – began gently to mop the blood from his bald septuagenarian bonce.

The flow began to abate, and it became clear that Dick would not die from blood loss. And as it did so, I had the leisure to ask myself what, in the name of God above, I was doing there. If this was what happened to the guys who did the training, what chance was there for the trainees? The faintest glimmer of an early-warning light went on in my mind.

The story was simple. Robert (a schoolmasterly figure with knobbly knees) explained it to me later. He and Dick had found a couple of light boats for us to paddle in, manhandled them out of the building and laid them on the pontoon. Dick had then returned to the boathouse to reconsider whether these really were the right boats. Perhaps one of them (the small one) was the right one, but the other one (the larger) was wrong. Or perhaps the large was OK, and it was the small one that was no good. Should they both be large? Should they both be small? Where was Wo

Chung? And as Dick had meditated upon these thorny problems inside, a gust of wind outside had suddenly lifted up one of the boats, and deposited it in the Thames.

Naturally, Dick, a man of action, catching this undiscussed movement out of the corner of his spectacles, had run at full pelt out of the boathouse, forgetting that, on one side, only the small door (height 5 feet 3 inches) was open. His legs and body exited the building smoothly and made for the pontoon. His head, however, struck the top of the door with an almighty crack and stopped. He came to a second later, and found himself lying on the floor with a hole in his scalp. Dick had come to us in search of succour, and in the meantime Robert and Wo Chung (who had just put in a fortuitous appearance on the towpath) retrieved the blown boat.

Dick's canoeing was clearly over for the day. And so, I rather hoped, was mine. I had been shaken by events and wanted to contemplate them over a coffee in a warm cafeteria a long way from Richmond.

Dick would have none of it. For once there was no havering. Norman, he declared, would take me out. Norman was a stolid man of forty or so, and very few words. Without any further fuss I was kitted out with a canoe ('No one falls out of one of these,' said Norman), a paddle and a buoyancy aid. Gingerly I placed the canoe in the water next to the pontoon, and tried to get in.

It was not as I had remembered. At eleven I had just sort of jumped aboard. The trouble now was that every time I pushed one leg into the boat, it tried to evade me, moving smartly and smoothly away from the pontoon, leaving me racked between ship and shore, clutching precariously on to dry land. Only when Norman firmly held the skittish canoe steady, did I manage to slide my legs and bum inside, and sit – for the first time in three decades – in a kayak.

I have watched the first wobbly steps of my own children, involving bruises and broken china. But they seemed as though fashioned out of rock, compared with how I felt in that canoe. It was not as I remembered it. In 1966 the canoe and I were one. Melded at the waist, we glided together down-stream and up-river. Now I quivered at the slightest shifting of the water. Hesitantly, feeling myself about to go in at any minute, I paddled precariously behind Norman as we headed slowly, stroke by stroke, towards Eel Pie Island.

On the way back I felt that I was getting the hang of it. Provided I concentrated absolutely on staying upright, and providing that – like a cyclist – I kept moving, I was OK. I tentatively tried some wider strokes, and stayed afloat. Then I laid the paddle flat on the water and leaned into it, and that worked too. I was like a cartoon chick finding his wings.

'This is great,' I shouted to the taciturn Norman, 'I'm really . . .' The rest of my sentence was drowned. This was because it was spoken underwater. Norman had wafted across my bows, my boat had touched his. Since I had stopped paddling I had no momentum, and I was taken by surprise. The sky and the water swapped positions, and there I was again, eleven years old, looking at the sky through three feet of the Thames.

Nothing that had happened to me in the long, short thirty years between river immersions was remotely as like that first wetting as this second one. The flailing, the pull of the clothes, the moment of doubt, the emergence from the deep, all belonged uniquely to the experience of sudden capsize. It was real *déjà vu*.

I broke surface to find Norman peering at me in pure wonder. He could not work out how I had come to be in the river instead of on it, nor how he was going to get me out of it. For my part I was irritated that he couldn't see that I was perfectly happy, that this was an inevitable part of learning to canoe, that I'd done this before actually, and that now I was going to swim sedately to the bank, pushing the upturned canoe in front of me.

Unfortunately, I had gone in almost in the dead centre of the Thames, and it was colder than I'd expected, forcing more breath out of my body than was comfortable. My swimming was heavier, more laboured than when I was a boy. I was in more danger. Over on the north side was a staircase descending into the water. I made for it, Norman nervously asking me, periodically, whether I was all right (this, apparently, is a survival technique). By the time I reached the steps I was almost exhausted and not at all looking forward to pulling the water-filled boat up the flight, and emptying it. Fortunately, at that very moment, Wo Chung, now walking home along the towpath, hove into view, and – smiling a little too broadly – soon had me and the canoe, rightside up, in the water. With extreme care, a badly shaken Norman shepherded me back to the pontoon. Shamefacedly I got changed, said my goodbyes and set off home. It had been a disastrous afternoon.

Dick didn't think so. Two days after my dunking the phone rang and the thin voice told me that he'd heard that I had fallen in (from a boat, he felt it necessary to add, that even he had never managed to capsize), and that he supposed that I must need his tuition more than ever. He therefore commanded me to return the following Wednesday.

Indeed I did go back, and – thanks to Dick – it got easier. Each week we'd go out for an hour or more, up to Teddington lock, or down to Kew: Dick and I, Dick, Robert and I, Dick, Robert, Wo Chung and I. Thanks to my capsize I was always treated with an exaggerated concern, as though I could need rescuing at any moment. I was almost equally anxious. Being rescued by the accident-prone Dick was not my idea of building up confidence ahead of the great journey.

It was obvious to me and everyone else that I needed a more intensive course in river paddling before I could credibly embark on a thousand-mile lone trip. I cast around until, on the Net, I found an organisation called Canoeright, located close to the River Avon. Their bright website boasted a team of skilled instructors who would tailor a course specifically to my needs. I emailed them, and a man called Bob emailed me back. Yes, he said brightly, after having consulted his instructors he could indeed provide the dates I wanted, on a weekend in mid-spring. It would cost £120.00. On their very own lake I would practise all the skills I needed to become a proficient canoeist. I imagined a stretch of blue, sunlit water, populated by a laughing armada of rookie paddlers in luminous paddlewear, each one attended to by one of Bob's athletic young men or women.

The camera lies but the Internet lies more, as I discovered

one Saturday morning. The HQ of Canoeright was a draughty warehouse, with a canoe shop at the front, and a plyboard loo that doubled as a changing-room at the back. Bob himself was a shabby man in his late thirties, tall and overweight, for whom speech appeared to be the most unnatural form of communication. He was Dick's polar opposite. So eloquent in cyberspace, he barely grunted to acknowledge my arrival that Saturday morning, and then left me alone in the dusty shop to admire his collection of unsold wet-suits.

After half an hour or so, a little, scraggy man called Jim drove up. Resembling the weedier of the Chuckle Brothers, Jim introduced himself in a broad Black Country accent. He was my instructor, he told me, and his sole aim was to make sure that I'd get out of the weekend what I wanted to get out of it. I told him that I wanted to get out of it the ability to paddle a canoe for a thousand miles without drowning. He nodded. We went into the warehouse to choose a canoe.

Jim evidently had attended the same unsuccessful speech therapy school as Bob, but had the added problem of poor hearing. If you said something to him that required even a second's extra labour on his part, then all of a sudden he'd be unable to hear you. Like when I made clear to him what kind of canoe I needed to be trained in.

I'd decided already that, on the journey itself, I would be taking what's called a touring sea kayak. These kayaks are long and thin, and quite hard to turn. Once you have them going in straight line, they pick up speed, which is vital for longer trips. Travel any distance by water and you have to make the most of your forward momentum; if the boat is continually moving off to the right and left, most of your effort is about steering. That's fine with white-water canoeing where you need to dodge rocks and turn into eddies. But there isn't much white-water on the Grand Union canal.

So when Jim picked for me a little, stubby, orange thing, and said that this would be the perfect craft, I was inwardly sceptical. I couldn't help noticing that it was the only canoe in the place that wasn't for sale, and was therefore, possibly, the only canoe available for training. Still, he was the expert – perhaps he knew something I didn't. We loaded it on to his car and made for the lake.

The lake was completely empty. There were no giggling kids, no athletic trainers, no splashing multitudes. On this cold expanse of tree-lined water there was nothing but me and Jim. So much for the laughing armada.

Jim slid effortlessly from bank to water, and then paddled off, leaving me to negotiate my own entry. Upon which I discovered that the orange canoe was a bastard. A bad-tempered, irascible thing, it over-reacted to everything I did. So, for every forward paddle I took, I had to add a couple of slowing and self-righting strokes to stop myself from suddenly turning full circle. This made the morning's work both slow and exhausting.

When lunchtime finally came, Jim brought out a packet of sandwiches and a flask. And without offering any to me he concurred with my irritable view that it was unfortunate that Canoeright provided no refreshments. 'They should at least give yow a cuppa,' he said, as he washed down his last sandwich with the last mouthful of tea. 'Yow need summink hot inside yow. Now, about the morning, have yow got what yow wanted out of it?'

The next morning Jim was a little late. I bumped into Bob in the shop, and this time he refused even to acknowledge my existence, walking straight past me and into some damp stock-room. Fifteen minutes later Jim arrived. I pointed out that Bob had failed even to nod, which was – in my view – an odd way to treat a paying customer. 'He's not much of a talker,' said Jim. 'Anyway we must hurry. Bob wants to take us down to the river now. So we'd better look lively.' I looked lively, and forgot to pick up the little strip of elastic that I'd been using to secure my spectacles to my head.

Half an hour later we launched our boats on to the Avon, six miles upstream from Stratford. And it was about twenty minutes after that that I again fell in, disastrously. Jim was urging me to try a manoeuvre that I couldn't execute, in a bit of the river where the water seemed very lively indeed, when – for reasons I still cannot understand – I found myself going through the old head-in-the-water routine.

Jim was amazed. I, meanwhile, was furious. I made for the bank, pulling the canoe and – as I tried to clamber up a pile of foul-smelling shit-like mud, sinking up to my thighs in a horrible ooze – I realised that £150-worth of spectacles was now at the bottom of the Avon. I swore, I shouted, I cursed God outwardly and Jim and Bob inwardly for their hurry and their incompetence.

Eventually, humiliatingly, I got back into the fucking orange canoe, and we set off once again. As with Norman, Jim followed the rule that the dry canoeist should get the wet one to answer questions every few minutes, to ensure that they are still alert and not slipping into a hypothermic coma. So, at unbearably short intervals, Jim (who had now given up giving me silly things to do) would turn in his boat and ask me, 'Are yow getting out of it what yow wanted?' Three more times I fell in, as Jim took me to the more difficult features of the river – such as the deer-wire slung across the water about two feet above the surface – which I had to negotiate without the benefit of my glasses. And after each dunking he'd ask me whether I was getting what I wanted.

I soon began to hate him. Of course I fucking well wasn't getting what I wanted. I was blind, demoralised, exhausted and wet. Furthermore, I was spending the whole day with a moron.

Worse, the experience was beginning to make me ask myself if this really was the journey for me. I seriously wondered whether I'd manage ten miles on the Thames or Severn, let alone a thousand. Perhaps I was just not up to it. I limped into Stratford, was picked up from a hypermarket carpark by silent Bob, and – sodden – driven back to the Canoeright warehouse. Fortunately I had a spare pair of glasses in the car, so I had no trouble writing Bob's cheque. 'Goodbye,' said Jim. 'I'm glad yow got out of it what yow wanted.'

A week later I received this email: 'Dear David,' it began,

I hope you have recovered fully from your two days exertions. I had a debriefing discussion with Jim after your course, as is my usual habit, and I think I have to pass on his concern that you are realistically probably not yet ready to undertake the trip that you have planned on your own. While the canals will probably not provide any serious challenge, the wider rivers, which are still quite cold, could land you in serious difficulty if you capsize and have no support from other paddlers. I do not want to take the wind out of your sails but as a responsible course provider I think we have a duty to express our reservations.

Best regards.

Bob at Canoeright.

This was more words in one email than I'd heard him say in two days; the Internet, it seems, is a force for liberating the terminally taciturn. People who can hardly bring themselves to acknowledge the existence of others in the flesh, for whom 'Hello' is a battle, become loquacious in instant print. It's always, I suppose, been true of some authors. Now guys like Bob are selling themselves as avuncular, good-talkin' types. It's progress for them. Not sure about how good it is for the rest of us.

So now virtually everyone thought that I shouldn't go (Bob 'n' Jim, Wo Chung and Norman), or that I wouldn't (Sarah and Dick), or both. Everybody, that is, except my mother and Jane.

My mother has always had a curiously unmaternal attitude towards my welfare. When I was six months old she was running downhill, pushing me before her in my pram, when she tripped and fell. The pram kept moving, picking up speed, until it hit the kerb. My mother recalls, fondly, seeing her baby, wrapped in white blankets, describing a high parabola over a hedge and falling head-first to earth in the garden beyond. It is her favourite story from my childhood.

Having failed on that particular occasion to bump me off, she used to send me to school if I was unwell, and – not believing in the concept of illness – express surprise when I was sent home at lunchtime with a diagnosis of chicken pox or measles. She once put me, at the age of seven, bareback on a horse and watched me fall off, head-first, on to the stone surface of a Scottish bridge.

Softness and privilege, however, did concern her. My mother was upset when I got into a grammar school, dismissive when I was accepted into Oxford University, and pleased when I was chucked out again within two terms. She has always hated mollycoddling. 'Of course he should do it,' she told Sarah firmly, when asked. 'Look at him! A bit of exercise and hardship wouldn't go amiss there. Be the making of him.'

The other great supporter of the venture was my friend Jane. Jane is a handsome-looking, big-jawed loner with whom I'd shared a house fifteen years before. She is one of those rewarding people who is tough with everybody, but is most brutal with her friends. For the last ten years she had been developing into a rock-climber and venture traveller, hanging off mountains by a couple of crampons, or sailing Lake Titicaca in a storm. If she's physically afraid of anything or anybody, then I've never noticed it. Jane is pitiless – mostly with herself.

When I told her about my plans, and after I had finally convinced her that I was serious (which took some doing), she entered efficient-expedition mode, and volunteered to organise the journey.

'I know about these things,' she told me, her jaw set to full jut, 'and you don't. We'll need a proper route map detailing exactly where you'll be every night. You must call once a day to fix your position. I'll make a list of what you'll have to take. Don't forget loo paper. I don't believe for a moment that you'll complete the circuit, but if you don't, it won't be my fault.' And she smiled. Grimly.

We sat down together and planned the journey in detail. My route would take me up the Grand Union canal, through the new city of Milton Keynes, then branching off to Leicester, north of which I'd join the mighty River Trent. From Nottingham I'd paddle to Lincoln, and from Lincoln to Leeds. The Pennines would be crossed on the Leeds to Liverpool canal. Then the idea was to split the difference between Merseyside and Manchester, passing down through Cheshire, on to the Shropshire Union. At Welshpool I could switch from the still waters of the Montgomery to the adjoining, fast-moving Severn, by crossing a small spit of land. From Shrewsbury, I would pass right down through Worcester and finally to Gloucester. After a brief interlude on the road, the boat would taste water again at Cricklade on the Thames, and then carry me the last 160 miles, through Oxford and above Reading, back to London and the Millennium Dome.

The project had been in gestation for six months. I was fitter, thinner, more muscular. I had better stamina and I could fall in the water without drowning. There was only one thing I lacked. A boat.

CHAPTER 3

The Subtle Knife

My canoe was beautiful. Jane had arranged for it to be delivered to a water-sports shop in west London, where it was fetched for me from a metal container full of boats.

It was exactly what I'd envisaged. From pointed stem to pointed stern she measured a majestic 17 feet, a *Queen Elizabeth* of kayaks, her lower parts pristine white and her deck sky-blue. Fore and aft of the cockpit were two hatches, held shut by snap straps, and then sealed by strongly elasticated latex hatch-liners. These were to house my tent, sleeping bag, camping stove, my meagre provisions, a watertight box for valuables, a change of clothes, dry shoes, a knapsack, toiletries and – of course – the loo paper. Being airtight they would also give me added buoyancy, making it more difficult even for me to capsize the boat.

In front of the cockpit a criss-cross of black rope offered a net for my drinking water and my maps. Behind, yet another, longer, arrangement would accommodate the spare paddles and my wheels.

These folding wheels, a dinky arrangement in aluminium and rubber, could, when unfolded, be slid over the canoe's derrière, coming to rest securely about a third of the way along her length. During long walks around non-negotiable obstacles I could put the boat on these wheels and then pull her along behind me. And there were many such obstacles ahead.

I practised on the lawn. With careful planning and packing I could get almost all of what I needed into the two compartments, and still have room for a copy of *Middlemarch*, the book with which I decided to fill the empty evening hours under canvas.

Getting myself in was more of a problem. The seat, with its adjustable back-rest, was too far forwards, and I couldn't sit and get my knees under the canopy. This was a potentially terminal problem, and a miserable scenario suggested itself, in which – after all this effort – I had to call off the trip because I was too big for my canoe. All the sweating, dunking and shivering for naught! That thought was enough to spur me into finding a spanner and shifting everything two inches backwards. It worked. My feet engaged successfully with the foot-rests deep in the boat's bowels, and we had lift-off.

Now came the naming. I invited my infants to suggest favourite appellations, but their nerves failed them after my negative reactions to *Stinky* and *Spice Girl*. The boat itself was an Orca, made by a company called Pyranha, but I didn't really want anything fishy. In the end her shape led me to borrow the name of a wonderful children's book by Philip Pullman that we'd just been reading. *The Subtle Knife* I called her, or *Knife* for short, picturing her bows, propelled by a man of grace and sinew, cutting their way effortlessly through the turbid waters.

One last time I went to Richmond, where the *Knife* was much admired as she formed part of a large party paddling down to Syon House. Dick was particularly taken with her compartments, and kept us amused for some time as he decided whether his flask of coffee should go in the front or the back.

But summer was coming in. The launch was set for the first of June, and I was as fit and experienced as I was going to be. On the night before my departure, the first anniversary of my dad's death, I invoked his questing spirit and reminded myself that human beings – even this one – are capable of extraordinary feats.

Supper was steak.

CHAPTER 4

The First Day

07.30 a.m. The first Tuesday of summer. Jane and I lower the loaded *Knife* into the black waters of the Paddington arm of the Grand Union canal. We are at Camden Lock, the newly trendy warehouses rising in front, and the detritus from yet another night's north London partying lining the canal.

The boat weighs at least seven stone. And I am bulked out with a red buoyancy aid, inside which a waterproof shoulder holster holds my mobile phone and a voice-activated tape recorder. This cunning machine is there to capture the many interesting and noteworthy thoughts that I shall doubtless have as I paddle northwards. At each day's end I will listen to a simply thrilling and authentic medley of impressions and incidents, and carefully note them down.

07.35 a.m. I make my hearty farewells to Sarah and the children, who stand by the waterside. They are bemused, a bit proud and a bit embarrassed. My oldest looks at the water with disgust. 'Are you really going?' asks number two. As Jane holds the boat, I gingerly slide my legs in. There is no one around. The cast-iron bridge, the neighbouring pub yard, the towpath past the old factories, will soon be full of young pilgrims to London's greatest market. But now only the early light shoves its way between the buildings of the Camden recycling depot, and catches the remains of polystyrene cups floating in the dusty water.

07.36 a.m. I pick up the paddle, push myself away from the low, dirty pavement, and – with two long strokes – I begin my great journey. I don't turn to wave as I leave because, so early in the day, this could be a risky manoeuvre, so I call my final salutations over my shoulder. I hear the desultory farewells of my children returning to me.

07.40 a.m. With Jane loping alongside me on the towpath, I leave Camden Town and slowly enter the straight run that passes, well below street level, through Regent's Park and beside London Zoo. Beneath the mesh of the Aviary, a few early cyclists and walkers are going to work. The drunks and murderers will not put in an appearance until nightfall, I imagine, when lots of dreadful things will happen next to the canal. Over half of all the dismembered bodies discovered in TV cop shows are fished, white and dripping, out of urban waterways. But right now the canal path is the province of the respectable and the fit, wending their carless, healthy ways towards advertising agencies and social work offices in north London.

08.00 a.m. Suddenly, without warning, the towpath ends and Jane disappears up a concrete staircase. I am now alone and in almost complete gloom, wobbling through the Maida Vale tunnel. This is, I can tell, a moment of significant danger. Canoes are not allowed through canal tunnels, but this is just about the shortest tunnel on the inland waterway system, and I can easily make out the light that is pouring in from the far end. But this doesn't mean that any narrowboat, ploughing on from the Thames towards Limehouse, will be able to see me, low and negligible as I am. Even the merest of touches from the fender of a powered craft will have me in the water, over 150 yards from safety and light. It's the first great challenge of the journey!

08.10 a.m. Sweating heavily I emerge safely from the darkness, among the moored, flower-covered boats of Little Venice. A heron, perched on a floating sleeper, fixes me with a sardonic eye, and pecks a gleaming fish from out of the water in one precise movement.

This isn't so bad! I have covered my first two miles, and it has taken me just over half an hour. I extrapolate. The whole trip is about 1200 miles and there are sixty days to do it in. I reckon on paddling around four miles an hour, because that's what you can do at a brisk walk, and canoeing surely can't be any slower. So, 1200 divided by 60 is 20, and 20 divided by 4 is 5. A mere five hours paddling every day, and I will easily finish the course; QED. That will leave plenty of time for encounters, conversations and visits. And four miles an hour is exactly what I've done!

For this first day I have planned a leisurely 13 miles, ending up at a marina in London's western suburbs. There I will leave the boat overnight, while I stay at some pleasant local family-owned B&B or small hotel. Later, when I hit countryside, I'll pitch my tent and live a simpler more unencumbered life. It's going to be wonderful.

Happily I hail my first two passing narrowboats. Their captains, silver-haired chaps, both wearing leather cowboy hats (1999s fashion for the well-dressed waterman), salute me rather apathetically. I'm disappointed.

08.30 a.m. The light reflected from the water dapples the underside of the Westway, turning the bottom of the ugly A40(M) into a Hockney painting. I pass a council estate; benign in the sun, with new seats laid out along the canal path. As Wormwood Scrubs floats away on my left, I stop and drink some water from the bottle. A teenaged policeman in white shirt-sleeves dallies for a moment. He doesn't get many canoeists down this way, he tells me. Not many dismembered bodies either, he adds, when I ask him. The white and green of Kensal Green cemetery, resting place of Thackeray and Trollope, slides past on the north bank. I feel all that research is paying off.

09.00 a.m. It's been ninety minutes now. The well-kept, paved canal path is giving way to a tatty brown ribbon, flanked by the rusty arses of factories. Corrugated-iron workshops, badly tarmacked carparks, old disused wharves alternate, with no signs to indicate the business that's going on inside. Somewhere round the front is a big sign, a reception, a telephonist and a security guard in a little hut. From the canal, you just have to guess.

09.20 a.m. Smells are emerging from behind the wire fences, and what smells they are. From one set of battered buildings comes the tangy whiff of tomato ketchup. A few yards further on the acid stench of salad dressing spreads across the water. Twenty or so more strokes and this is supplanted by a strong chocolatey smell. What strange industrial process, I wonder, can account for this? Are there forms of paint or chemical manufacture that perfectly – but accidentally – replicate the whiff of tomato sauce and chocolate? I pull in and glance down at the map; this tells me that I have just passed the Heinz and McVities factories. The smell that I had thought was like ketchup, is ketchup. Oh.

09.30 a.m. Two hours in, and the canalscape is made up of the backs of houses, punctuated every now and again by a failed attempt at civic restoration: a red-and-purple-bricked garden, with a deserted picnic table, now graffiti-covered and surrounded by broken glass. It must have seemed like a good idea, five years ago, to spend a couple of thousand on a canal corner, but it appears there has been no follow-up; no money for maintenance, or for someone to come along and clean up. The drunks and the teenagers have taken over.

Ten yards away from me, an Asian woman in a beautiful sari appears by the bank, at the end of a terrace of small houses, and tosses a large, mauve bag of rubbish into the canal. I wonder what else is in here with me. So far I've seen no drowned, bloated cats or submerged joy-ridden bangers.

All the canoeing handbooks and the Internet newsgroups warn against something called Weil's disease, or leptospirosis. This is a virus, carried in rats' urine. And England's rivers and canals, apparently, are awash with rats' urine. Just about every rat in the country, when it hears nature's call, goes down to the waterside, cocks its little leg, and adds its contribution to the English waterway system. If the unwitting canoeist or swimmer has an open graze or wound, and some of the rat-donated virus is floating around, the consequences can be fatal. The first symptoms are a bit like those of flu: high temperature, sweating and headaches. But the next stage, if untreated, can see liver or kidney failure and –

in five or so cases a year – the Big D. The answer, I think is, as ever, not to swallow.

11.00 a.m. I am getting tired. The muscles in my back and shoulders are hurting, and my paddling is becoming slow and even a bit erratic. I count twenty strokes and then rest while my momentum takes me forward, then twenty more.

12.00 midday On a path near a power station, I find a low bank and, grasping a clump of grass, struggle out of the boat. I'm in either Perivale or Acton. It's lunchtime, and women workers are crossing the footbridges on their way to do some shopping, while the men congregate in the tarmac carparks and smoke. I smile bravely at the women, and the older ones smile back. I eat a banana and drink some water. Over four hours, and 10 miles completed. Well below the rate I've set myself but, still, it is only the first day.

12.15 p.m. Getting back in, with one of my legs inside the canoe, the *Knife* decides that it's time to go, and pushes strongly away from the bank. I am now suspended, groin first, over a widening expanse of dirty water, and it's only a despairing grab at a fistful of dandelions that saves me. But my confidence – essential to getting into a kayak – has gone. I ask a passing, bemused Asian woman in a business suit to hold the boat for me while I tip myself in. She can hardly say no to someone so recklessly willing to look ridiculous. But even so, she looks relieved to be on her way.

1.10 p.m. Now, unwilling to get out of the boat again, it's just a matter of keeping going till I reach my destination – the lovely-sounding Willowtree Marina. But it is pure plod. Factories alternate with suburban council estates to left and right, my view of them blurred by the sweat trickling into my eyes. My back and thighs add their complaints to those of my other muscles. Every other stroke I have to lie backwards, resting my kidneys on the back of the boat, to try and get some relief. For more than an hour

I have inched down the grey streak, complaining loudly to the occasional moorhen that skitters out from the banks ahead of me, and scattering the water with curses. The marina should be around here somewhere. A tall skinhead and his girlfriend lounging in a park demand that I give them a turn in the canoe. When I smilingly refuse they lose interest and begin kissing again.

1.30 p.m. No sign of the marina. I have certainly covered the distance. Surely I can't have passed it? I come to a halt by the grassy towpath, temporarily defeated.

1.31 p.m. I see, on the opposite side of the canal, an arch. I'm there! With a boyish surge of energy, I shoot across the water and into the sunny basin of a lovely, spanking new boatyard. All around me brightly painted narrowboats ride their moorings. Straight ahead is a red-brick pub-restaurant, with a couple of drinkers sipping shandies under sun-umbrellas. I paddle up to the slipway, put my feet into the water and stand up.

I am now liberated from the water and from the soggy confines of the canoe until tomorrow. Morale soars. I park the boat in a corner of the yard, change discreetly in the shadow of a cruiser and fill my knapsack. I secure the *Knife*'s hatches, congratulate her on her first day out, and saunter down to the pub.

2.00 p.m. Over my pint I consult the map. I am in a place called Yeading. Very few English place names begin with a 'Y'. Just Yeovil and York really. The rest sound as though they are being pronounced by someone with a speech impediment. Next stop might be Yedcar, Yipon or Yomford. It all adds to a certain sense of disorientation; Yeading is somewhere you would never go by car, because you would never take the Yeading turn. It is the kind of place you could only arrive in from the water. Or live in.

And where, exactly, might one stay in Yeading? The red canal guide, which all narrowboaters carry with them, suggests a Travelodge just down the road. When I call on the mobile they tell me all their rooms are taken. I can hardly believe it; a

Tuesday night, and the Yeading Travelodge is full! Still, it's only two o'clock – plenty of time to find alternative accommodation.

When pressed, the receptionist recommends the Ibis Hotel, Heathrow ('That's quite nice'), so I call there. Yes, they have a room. In the marina shop, which is closing since it is now nearly three in the afternoon (and what a warm and close afternoon it is!), the woman selling postcards and bilge-pumps tells me that I will have to get a cab to the Ibis, and helpfully calls me one. While I wait for it to arrive I have another pint, and watch the shaven-headed men with beer guts and mobile phones loudly indulge their girlfriends in green cocktails.

4.00 p.m. The Ibis Hotel is a large, beige-coloured box sitting almost within the perimeter of Heathrow airport, and miles away from civilisation. It's the sort of place where cheapskate airlines put passengers up when the flight to Djibouti is delayed for three days. Vast amounts of luggage bumps its way in through the doors and up stairs, or out of the doors and into buses and taxis. The receptionist looks sceptically at me in my blue shorts, gripping my small black foldable rucksack, and sends me up to the fifth floor.

5.00 p.m. My first home from home. The room is a dreary square, reminiscent of my student hall of residence, except without the cheesy Pre-Raphaelite poster and the dirty underwear. There's a view of far-off jets and a hangar through one small, double-glazed window, a picture of flowers, three biscuits, a TV, a wardrobe, a desk and a small bed. I am now trapped here for the next fourteen hours. I'm too knackered to go and look at the planes. I have nothing to do, but wait for supper. Oh dear.

No, not quite nothing. I remember the tape. I should have recorded at least an hour's worth of live wit, aphorism and anecdote. That will keep me entertained.

5.40 p.m. I have rewound the tape and switched the machine on. At first there's nothing. Then, very faintly, I hear myself bidding farewell to Jane at the tunnel. For the next hour all that can be discerned is the splish and then the splosh of my paddles. It reminds me of an aromatherapist I once visited, who insisted on relaxing me with a tape of sea-sounds. These consisted of lapping waves, and the occasional 'berloooob' cry of a whale.

Anyway, my tape sounds just like hers, except mine has swearing. 'What the fuck am I doing here?' for instance. And, 'Whose fucking idea was this?' Most poignant of all: 'Twelve hundred miles? I'll be lucky to make it to fucking Watford.' Such fascinating observations as I've made during the trip (and there aren't many) have been lost.

What time is supper?

6.30 p.m. The earliest that they serve dinner. Downstairs the wall-menu offers the choice between 'Steak or buffet'. It strikes me that this is the kind of ridiculous decision that only budget hotel managers can force you into. What other possible dilemmas lie ahead of me? 'Bacon or breakfast'?, 'Underpants or evening dress'?

I can't be sure what they mean by 'buffet', but I know what steak is. I choose steak. A tiny Filipina brings it to me, and I linger over the peas as long as I possibly can. Eating is, at least, an activity.

07.30 p.m. Upstairs again. It's hot and humid and strangely dark. The weather is closing in, as though there is going to be a storm. I call Sarah and tell her that I am fine. I speak to the children and find a lump in my throat – the same one I used to get when Lassie died in films. Then I call Jane. She congratulates me brusquely on surviving the first day.

08.00 p.m. All human contact for the day is now over. I sit, naked, at the desk, and write a postcard home. Looking up I catch sight of myself in an unexpected mirror, a sad, startled Lucian Freud nude with blue-tinged skin.

3.15 a.m. My sleep has lasted only four hours before the most savage electrical storm propels me awake. Rain thuds against the double glazing, and sheets over the distant, luminous white planes.

Within minutes the hotel carpark is awash, and late buses bringing delayed nocturnal Djiboutis to the hotel send up plumes of spray as they brake by the doors. And I suddenly remember my poor canoe. She is sitting, right side up, in the Willowtree Marina, filling up with storm water. What if it's like this tomorrow? What if the canals burst their banks? What if I can't get back to sleep?

I am not, I think, a natural traveller.

CHAPTER 5

To Watford and Beyond

By eight o'clock the next morning I had left behind the airport nation of Heathrow – as big as Luxembourg and populated entirely by people from Asia. At the marina I tipped the water out of the *Knife*. To my great relief she seemed to be completely undamaged and unworried by her soaking.

Together we skirted round a couple of swans on the slipway, and were soon back, making speed bravely, down the dull strip of the canal. Off to my right, obscured by nondescript interstitial vegetation, was central Southall. Before me lay outer suburbia, and Middle England.

After an hour of this I passed under the Ball's Bridge, and turned right into the main Grand Union canal, the first great thoroughfare of my journey. It looked exactly like the canal from which I'd just emerged.

I soon found myself behind the first boat that I'd seen on the water since early the previous morning. It was a slow, chuggy thing, with only one man on board: a thick-set bloke with sideburns, wearing the violent green of British Waterways. Every few yards he would leave the tiller, and, with a hook on the end of a long pole, fish large bits of rubbish out of the cut.

He was the dead dog patrol. While I watched, Sideburns caught two kids' tricycles and a number of large boxes. As he poked and lifted, so his boat, unsteered, headed slowly for the bank – only for Sideburns to rescue it at the last moment, before it could plough into a factory wall or the crumbling towpath. He had it down to a minor art.

The vista now was one of endless factories. From high above, in an overgrown forecourt, a young man yelled at me in the hoarse sing-song of the English football fan: '*Row, row, row ve boa'!!*' Then he got bored, and left the rest of the song unsung.

After him, there was no one about. No one on the path, no one on the water. Just ducks. It was weather for ducks, drizzly wet above and wetter below.

Five miles more and, as the rain insinuated itself down the neck of my waterproofs, I arrived at my very first lock, the white ends of the lock paddles gleaming through the grey-green.

Cowley lock is about half a mile from the M25, but it could have been twenty; there was no moan of distant traffic. Two small cottages sat by the pound. As I approached the bank, warily, a bearded, smiling man, also in British Waterways green, came down to the water's edge, and helped me out as though this too was part of his job.

He was the lock-keeper, he told me, and then went off to assist a narrowboat that had now appeared on the other, higher, side of his lock. A pretty woman with a baby stood at the gate of the second cottage, as though posing for a Victorian artist.

'How far are you going?' she asked me.

'Burnley,' I told her.

'That sounds a long way,' she replied, 'especially in this weather.'

But I didn't feel that it was such a terrible distance, not with such pretty women and friendly lock-keepers to help me. Before returning to the canal I sat in front of a cottage, ate a banana and phoned Jane to say that I had made it through the first big obstacle.

There were many more ahead. Locks are how canals go up and down hill. The Grand Union rises from sea level at the Thames, to 380 feet, as it crosses the Chilterns near Tring, in Hertfordshire. Because water has difficulty running upwards, fifty or so locks exist to lift or lower boats to the next level. If they're going up, they open the gates, enter the lock, shut the gates again, and activate a mechanism to let water in. The boat rises. When the water in the lock and outside are at the same level, the gate is opened, and the skipper and his crew sail off to their next damp destination.

And if they're going down, obviously, the water is let out. Every time this happens, between 70,000 and 200,000 gallons of water flow down into the canal below, eventually ending up at sea level. This is water that needs to be replaced or the canal will run dry, so every canal has huge reservoirs from which water is pumped to the highest points, just so that narrowboaters can go downhill.

Canoeists are not usually allowed inside locks: there's too much rushing water and danger. So they have to carry their canoes around. Each time I came to a lock I would have to get out, lift the *Knife* out, slide her on to her wheels, drag her up or down the incline beside the lock gates, take the wheels off again, and manhandle the whole lot back into the water. This last part I managed all by myself and without mishap. It was all right, I thought, as I made northwards from Cowley lock. I could do this. My spirits lifted.

It was 3 p.m., the sky had been heavy and grey for an hour, and a nasty wind was rising. My shoulders and bum were very sore again, as I spotted the entrance to the Harefield Marina.

As I paddled in, the storm broke. Within five seconds I was soaked, the rain being thrown sideways at me, as though I was a comic turn in a vaudeville act. I laboured against the deluge, my eyes full of water, looking for the slipway.

'Oi!' shouted a voice from a moored narrowboat. 'This is private property!' I could barely make out the voice's owner through the deluge.

'Is it?' I almost shouted back, 'Well I'll just die then, shall I? Just roll over in the water right here and drown? Would that be all right?'

Instead, I paddled closer to the bank, and shouted above the slap of rain on water to explain that I'd called earlier, and been told that it would be OK for me to leave the boat here overnight.

'There's a slipway right over there, by the trees,' the voice gruffly directed me. Sure enough, once I'd pierced the curtain of rain-water, I could see it sloping up the bank. I drew the boat up beside a large bush, and waited for the rain to abate before changing. After twenty cold minutes the deluge stopped.

Lined jogging pants make a nice change of clothes, but don't try and get into them when your feet and legs are damp. I was hopping around, one foot snagged against the lining, my ghostly white buttocks describing jerky, but luminous paraboli against the dark foliage, when a middle-aged woman taking advantage of the dry intermission walked past with her dog. 'Nice day,' she said, ignoring – in that English way – the fact that the moon was very full that afternoon.

In the gloomy brass-fitting-festooned marina office, I asked about local accommodation, since there was no way I was pitching a tent in monsoon conditions. 'Yeah,' said the man in the office, absently, 'there are loads of B&Bs in the village. Just turn right, then left, up the hill and you're there.'

It took me twenty-five minutes to walk up the wet hill to Harefield village. The epicentre of this uninteresting place was a large pub, upon which hung a banner announcing 'Saturday night is CURRY NIGHT – £3.45'. If that was what Saturday night was, I thought, it did not bode well for Wednesday.

And, of course, there was nothing. The pattern was set. There were no B&Bs, no inns, no hotels. At a newsagent's I was directed to a building just three doors down, which the girl said was definitely a hotel. But the sign outside declared that it was now a hospice, and gave its founding date as three years earlier. I opted not to stay there.

I enquired at a minicab office. There was a B&B, they thought, in Northwood, three or four miles away. Or maybe, there again, there wasn't.

I was standing miserably on the pavement outside a grubby tea shop, cursing the casual liars down at the marina, when a red bus slid to a stop beside me. It was the number 331 running between Ruislip and Uxbridge stations, both of which I knew to be on the far ends of the London underground system.

A fierce, but very short, internal debate ensued. Going home for the night didn't count as giving up, because I'd be back on the water the next day, said one voice, its tones soft with the seductive suggestion of my bed, my books, my refrigerator. Oh yes it did, said another, more muscular voice, which sounded very much like Jane's. You can't just bugger off back to wife and kids whenever you feel like it.

I listened carefully to them both for about thirty seconds, then I got on the bus. An hour and a quarter later I was back in north London. When I arrived home Sarah was surprised and not pleased. Jane phoned, expecting to find Sarah, and was also surprised and not pleased. I solemnly promised that I would be back on the bus, early the next morning, to Harefield and the North.

It was Day 3, and the 331 was full of silent, sad passengers. The route took in both the Harefield and Mount Vernon hospitals. I remembered that week, almost exactly a year before, visiting my dad in the final days of his life. The last words I heard him say were, 'I feel bloody lousy.' That night he became unconscious, and the next five days were, I now realised, simply the period in which his carers prepared us, his family, for the inevitable. Maybe the haggard woman next to me was going through the same thing now.

The Subtle Knife was crawling with slugs when I reached her, and I picked them out morosely. The air was still slightly chilly, and rain threatened from the east. But today was a short day's paddle – just eight miles to Watford – and I'd already decided to go home again that night. It would be OK, and it would be the last time.

At a place called Copper Mill lock, south of Rickmansworth, I came across my first boaters of the day. I'd just dragged the *Knife* up a steep bank and round the lock, when a couple of ladies in late middle age appeared and began opening the upper lock gates, one on either side. A moment later two narrowboats followed, squeezing into the lock side by side, each skippered by a grey-haired man: one thin and one fat.

As they passed me, the fat man shouted to the thin man, brightly, 'I say, has she been in before?'

The thin man seemed not to hear. 'What?' he shouted back.

'I said,' screamed the fat man, 'has she been in before?'

'Oh,' replied the thin man, tetchily. 'Yes, actually. Birmingham: nineteen seventy-one.'

I looked at his craft. Long, elegant, with a copper smokestack and her name painted in bright colours, it seemed most unlikely that she'd been in mothballs for twenty-eight years. That didn't make any sense. But what then was the big bloke referring to?

Then something about one of the women caught my eye. Her slacks and tan anorak were clinging to her limbs, her hair was plastered to her forehead, and her eyes held an expression of defeat and resignation. This was the 'she' who had been 'in' before, when Edward Heath was Prime Minister and Donny Osmond was at number one. Now it had happened to her again, in front of the odious fat man, his dry wife, and the peculiar chap sitting, open-mouthed, on the path next to a sky-blue canoe.

Sorry though I was for her, I had my own problems. I might have set out with the intention of discovering England, but I found I was spending all my time thinking about only three things. When I came to the next lock would I be able to get out of the canoe? Once I had got the canoe out of the water, would I be able to get it round the lock? And, once I had managed to manoeuvre it round all the obstacles, would I be able to get in again?

No two locks, I was discovering, were exactly the same. Some had nice, low, easy banks where it was a doddle to get out; but most presented some kind of difficulty. I became an expert in all of them. There were low banks, and there were high banks, where it was necessary to grab hold of projecting stones or clumps of grass and hold on for dear life while Fosbury-flopping out on to dry land. Some banks were made of crumbling concrete, offering nothing for the fumbling fingers, but scraping my knees to a bloody pulp as I hauled myself ashore. Others, fashioned out of old railway sleepers, would leave splinters in my hands and forearms. Long grass might look best, but it was full of nettles and thistles. And any surface was likely to be liberally coated in dog-shit, goose-cack or duck-dos. But the most dangerous were corrugated-iron lengths, pushed edge first along the banks. These I had to slide over, hoping that my weight would at no point leave me bearing down, testicles lowest, on to the wicked serrations.

So I would paddle along, sightless between the high canal banks, dreaming of nothing other than secure grassy portages.

In addition I began to discover the variety of man-made impediments that had been deliberately placed in my way on land. The most common was a pedestrian-only railing gate, of the sort that obliges you to shuffle sideways round it. These necessitated lifting one end of the *Knife* five feet or so on to the very top of the railing, sliding her to the point of balance, and then dashing round the other side — holding her steady in one hand — ready to catch her as she slid, suddenly, down on the other side. At another lock, the gentle slope had been thoughtlessly replaced by a steep post-modern ziggurat, which I negotiated only by ruthlessly impressing a jogging South African into my service. At still others there were flights of brick steps that went round sharp corners, forcing me to inch the boat around them, first from the front and then from behind.

I entered the Bridgewater Basin Marina at two, changed, stowed the gear, bade farewell to the *Knife* and practically ran for the tube. The distance that had taken me three arduous, sodden days in a canoe, took exactly forty-seven minutes by electric train. It was just time enough to read a discarded *Daily Mirror*. On pages 4 and 5 there were three stories close together. One was the tale of a man who was playing football in his own garden when he slipped and fell backwards through a conservatory, severed an artery and bled to death. The second concerned a ten-year-old who choked on a peanut and died. The third was also about choking, only this time it was a toddler on a lollipop.

In my own bed again that night, I woke at twenty-minute intervals from dawn, full of dread and foreboding. By the time I stopped paddling this evening, I would have finally disappeared from returning distance; I'd be completely alone. The seductive voice would be dumb.

The rain was quite heavy by the time I arrived at Croxley Green station. As I walked down towards the canal, I found myself assisting a middle-aged man to find an industrial estate that I knew was close to the boatyard. Jitu was a small, delicate-looking being in his early fifties. He was, by profession, a book-keeper, and he was to be interviewed for a cost-controller's job at an engineering firm. He had travelled up from wet, grey Wembley, but he had been born on the warm spice island of Zanzibar, where the breezes blow in from the Indian Ocean and ruffled the palms. Politics had made him leave, when still a child.

'Things were good under the Sultan,' he told me. 'Little houses, little streets, pineapples. All gone.' He sighed. The new rulers, the Africans, had exhausted the land. 'Now nothing grows,' he insisted, somewhat implausibly.

In Europe the Kosovo war was coming to an end, and Jitu wanted to know what I thought about it.

'It doesn't matter anyway,' he said, quietly. 'There will be a great world catastrophe in September or October. I know it. That is why I am not hurrying to this interview.'

And for one mad moment I actually hoped Jitu was right. Because, if he was, then there wasn't much point continuing on this journey that I was beginning to hate.

Back in the boat, I was conscious of passing out of the city and its suburbs. Now everyone I saw, on towpath or afloat, was white. Today was the first day in which I had to cover my full quota of miles, and no fewer than twenty-six locks stood between me and the summit of the Grand Union canal. My previous highest daily tally was five. At the third lock I was dragging *The Subtle Knife* past the gates, when a little tubby man on a boat going my way kindly offered me a lift. We loaded the canoe on to his flat roof, and I helped his wife close the lock gates as he took his craft to the bank beyond.

For an hour or so, I sat up there beside my round friend as we passed through the beautiful Cassiobury Park. And I suddenly realised how little I had been able to see from the kayak. Sitting in a canoe, there is only the thickness of the plastic and your pants between you and the water. From arse to eye you may be about, say, three and a half feet tall. But the banks on either side are rarely less than three feet above the water. Add the merest summer's thrust of canalside plant life, and you can see absolutely fuck-all.

Really, you might as well wear a blindfold. But I hadn't known it till now. It was a hell of a jolt.

My hosts' names were Richard and Olwen, both in their early sixties. Richard, with his glasses and reticent smile, was a dead ringer for Mole in *Wind in the Willows*. A former BT engineer, he had been, he told me, a 'willing casualty of privatisation'. With his pay-off he had bought the boat he'd always wanted. Now its pocketa-pocketa engine transported its doilies and brasses all over England for fully six months of the year.

We drank coffee and ate biscuits while Richard steered, and Olwen went to open the lock gates. Remembering the half-drowned woman from the Copper Mill lock, I asked Richard whether his wife liked the boating life as much as he did.

'It was like wind on a stone,' he replied. 'I had to wear her down over ten years, but now – would you believe it? – she's a bigger enthusiast than I am!'

A few minutes later I asked Olwen if she thought women enjoyed the canal life as much as the men.

'No they don't,' she answered, quickly and emphatically. 'You don't meet anyone for more than five minutes. I'd rather be at home.'

At King's Langley we passed the Ovaltine factory, and – almost under the shadow of the M25 – we parted company. I had hardly hit the water and gone round the first bend before a rainstorm came out of nowhere and, once again, I was wet from scalp to stern.

Now it was just a matter of jaw-clenched determination. With the wind up, and the occasional rumble of thunder, there was no one out boating and no one hanging around at the locks to help me carry the boat. At lock after weary lock I climbed the banks, dragged and lifted the canoe up steps, over fences, and back into the drop-circled water. Twice, teeth gritted, I pulled the canoe past comfy lockside pubs, whose warm patrons looked out at this dripping vision, and giggled. By early afternoon every muscle in my back and arms, from my trapezoids to my psoas, was in agony; my legs and elbows were covered in grazes and cuts, the diluted blood streaking my limbs. I looked like Dick.

Somewhere near Hemel Hempstead the towpath next to the lock disappeared up a steep muddy incline, and over a road bridge. I put the *Knife* on her wheels and, for the twentieth time that day, pulled with all my might. I had just got to the top, by the road, and was thinking about how much time I had to cross the road with a 17-foot boat, when my foot slipped, and the rope tugged free from my grip. With horror I watched the *Knife* career back down the slope, picking up speed. As she trundled downhill, a white van full of young men zoomed past. 'Whayayayay!' they shouted joyfully, and sped on.

I scrambled down the bank, and discovered *The Subtle Knife*, balanced, as in a comedy movie, right over the edge of the canal. I grabbed hold of the rope attached to her bows, and started to climb all over again. When I got to the road, I crossed at my own speed, defying any car to hit me.

Naturally, it was just after this Sisyphean low point that a new and unlooked-for danger presented itself. Most swans are OK most of the time. Actually, they quite like people because people give them bread, and swans are too bloody lazy these days to get their own food. Once, perhaps in a more robust age, they fended for themselves, but now they prefer, if you'll forgive me, to go swanning around, with their snooty beaks in the air, looking gorgeous. But something comes over a swan when it has cygnets in tow. Add a couple of bundles of straggly grey fluff to a swan family, and the chances are that the male will become homicidal. He will hiss, arch his feathers, swim towards the threat and, if all that fails, he'll rear up on his legs and beat his powerful wings all over his opponent. Since, at that point, he can be standing at least four feet in the water, and since each wing-beat is equivalent to a blow from Chris Eubank's left fist, this is bad news for canoeists.

Fortunately, not all male swans, *en famille*, mistake kayaks and their occupants for swan-predators on the hunt for cygnet supper. Only the particularly brave and stupid ones do, but it is hard to tell which is which from a distance. In very broad stretches of canal or river it may be possible to bypass any psychotic swans by paddling over to the further bank. But swans prefer to gather at places where the water narrows, like under canal bridges or at jetties and slipways. Three or four times already I had actually got out of the boat and walked around a particularly angry-looking male, rather than run the risk of being dumped in the water with a broken arm by an ugly duckling's doting dad.

But just outside Berkhamsted, with the rain temporarily lulled – exhausted and humiliated – I came across a swan family in a narrow section where there was nowhere obvious to land. The mummy and baby swans were swimming by the bank, where a heavily pregnant woman, a cutesy toddler and a little grey-haired old granny were tossing occasional bits of bread into the water. As they saw me, the pregnant woman stopped and pointed at me. The toddler stared.

I decided to go for it. Taking the far bank I put on some speed, hoping to get round the male swan before he understood what I was up to. It was no good. Spotting me out of the corner of his evil eye, he swam towards me, slowly – the equivalent of 'Where do you think you're going, mush?' As he came closer I paddled as fast as I possibly could, thinking that it would be clear to him that I presented no threat. He passed out of sight, behind me.

And then I heard, and almost felt, the beating of his wings on my neck. The bastard was giving chase, and in a second or two I would be in the water with a pneumatic bill taking lumps out of my face.

'For God's sake!' I screamed at the women. 'Throw it some bloody bread!'

Startled, they chucked half a loaf in the water, and the noise from behind me subsided as Mr Swan considered whether to attack the aggressive bread. My chest bursting with fear and adrenaline, I paddled away, determined not to take that risk again. From now on all swans were potential capsizers. They had all become my enemy.

I passed through Berkhamsted – a historic place I had been looking forward to – and saw nothing except high banks. Beyond, no one else walked on the towpath, save for one young bedraggled man with a beard, who had a wheelie-bin strapped to his back.

'Hello!' I called to him, unwisely.

He stopped and looked at me, and gave me a nasty smile. 'Have you seen a body in the water?' he asked.

'Nearly,' I told him, and hurried off.

And then, at last, I was there, the Cowroast Marina at the very summit of the Grand Union. I had covered over twenty miles, ported nearly thirty locks, suffered one near capsize, had my canoe attempt to run away, been attacked by a swan, and was covered in water, bruises and blood. At that moment, however, I was exultant at having reached my destination. I had pitted myself – absurdly – against the worst set of impediments that a canoeist can face, and I had made it.

I changed and walked along the towpath and up some steps to the Royal Hotel in Tring, an old inn, where I checked in, shoved my filthy, sodden clothes in the sink and fell, almost catatonic with exhaustion, on to the bed. An hour later I washed my dozens of abrasions and cuts in the bath, and went downstairs again.

It was Friday night, and a youthful clientele were gathering to eye each other up and get drunk. The boys congregated in one bar, the girls in another. One seventeen-year-old vamp, in long black coat and a short silver shirt that showed her creamy stomach and cheeky navel, swung in with a 'who gives a f— ?' expression on her lovely face. 'It's Miss Deborah Thomas!' said a boy, in the tones of a butler at a ball. I wanted to be young again, to gather in pubs, and to be vulnerable to the developing wiles of Miss Deborah Thomas. I ate my fish pie alone, my exultation evaporating. Four days gone. Two months to go.

On Saturday morning I woke up, had breakfast and abandoned the whole journey, in that order. I phoned Sarah and said I couldn't go on. Could she ask Jane to come and get me? I'd been a fool. It was over.

CHAPTER 6

The Journey Abandoned

I'd known the game was up from the moment I awoke in the inn bed, looked over at my shorts drying on the towel rail, and felt the sheets tug at the scabs forming on my legs.

It reminded me of the many times when I'd given up smoking. The prospect of those days stretching ahead into medium infinity without the pleasure and consolation of nicotine had been unbearable. Until, finally, the thought of lung cancer or of standing on pavements outside work with the other addicts, was even more unbearable.

Now, despite my victory over the elements the day before, the idea of repeating it all week in, week out, was appalling. I'd done all this lock and drag stuff once, said the seductive voice, what the hell would I gain from doing it all again? What more, for instance, could I learn about wetness? I had been wet for four days and sixty miles, experiencing wetness in virtually all its possible forms. The Inuit, we are told, have a hundred words for snow, because that's all there is in the Arctic. And the English are the same about the quality of water all about them. Since setting out, I had been moist, damp, dripping, soaked, sodden, sopping, drenched, wringing, waterlogged and saturated. I had sat for up to three hours with my crotch in the cold canal water slopping about in the bottom of the canoe. What more was to be said?

And what, the insinuating voice asked softly but insistently, was the point of it all? The journey was surely futile. I had seen nearly nothing except canal banks. I had met almost no one except for Richard and Olwen and the loonie with the wheelie-bin. Despite all the offers of help on the newsgroups, I had not yet encountered a single e-narrowboater. My poor canoe now had two holes in the first layer of its external skin. All I had done was paddled and ported. I was an expert, the voice insisted, on the structure of the Grand Union. I knew which sections were rewalled in 1931, and which bits were not done until five years later. But towns, suburbs, people had all dissolved in the rain, and were nowhere to be seen. The idea was flawed. I was flawed. That didn't make me a bad man.

My internal Jane held out for a while. I had just scored a major triumph and got through one of the worst days I was likely to experience. Such journeys were always hard at first, but they got easier. Loneliness was part of the deal, it was what made the traveller change from the thing he was to the thing he became. I should persevere. Besides, said internal Jane, what about external Jane? She'd arranged the canoe, got the paddles, studied the maps, and posted information on to the Net. She would kill me with contempt. And the publishers who'd been gulled out of their advance by an absurd and optimistic assessment of my fitness to undertake this journey; an advance which had already bought a new kitchen? How about my entire family, my colleagues at work, all those whom I had blithely informed of my impending adventure? Was I prepared to look such a complete arsehole? Surely not.

Going on was intolerable. Giving up was unthinkable. But what, asked the first voice, about forced retirement? If I were ill then I could stop with honour salvaged. I needed the equivalent of a sick note. Perhaps some digitalis growing beside the canal could be used to simulate a mild heart attack? Too risky. How much digitalis was enough? Or too much? I'd no idea.

So I started seriously to consider the possibilities of a virtual journey. The papers had been full of the story of the Swiss man who had managed to convince the literary world that he was a Holocaust childhood survivor, when in fact he had spent his early years surrounded by chalets and Toblerone. He had won prizes and made a fortune before he was found out. There had also been several cases of American Pulitzer prize-winning journalists whose incredible voyages into the darkness of the human soul turned out to be entirely made up.

Would it be possible to write a book about having made a journey, without having actually made it? I'd done a fair bit of research and already paddled on river and canal. With a bit of imagination and a liberal use of guidebooks, might I not be able to construct a plausible adventure, and populate it with boaters, eccentrics, clerics, grandpas, farmers and call-girls? Others had done it. Did you actually have to paddle through, say, Newark, in order to write about it? It was pretty evident looking through some travel books that the encounters in them were, to say the least, reconstructed.

Encouraged though I was by this scheme, and despite feeling desperate enough actively to consider it, in the end I was defeated by its impracticability. Its success would depend on my hiding at home for nine weeks, staying out of sight and never going out, on phoning Jane every night and pretending to be at the next point on my journey, on Sarah and the children lying about me to everyone they met. And Sarah would have to drive me to my various planned rendezvous with angry Jane; I would arrive an hour early, distress my clothes, wet the boat, smear mud on my face, and complain of hardships undergone. But she'd know.

All I was sure about was that I could not go on. Somewhere in the last twenty years I had metamorphosed into the ultimate metropolitan, a soft-bellied lounge lizard. Worse, I had become a martyr to self-pity; the unfairness of my situation welled up inside me, like a deep and terrible sadness. My sympathy for myself had a pure, undistilled quality, which hurt like hunger.

I had learned something about myself in those four days, but I didn't like what I'd discovered. Searching for the rugged man of adventure within, I had only caught sight of him on a couple of occasions, turning a corner in the far distance. I'd hoped to leave Mr Storm behind, and become a perpetual, omni-competent Sunny. Instead, a third, pathetic person was taking over: Mr Drizzle.

Down at the marina I sat by the *Knife* and waited for Jane.

The Grand Union Again

CHAPTER 7

The Journey Resumed

It was two days later; Jane was driving me back to the water and giving me the lowdown on the particular challenges that I faced.

'You have the attention span of a gnat,' she said. 'Always have had.' She glared at the road ahead. There was a silence. Then she added, 'If anything takes longer than five minutes you get bored.'

'I . . .'

'One moment you're there, the next you're gone.'

'On the contrary,' I said, 'I am capable of prolonged periods of concentration.'

Jane snorted. 'As in?' she asked.

Well, I said, I could play computer games for hours on end, and sit at railway stations waiting for very late trains without complaining, as long as I had a book. When it came to that sort of thing I was a Stoic.

Jane kept driving and said nothing more. I don't know what conversations she and Sarah had had on that Saturday, but I was guessing they involved phrases like 'bitten off more than he can chew', and 'we can hardly tell the publishers to come round and remove our kitchen'. At some point, while I was waiting in Tring, they had worked out a strategy for handling me.

The strategy was a good one. After a bit of bullying by Jane they changed tack – the nasty cops, in general, being replaced by the nice cops. They encouraged me, telling me I had done well in unseasonably bad weather. They told me that I looked thinner and more muscular already. And then the killer blow: they said that if I didn't go back, then they wouldn't hold it against me. I had done my best, but never mind; some people are just more limited than others.

This exquisitely aimed thrust at the heart of my pride succeeded where all else had failed. It was one thing to be shunned, it was quite another to be pitied. That was my job.

So here I was, on a bright day when summer seemed at last to have begun, heading towards the *Knife* and the resumption of my journey.

The thing is, Jane was right. It wasn't the hardship, or the wetness. The real enemy was my extraordinarily low boredom threshold, a personality trait that I share with idiots all over the world. Lock after lock and life seen from three feet below street level had added tedium to the process of travelling itself. I felt the monotony of evenings spent on my own, like the one at the Ibis, as though I was suffering from a physical pain. The swift-flowing, low-banked rivers would be different, I told myself. Taking longer breaks in places like Lincoln, Leeds and Worcester would give me something to look forward to.

The feeling that I had when I was reunited with my pretty boat and her familiar hatches was one of relief. Of course I could do this. My dad had run half-marathons at seventy, had taught himself German at seventeen so that he could read Goethe in the original. I knew now that I was not the rugged adventurer that I'd hoped to become, and that I'd always be weak and on the verge of surrender, and that there would be bad moments ahead. But what the hell? The worst that could happen would be that I'd give up again.

'Oh no, you won't,' said Jane.

CHAPTER 8

Milton Keynes

If you want to know how the English lived on the cusp of the last millennium, then visit Milton Keynes. Hidden by trees, and announced only by their pantiled roofs, lurk little settlements of one- and two-storey houses, arranged around closes and avenues in arbitrary and irregular relationship to each other.

Like the small-holdings of Saxon villagers, each little house has a garden, where hanging baskets and rockeries take the place of chickens and cabbages. These settlements are mostly called 'parks': Downhead Park, Giffard Park, Willen Park. There are no shops in them, no places of work, nothing but the houses themselves, separated by lawns and wooden fences.

The Grand Union canal enters Milton Keynes from the south, describes a great curve close to its centre, and departs to the west. For most of the ten miles that the city and the waterway keep each other company, you would never guess that England's most notorious new metropolis is within cooee-ing distance. There are a few more bridges, every few minutes there is a glimpse of an estate of tiny semis, and − once or twice − a modern dome or a pale brick public building: a sports hall perhaps.

You will not find a waterside cathedral, old wharves, an opera house, some grubby slums, or a tower topped with penthouses.

By the narrowboat marina near Peartree bridge, a crescent of two-storey houses in brick and wood sweeps down to the waterside, each with a balcony overlooking the slate waters of the canal. And that's where I made landfall. Two miles or so from Peartree is a windswept plateau where the strange heart of this city beats. In the early 70s, before the long, glassy buildings appeared up here, some 40,000 people lived in the villages and small towns of this part of Buckinghamshire. Now there are a fifth of a million, and the figure rises by 3,000 each year. New plans were announced recently that will add another 80,000 people by 2010.

Milton Keynes horrifies some sections of the media, the young ultra-sophisticated urbanites who like to eat in restaurants where syringes and bandages are part of the décor, and who would rather live in Manhattan or Tokyo than anywhere else on the planet. They loathe MK. All they know about it is that once concrete cows stood in one of its meadows, and that children on bicycles with balloons were used to advertise its virtues in the 80s.

Certainly, the main square by the station, a great, windswept, featureless expanse, is not easy to love. On the day in mid-June that I stood in it, I was the only human being around. A hundred yards off was the railway, and in another direction a series of long, low, angular buildings lined the near horizon. I had no idea what they might be.

To add to the unanswered question of what the square was doing there, was a second query: 'Why are these things in it?' For by way of decoration there was a full-sized locomotive, and a 10-foot statue of a troll, apparently picking the nose of another troll. Around the square stood twenty or so flagpoles, on which the only flags wagging in the wind were the red dragon of Wales, the cross of Norway, and the sepia company logo of that huge, ubiquitous finance, banking and insurance company that I shall call the Magnanimous and Providential. Maybe the troll was a fraternal gift from the Norwegian branch of the Mag & Prov, and mutual nose-picking was a sign of successful business partnership inside the Arctic circle. As for Wales; there was no clue. Perhaps it was Welsh week here in new Buckinghamshire. And perhaps it wasn't. Arbitrariness, I was discovering, is a characteristic of English provincial life.

From one side of the square I walked down to the Milton Keynes main drag. It is boldly utilitarian. At ground level mirrored buildings ran along its length, interrupted periodically by vast intersections with other large roads, similarly lined. Half of everything here bore the rectangular logo of the Mag & Prov, slapped discreetly on its trademark building design – russet brick, gabled roof, shiny metal and glass doors that opened with a swoosh.

Standing away to one side of each set of swooshing doors were, at last, some people: tiny knots of smokers in white shirt-sleeves or trouser suits, simultaneously happy and guilty to be spending five minutes away from reconciliation, or claims, or personnel. The Mag & Prov had given them a choice between smoking and promotion. They had chosen smoking.

The other side of the street was so far away that I could barely see it. Next to where I was standing was a strip of car parking for the Mag & Prov middle brass. Alongside that was another, thinner, raised pavement, upon which stood the occasional bus stop. Only on the far side of the bus-island did the actual road begin. Then the sequence repeated itself: bus stops, car-parking, pavement, mirrored buildings. All in all, the street was probably about 40 yards wide. And just before the tarmaced road proper, I could see a sign reading 'Pedestrians do NOT have right of way'.

These signs are famous in Milton Keynes. Motorists interpret them in only one way: if they kill a pedestrian here, then they are legally absolved. In the days of bad King John, outlaws (mostly Saxon rebels and starving villagers) could be bumped off by any old serf without blood money having to be paid. If you saw an outlaw in the woods you could just take your stave to him and knock his brains out. Eight hundred years on, if you were driving around here and some pedestrian forgot – or had ignored the clear warnings – that theirs was NOT the right of way, then it wouldn't be your fault if there was a collision. This might explain why I hadn't seen many people – pedestrians were afraid to venture out in this hit-and-run haven.

Criss-crossing beneath the big roads, however, were half-hidden miles of pedestrian underpasses, landscaped with little lawns, weeny trees and flowers. Under one of the bridges sat a blond boy of about seventeen, well-dressed and with a pleasant smile. In London the panhandlers are mostly mottled drunks with scabs on their foreheads, who say 'Wheurgh' and stick out their three remaining fingers. But here in spanking new MK we had a spanking new beggar.

And sure enough, from a converging underpass emerged a young woman who made a beeline for the blond beggar, and gave him two quid – four times the going rate in the metropolis. They had a brief conversation in which, no doubt, he told her that he was having difficulty in keeping up the payments on his Harley-Davidson, and she sympathised and then departed. So I gave him £2 as well.

I finally emerged from the semi-underground, into the bright light of midday, and found myself outside a large three-storeyed building in glass and gun-metal grey. I had walked half the length now of Midsummer Boulevard, as the main road was called. The name was clearly a homage to England past, but I'd seen no maypoles, no varlets selling tat and cucumber from stalls along the roadside, no fire-eaters or jugglers, no soldiers walking their maidens, no wandering tinkers, almost no one at all. And then I entered the building by a modest door, and all that changed.

Milton Keynes shopping centre was the first really great English mall. There are plenty of others now, but this one was the earliest attempt to provide in England what Californians and Floridians had been enjoying for decades. The entrance led me directly on to the ground floor of a large department store. Outside there had been nothing; inside there was everything. There was the melodic hum of distant muzak, accompanied by the million small electronic burps and farts of mobile phones, pagers and cash registers. A foot away were forty kinds of umbrella, from great golfing pagodas to flick-brollies that open savagely at the press of a thumb. A little bit further on, antiseptic-looking women – first cousins of air stewardesses – surrounded by crystal bottles and green liquids, sprayed perfumes at each other and grinned. Signs pointed towards food halls, menswear, cafeterias, electrical goods and exits to the rest of the shopping centre.

The department store gave on to a vast indoor hall, lined with two storeys of every kind of shop. These 50-foot high corridors were home to a straggling line of incredibly tall, etiolated cacti, which murmured slightly and bent their limbs in a non-existent breeze, beneath which the previously invisible people of Milton Keynes had magically materialised, as though teleported from their pantiled Parks, miles away. Here they all were, mums and teenagers, toddlers and grandpas, sitting on wooden benches, peering distractedly through windows, sipping cappuccinos in not quite al fresco, not quite pavement cafés, strolling slowly, singly and in groups.

Socially the mall seemed to play almost exactly the same role as did the Great Hall of a Saxon earl a thousand years before. Here were light and entertainment and company. This was the only place to be, if you didn't want to sit, alone in your wattle-and-daub hut and contemplate the cow-dung fire, or watch daytime telly. This was market, feasting, entertainment, all the attributes of the lord's dwelling place, rolled into one. Even the fire brigade and the girl guides had stalls here, and here the cancer charities sold their flags. You could live here, and never want to go anywhere else.

An older friend of mine once lost his wife in Milton Keynes shopping mall. One day in the mid-80s, he came down with a terrible headache, and went home early. No wife. She eventually rolled in – just before the kids – at 3.30. She was surprised to see him. She'd had lunch with a girlfriend at the cafeteria in John Lewis's department store. The trouble was that my friend had been in the mall that weekend, and seen that the John Lewis cafeteria was closed for refurbishment for the next four weeks. And all of a sudden he knew, without a doubt, exactly what his wife had been having for lunch. He just didn't know whose.

How many other brief encounters, I wondered, had taken place in the five department stores, twenty clothes shops, a dozen food places selling exotic breads and spices, dozens of weird sweet stalls laid out on ye olde golde-painted cartes, toyshops, mobile phone emporia, fifteen bistros, two computer vendors, eight electrical goods outlets, seven shoe-sellers that made up just the North Hall?

I still had the South Hall to explore. While most of the names were familiar, I also found out that mega-malls provide homes for a kind of store that could not survive elsewhere. I wandered, footsore, into an intriguing looking shop. At the front, near the door, it had some neat-looking gifts for kids, including Make

Your Own Volcano. Then there were presents for grown-up children, like desktop golf sets, metallic puzzles and stress toys that you could squeeze.

At the back was the adult section. And here, perfectly accessible to children, were saucy wife-swapping games with names like Foreplay. I supposed that they were strip-quizzes, or truth-or-dare games, to be played when hubby was at work in London. There were the inevitable chocolate genitalia, without which no office party in any office where cretins work would be complete. And there was a stress phallus, a soft squeezable penis, presumably for female executives who had had enough of men for one day.

Nearby was a discount bookstore. Since I would soon join the ranks of English authors, I took a look at how some of my fellow writers were doing. Not well was the answer.

'We shift what no one else wants,' the assistant told me, when I questioned him about the economics of selling new books for next to nothing. 'They're of no value to Hatchards or Dillons, so they ship them to us. Look. Two pounds for Ian Botham's trip round Britain. It can't be bad, can it?'

Yes it can, I thought, for Botham.

In the middle of the Great Hall, an exit led to a small open piazza. There a fountain splashed in the sun, while a group of bronze statues gambolled near some bushes. But these were no tributes to city founders, military heroes or dead royals. Instead there was the likeness of a dad with a small child on his shoulders, a laughing boy on a bike, a happy mum with a pushchair and a granny squeezing a stress phallus. No, I lied; she was preserved for ever walking a dog. These democratic statues – The Burghers of MK – represented the triumph of the citizen consumer; an idealised version of the very people who now sat in the square and looked at them. They said, 'We shop, therefore we are the bosses now.'

I sat in the square, beneath the modern metal Anglos, and suddenly the heretical thought came to me that this was all just fine. The food halls were full, not of ersatz rubbish but of desirable breads, of organic honey, of home-made pasta sauce, of coffees and teas from all over the world. For the first time that

I had ever seen in England, there were baby-changing facilities in the gent's toilet. The gents! No more laying junior down on a flimsy loo seat, or begging passing women to change your child for you.

And most of the folk I saw here were happy. Despite the temptations and the occasional silly shop, they didn't creep around in a zombie-like state of shopaholism, of gift addiction. They gabbled and scrutinised and smiled and wheeled their kids to and fro, and met their lovers in John Lewis's cafeteria.

I took a taxi back to the marina. As we drove I wondered, was it such a terrible thing to want to live in a place like this? The theatre was showing something by Shaw. The eleven-screen multiplex had all the latest Hollywood movies, plus a goodish British film. A classical orchestra was playing in a community hall. The Open University were hosting a festival of some kind, sponsored by the Mag & Prov. You could cycle all the way from the canal to the mall using the underpasses. And, wherever you lived, there'd be a bit of garden, a communal front lawn, a fringe of trees, and a kids' playground. Were you really to be disdained because you added your own carriage lamp, or a gnome or two?

Bright with this surprising enthusiasm, I questioned the middle-aged taxi driver about life in the new city. Was it as nice as I was beginning to think?

There was a silence, then, 'It's a good place to . . .' His voice trailed off.

I waited a moment. Then a moment more. But that was it. I tried a different question. What was it like to bring kids up here?

'Hmm,' he began. 'Well, the schools are certainly . . .' And once again his sentence petered out in a long, gradually dying sigh. I found this aggravating.

'So,' I said, 'would you say that . . .' And I too abandoned the sentence halfway. A minute passed, and the marina was now in sight.

'Would I say what?' demanded the driver, a note of irritation in his voice. I shut up. I didn't want him knocking over any pedestrians.

We arrived beside the water. I bid him good . . . Paid him his . . . And got out of the . . . The Midlands awaited.

CHAPTER 9

Danelaw

No boats followed me out of the once more invisible city. It was, at last, a bright, clear day with no wind. For two miles beyond the old town of Wolverton, the canal ploughed a straight course, the towpath becoming a reed-lined track along which the occasional dog-walker or new town jogger would accompany me for a dozen yards or so.

Like a Dutch landscape painting, the canal's shiny surface would, from time to time, reflect a single tree on the bank, outlined against the sky. On the other side, at last, the sharp, high definition of the canal faded, and meadows tumbled down to the water's side. At their soft edges, meandering down to drink or bathe, were job lots of sheep, Canada geese, cows and swans. My heart lifted, and I hummed a merry tune. I had been six days on the water, on and off, had covered ninety canal miles, and the weather was kind.

Soon I was on my own again, as the waterway bent to the right, and headed sharply north-east. Suddenly the water narrowed abruptly, and ran between low iron walls. I was on a viaduct, high above the Great Ouse river, flowing towards Bedford, East Anglia and the spot where, thirty-three years earlier, I had shivered on the bank.

A notice told me that I was paddling out of Buckinghamshire, and into Northamptonshire. And, as it happens, out of Saxon England and into the lands of the Danelaw. Sadly, there was no notice for that. Once again it was my recently acquired erudition I had to thank.

A thousand years ago, before ever a canal crossed the Ouse, a large forest called Bruneswald described a long, soft-edged rectangle across the bottom of the East Midlands. Through it ran the already ancient stones of Watling Street, built by the

Romans eight centuries earlier, heading for what is now the Watford Gap. Today, Watling Street is the A5, and it, the canal, the main south-east to north-west railway and the M1, all move towards each other, converging at a point between Daventry and Northampton. There the lorries thunder to the right, the trains blast past on the left, and – at four miles an hour – narrowboats and the odd mad canoeist tonk along below.

Along this line, to the south and west, was the Wessex of Alfred and his successors. To the east and north the land was settled by the Danes. You can tell roughly which was which because Saxon villages and towns had names that end in -ton, and Danish ones in -by, -borough and -ness.

These Danes came here first as raiders. In the late 800s King Ragnar Lothbrok was captured by Osbert of Northumbria and killed, so they say, by being thrown into a pit of poisonous snakes. These serpents can only have been specially imported from abroad; since it would take an appallingly long time to die if the pit only harboured those inoffensive native English adders. Being devoured by geraniums might be marginally quicker.

Anyhow, the angry sons of Ragnar, Halfdan and his brother, Ivar the Boneless, brought their Danish hosts over, and started some serious laying to waste of eastern England.

Hosts in those days weren't very big. A king, a dozen thegns, a berserker or two, a score of mad axemen and a hundred muddy peasants with billhooks, and you had your host. That was enough to do most of the fighting and pillaging required; there weren't any soaring, stone castles – just earthworks and palisades round the biggest places.

Of course, when it was written up afterwards by some monk in a draughty scriptorium, the tales of martial deeds got bigger and bigger, and thousands were said to have been slain on either side. Brother Propontius of Jarrow, or whoever, wanted to be famous for writing a classic, not some minor chronicle of everyday rapine. Not for the last time, the Church used its monopoly on written communication to gild the lily. To own the lily.

Then the Danes decided to stay. Loads of them shipped over from the cold, sand-duned coast of Friesia and set up home in the east. Periodically they would raid into Wessex, in an attempt to take over the whole island, and the Saxons would push them back into East Anglia and Lincolnshire. Over a century or so the country became two distinct places, one full of Athels and Eds, and the other ruled over by Grims and, of course, Cnuts.

The former land is now, essentially, known as the Home Counties. The latter was the Danelaw where the law was, um, Danish; the Home Cnuties if you will. The Saxons had witans and burghal hidage, and were a little more pro-European and conformist, whereas the Danes had wergilds and wapentakes, and tended more to belligerent individualism.

On the line between Danelaw and Wessex, the line that I was now travelling, the English language was born. There weren't any border posts on the old roads, no leathery Viking in a horned helmet (which they didn't wear in any case) would stop you at Rothersthorpe and demand to see your parchment. Years of raiding and settling had mixed the population of the area thoroughly. To the Europeanised tongue of the West and South Saxons, were added the gutturals and sentence structures of south Scandinavia. The kingly lines of England and Denmark intermarried and quarrelled and fought wars and intermarried again. Over time the Saxons became stronger, and the Danes assimilated.

That didn't stop one Saxon monarch trying to sort out a final solution to the Danish question. Ethelred the Unready – whose nickname means 'badly advised', rather than 'ill-prepared' – embarked on the last-known bout of ethnic cleansing in English history.

On St Brice's Day, 13 November 1002, Ethelred ordered that all the Danes be put to death. In large parts of the country, such as Lincoln, Nottingham, Leicester and York, Ethelred's writ did not run, and no one got massacred at all. But elsewhere, usually in places that have returned Conservative MPs since the war, some unfortunate Scandinavians did meet their makers. In Oxford, for instance, they killed Gunnhild, sister of King Sweyn of Denmark, which put her brother into pillaging overdrive.

Within sixty years, however, the rivalries between the Cnuts and the Athels became academic. The Norman occupation of England following the battle of Hastings was as thorough a change of ruling class as any Marxist could ever wish for. Out went the old aristocracies, the old priests, the old witans, and in came swanky new stone castles, Romanesque churches and trendy new names for what we eat: mutton, beef, pork and – of course – profiteroles. All the same, for 300 years after the Conquest the customs of Danelaw were different from those on the other side of the line.

So I mused as I edged along the canal. I was now entering a more populated stretch, populated by boaters, at any rate. Some, moored at picturesque spots along the waterway, were obviously from Saxon stock. Like the long green boat with gold lettering, proclaiming, 'Ted and Jenny Bottom. Exuberance. Newport Pagnell'. Or, 'Arthur and Winnie Darling. Passion-flower. Watford'.

Some of these moorings were permanent, and had been turned into bijou small-holdings, with tiny daisied lawns beside the boat, and crazy-paving paths marking the four feet from water to service path. On the lawns, grey-haired narrowboaters sat in camp chairs drinking tea, while their spouses were to be heard bustling about inside their chintzy craft, listening to Radio 2. The ones outside returned my greetings cheerily enough, but quickly went back to *Waterways World* or the latest Dick Francis.

At other spots I encountered very different canal folk. Every now and again, usually opposite where the towpath had become ragged and overgrown, I would find myself gliding past a hippie boat.

There would be no gold lettering, no lawns, no Dick Francis. On the bank an old armchair, its insides spilling out, would lie beneath a tree festooned with plastic bags – food, I imagined, hung out in the shade by someone who had no fridge. Large dogs hogged the armchairs, while rat-haired young men with no shirts fiddled with ancient machinery nearby. In the sterns of the rusty boats, beneath red and black flags flapping from bamboo poles, beautiful young women with wild, red hair would languish, smoking roll-ups or breast-feeding babies, or both, and airily ignore my hellos.

These were the spiritual descendants of the Danes. Unbiddable, rebellious and self-regarding; admirable and distressingly selfish at the same time. They wanted a world in which all lived together in communal harmony and in which they were entirely left alone. Such worlds are hard to come by.

Towards late afternoon I ported several locks, and came into the canal village of Stoke Bruerne.

On the whole, English villages pre-date canals, most of which were built between 1800 and 1900. So the cut is hidden away at the back, or on the edges of settlements. But, at some point, Stoke B. had been laid down beside the waterway, as though its main business was the canal – which, for a while, it had been. Once there had been a school here for the children of the thousands of boatmen and women who carried goods from Birmingham to London. And a little clinic, and several shops.

The main street still ran either side of a lock, requiring visitors to cross the lock gates to get from one side to the other. But now there was just a museum here (which closed at almost exactly the moment I arrived and opened at the precise second I left the next day), three pubs, two restaurants and one bed and breakfast establishment. You can buy forty sorts of beer in an average village these days, but where on earth can you find a plug?

My night was to be spent in a thin, wharf-side cottage, with a large, florid, wordless man in a tie and corduroy trousers and an invisible woman, whose voice always emanated from a next-door room. Upstairs, at the end of an ancient corridor, was a small room with the canal visible out of one window, and a cottage garden in full flower out of the other. I lay down briefly on a sagging single bed, and reflected that, though it hadn't been a bad day, how much better tomorrow would be if someone actually spoke to me.

Just about no one had. Not properly. The hippie women hadn't called me aboard to smoke ganja, to plan anti-motorway protests or to enjoy a lentil somosa; the narrowboating classes had failed to invite me to bide-a-wee and drink tea with them on their lawns. Dog-owners smiled, joggers grunted, serious walkers halloo-ed, but they all moved swiftly on. Why were the English so uncurious? This was especially puzzling, because, even after a week, I could see that I was clearly unique. There were no other canoeists on the cut; indeed, I hadn't seen anyone in an unpowered craft since leaving Camden Town.

And it wasn't just the English who were apathetic. For a couple of miles I had played catch-me-up with a boat crewed by four elderly Norwegians (the flag gave them away), who snurdly-hurdled happily away to each other as they worked the lock gates, but who became unaccountably taciturn whenever I hove into view. Maybe it was me.

I got changed, and went to the Boat Inn, bought a pint and sat outside in the early evening sunlight to reflect upon my lack of social success. When I thought about it, the only people who would initiate any kind of contact with me were the wags – waggishness constituting, perhaps, the greatest curse of the English.

I hate wags. Being a wag involves the casual slighting of friends and strangers at the minimum of cost to oneself. Related to the na-na-nanana of childhood, and much more prevalent in men than in women, it is a product of extreme self-consciousness, mixed with defensiveness and hostility. A wag takes nothing seriously. At least, nothing that someone else takes seriously. Pubs are full of wags. So are football matches. A wag will not ask you where you are going in that canoe. Nor will he offer any assistance as you pull a ton of kayak out of a canal, up a slippery 45-degree incline and round half a mile of locks. Instead he will observe – as you pass him, dragging six metres of reluctant plastic – that he thought the whole point was to paddle the thing! Haha! Hahaha!

And sure enough, at the next lock, a brother wag has – quite independently – thought up the same hilarious joke. Each time this happened to me, Mr Sunny would give the offending wag a weary, but apparently friendly, little smile. Mr Storm, however, was all for dropping the boat, grabbing him by his lapels, and hurling him into the greasy waters, with the utterance, 'Hahahhaha!' ringing in his shortly-to-be-drowned ears.

Unfortunately I was too desperate to talk to be rude to anyone. After just a few days, the slightest signal from any non-wags anywhere that they might be prepared to engage me in conversation, had me stopping and preparing for prolonged verbal contact. A slightly enthusiastic, 'Hello, there! Fine weather for it,' and I'd be alongside that vessel in a twist of hips and a flash of paddle, a host of sure-fire discussion-provokers springing to my lips. '*Potty Trained*! What an original name for a boat! And do you really come from Leighton Buzzard, as it says? I passed though there the day before yesterday. Very high, the banks round there, aren't they?'

But the English can also spot a talker a hundred miles off. I can do it myself. In any other culture the Ancient Mariner would have been asked into the wedding feast, and cajoled up to the microphone to tell his story of unusual horror. But in England we would far rather sit through a night of best-man waggishness, than hear long, gripping tales of albatrosses and curses.

So here I was, seven days into my journey, and I had become one of those garrulous incontinents that I had always sought to avoid. I was the bore that everyone could see coming. 'Oh, God,' they would groan, inwardly, 'please let him go and bother Len and Doreen on *Freedom*.' So bad had things become that, several times in the last few days, I had caught myself initiating discussions with terns, moorhens and ducks. I drew the line at swans.

So, in the restaurant that night, I felt very lonely. And, to make things worse, as I was finishing the soupe du jour, a wag, his wife and another couple arrived. The small rat-faced wag, in a yellow cardigan and red tie, stood at the door looking around the room for wagging opportunities. There was none.

They were shown to their table and Mrs Wag sat down first.

'Every time,' said the yellow wag in exasperated tones that the whole restaurant could hear. 'Every time. She'll grab the bloody window seat every time.'

He laughed and – relieved – the other man laughed too. But I could tell, from the sagging of her shoulders, that his wife wanted him dead.

Outside again, at 9 p.m., too early to go to bed and still warm and light, I supped another pint, while a few yards away the Norwegians excitedly examined the lock mechanisms for the umpteenth time. 'Snurdle hurdle?' asked the one with a beard. 'Hurdle snurdle,' one of the women replied.

Two young girls and a crop-haired boy of about seventeen passed on the other side of the canal. As they drew abreast of a swanky-looking restaurant, the boy suddenly put his hands to his mouth and shouted, for no reason that I could deduce, 'The chef's a wanker!'

The Norwegians looked at each other. 'Winker?' asked the woman. 'Wanker,' replied the one with the beard. I finished my beer, got up and sidled towards them, ready to pounce and engage them in etymological discourse on the importance of the word 'wanker' to the modern English vernacular. But these successors of Harold Bluetooth and Sweyn Forkbeard, though elderly, were too quick for me. They were already well on their way towards their boat, and bed. At ten o'clock I followed them.

CHAPTER 10

Into the Darkness

And so, into the darkness. The Blisworth Tunnel, at 3057 yards, is the second longest in the British canal system. It's one of those 'feats of engineering' that kids always quickly skip through in school history lessons, along with the Spinning Jenny and that thing for turning turnips. And then, when you get a bit older, you begin to realise that the Iron Bridge, the Great Western and the Five Lock Rise at Bingley were all genuinely a big deal. They made us what we are today. So you start watching TV programmes in which an old Northerner with a winky eye travels round old brick kilns, and you wake up in your armchair at midnight and know that youth has fled.

This particular big deal was completed in 1805, when there were just men and spades. The Grand Junction canal itself had been opened five years earlier. For those five years the boats had come to either end of Blisworth Hill, had been unloaded, and their cargoes pulled on tramlines by horses for a couple of miles. But in the year of Trafalgar the tunnel was completed. There was just room for two narrowboats to pass in the unlit tube, and no towpath for the horses. So, in the long years before the diesel engine (steam engines being, on the whole, too big for canal craft), the unpowered boats were 'legged' through by men.

While the horse was led over the top of the hill, a couple of guys with mutton-chop whiskers would lie, one on either side of the sloping roofs, and propel the boat through the mile and a half of ill-lit darkness, simply by pushing against the sides of the tunnel with their legs. It wasn't just physically demanding, it was pretty disgusting too. The roof of the tunnel itself would be perpetually wet, covered in slimy algae, and small waterfalls would occur down through the ventilation shafts bored at intervals along the way. Yet great cargoes of coal, porcelain and charcoal were transported in this fashion, by no more than a couple of pairs of muscly Victorian thighs, day in, day out, for the whole of their working lives. No need for Legs, Bums and Tums classes back then.

You can't 'leg' it through the Blisworth. Even with a head torch, the chances of successfully passing a sequence of powered boats going in the opposite direction, without landing up in inky black water a mile from safety, are pretty small. So it's forbidden. Completely. But you can hitch a ride. We sat down by the Stoke Bruerne lock, the *Subtle Knife* and I, and I stuck my thumb in the air.

A week earlier, just after I had started out, Jane had received an email from a woman who lived by the canal. My incentive for getting through the tunnel as quickly as possible was to meet her.

'Having done some days of canoe camping in the past,' her email started, 'I know having a shower is nice. So if David would like to stop by (new house just beside the canal with new landing) bath, shower and/or bed is available.' It was electronically signed by a 'Patricia Robinson'. The address was somewhere within a good half day's paddling of the end of the Blisworth.

As I waited by the lock for a lift, my mind began to range, in an undisciplined fashion, over just what kind of a person Patricia Robinson might turn out to be.

The 'in the past' suggested maturity. So I expected someone over thirty. The lack of a 'we' in the message, as in 'my husband and I know that having a shower is nice', spoke of a woman living on her own. The very fact that she was using email said that she was an educated person. And the mention of the shower meant that she wanted to see me naked.

So Patricia mark one was a thirty-five-year-old divorced nurse. After my shower, we would sit in the living-room while, over a Cointreau, she showed me old photos of her in canoe, running the Usk. The topic would evolve into the strains of paddling. 'Of course,' she'd say, matter-of-factly, 'I trained in physiotherapy, and I can tell from your posture just how tight those poor thighs are. Why don't you lie down? I'll fetch the oils.'

There was no time to enjoy this fantasy before it was replaced by its polar opposite. I am greeted at the landing stage by a woman in a mask. In a cracked voice she explains that she was mutilated in terrible car accident while travelling to London for Princess Diana's funeral. That night I awake in the strange bed to find a nude woman with a perfect body standing next to me, her face in the shadows.

'It's been so long since I met a man,' the voice croaks, and she steps into the light, to reveal that she has one eye and no nose. 'Ah, but I can see that you're repelled. What a shame. I will put the mask back on.' The next morning she drugs my Earl Grey, and keeps me tied up in her bedroom for two months, during which time she alternately ravishes and assaults me, until Jane arrives with the police. Thereafter, every day, she emails me from the secure asylum, through the gates of which she can never safely be allowed to pass again.

I was so taken by this image that I almost missed a lift. I came to as the *Bella* nosed into the lock below me, and a wiry, tall, elderly man hopped off and took his windlass to the lock's winding gear. Yes, it was fine, he told me in the tongue of the West Midlands, to stow the *Knife* on the roof. The *Bella* was travelling to the junction with the Northampton arm of the Grand Union, a mile or two beyond the tunnel, and I was welcome to stay with her till then.

The *Bella* was a hire boat, which meant that she wasn't covered in cute little stencilled paintings of flowers and vines, or brass plaques or canalesque knick-knacks. Instead she was floor-to-deck wood-imitation formica, with a functional little kitchen and sitting-room/bedroom fore, and the engine and loo aft. She was also decorated with the colours of quiet despair.

Eric, Dorothy and Kenny were friends who lived next door to each other in Rugby. Eric was the windlass-wielder. Once rangy, he had – while retaining considerable strength – now become long, creaky and cadaverous. I would guess his age as being the late sixties or even older. Eric had been a boater since long before retirement. Many happy summer's days had been spent by him and his wife, Dorothy, pottering around the canals of England, many good nights passed moored under the stars in places as exotic as Llangollen and Stratford-upon-Avon. So what could have been more natural than, when discovering that Kenny was down in the dumps, that Eric should have organised one more trip down to Stoke Bruerne and beyond?

No one said it out loud, but the trip had obviously been a disaster. Three days earlier Dorothy had come down with a gippy tummy, and had spent the best part of the journey either trying to persuade Eric to turn back, or sitting on the miniature loo next to the engine, her insides turning faster than the propeller. She was now reduced to a state of pained sullenness, foreign to someone clearly of a generally uncomplaining disposition.

The third crew member's condition was worse. A round, furry little man with glasses, Kenny was in obvious and continual pain. He moved around the boat with difficulty, and getting on and off the *Bella* required great effort. The reason wasn't hard to discern. On his wrist Kenny was wearing a copper bracelet – the universal badge of the chronic sufferer from arthritis. Kenny had it in his shoulder, in his hip, in his knee, in his ankle, in his wrist. And it was, he admitted, particularly bad at the moment. Now, unable to help with the locks or to steer the boat, Kenny was forced to sit in the front of the *Bella*, like a doleful figurehead, a squat albatross. Forget the Flying Dutchman, here was the Miserable Midlander.

So Eric's outing had gone badly wrong. A possibly final attempt to re-create past idylls was over. The spirit had been willing, but the flesh was too enfeebled, and the *Bella* was now making for Rugby again, the planned trip curtailed by three days.

As we entered the Blisworth, Eric steered, Dorothy made tea, while Kenny and I sat below and talked. As we spoke, boats passed us, their single lights winking, cyclopean in the pitch-black. It was like the tunnel of love. We rested our coffee cups on the formica table, as – encouraged by the intimate atmosphere of the shared cabin – I drew Kenny's life story from him.

Kenny had been born in Kent, and brought up near Maidstone between the wars. His dad had been a professional cricketer for the county. When Kenny *père* retired from playing the game, shortly before the war, he went into umpiring. This he gave up, Kenny said, 'because of the aggro'. Quite how bad cricket hooliganism was in the late 30s is a matter for others to research, but Kenny's dad then became groundsman and cricket coach at Rugby school, and the family moved to the Midlands. They had been offered a tied cottage by the school. They didn't take it.

'It had gas lighting,' said Kenny, 'and that wasn't what Mother was used to.'

I didn't press him on why his father was 'dad' and his mum was 'Mother', but the impression was created of a powerful woman who was the true guardian of the family's social position.

They'd all gone now. 'I don't have anyone any more,' he volunteered. 'I was married for forty-two years. And then she died in 1995. Cancer.'

He seemed so alone that I asked him whether he mightn't have preferred to go first, rather than be left behind. Kenny looked at me as though I had been watching too many American movies. 'Not really, no,' he said, rather tartly, and changed the subject.

He had been about to sell his bungalow, the one next door to Eric and Dorothy, but then, out of the blue, his daughter had left her husband, and moved in with the two children.

Kenny chuckled. 'I expected to be alone, and all of a sudden I wasn't. My daughter didn't expect to be alone, and all of a sudden she was. It's funny, really, how these things go.' Maybe not so funny, I thought, remembering my dad.

It took us forty minutes to get through the Blisworth, and a mile or so later the *Bella* moored against the towpath. I took my leave of the three unjolly boaters, who were by now sorry to see me go. It was a pattern that I'd see repeated a number of times on the journey: I'd ruthlessly talk myself into a lift, which would be reluctantly granted. Then we'd get talking, and the (usually elderly) boaters – and the women in particular – would be surprised then gratified to be asked questions by someone young enough to be their own son. There'd be tea and biscuits, and then – by the time we had to part – invitations to stay a bit longer, or suggestions of meeting up further along.

Back in the *Knife* and chugging along at a decent lick, I began to notice how little estates of Barratt's houses were now periodically, and for no obvious geographical reason, putting in an appearance at the canalside. Some of the semi-detacheds would give directly on to the water, a little series of yellow stone steps coming down from the house, the patio occasionally populated by a Narnia-style lamp-post or an iron flamingo. Sometimes a housewife would be in the back garden hanging out her smalls, and would carefully not look in my direction as I passed.

Four or five miles from my rendezvous with fate and Mrs Robinson, just by a boatyard, I came across a huge billboard situated directly on the left bank of the canal and invisible to anyone except those on the canal itself. In large black letters on a white background it said:

THIS IS A WORKING BOATYARD, AND HAS BEEN FOR 25 YEARS. THIS MEANS THE SOUNDS OF BOATS BEING MADE AND REPAIRED. SO THERE IS NO POINT IN COMING TO LIVE OPPOSITE AND THEN COMPLAINING ABOUT THE NOISE. WHY NOT LIVE SOMEWHERE ELSE?

Sure enough, there on the right-hand side of the canal, was a brand-new terrace of grey-brick houses, with little balconies overlooking the waters of the Grand Union. 'Come and abide in the waterside tranquillity of Waterlily Close,' publicity flyers and estate agents' blurbs had doubtless said. 'Commune with the vole and heron. Watch the sun rise over the reeds. Experience perfect silence, broken only by the rushing wings of the kingfisher.'

And then, early one Sunday morning, when all that one ought to hear is the gentle plashing of the moorhens, an infernal metallic din fills the distance between Wharf Cottage and the boatyard, just ten watery yards away. It's the sound of Fred, Darren, Wayne and Jason Boggins working on an emergency repair to a narrowboat from Alevechurch. And they were here first.

Towards late afternoon, at a spot where small cottage gardens came down to the water's edge, I saw her standing on the bank; a woman with short greying hair, spectacles, sensible shoes and slacks.

It was Mrs Robinson. No mask, no lascivious licking of the lips, no obvious mental imbalance. She helped me draw the *Knife* up the bare lawn of a brand-new glass-and-brick bungalow, all windows and aspect, to an area of scrub and gravel in between her garden, and the raised bank of the old A5, the Roman Watling Street.

Once inside the bungalow I followed her into the kitchen-diner, padding damply across a vast expanse of varnished wood floor. There was practically no furniture inside, and very little of the usual detritus of life: bins, plates, photographs, ornaments, bookshelves. On a small desk stood an open lap-top, the one from which the emails emanated. The house, like Patricia herself, was clean, economical, hospitable, withdrawn and, above all, melancholy.

'Do you want a shower?' Patricia asked me, in the accents of North America. She showed me to a sparkling new bathroom. 'You must tell me whether it's any good or not,' she said, adding, 'I've never used it.'

It was better than good. The shiny head disgorged a power-stream such as only the Americans install, one which washes away both dirt and sins, leaving you smelling only of jojoba. As I lathered myself from nape to knee, no strange footstep halted outside the door, no foreign hand tried the door, no blade sliced through the shower curtain. It was all spectacularly safe. And by the time I had changed, Patricia had set a small table with food enough for an Oxford boatcrew: a whole melon, a huge chicken casserole, an entire Black Forest gateau, and a bottle of white wine.

We sat down to eat, and – after telling her a little about my journey – I asked her about how she came to be here, alone, in a bare house by an English canal, an ocean away from her home. The story that this kind, intelligent, almost puritanical woman told me was one of the saddest that I had ever heard.

Until eighteen months before, she had been married to a man called Bill. 'We were college sweethearts, actually,' she smiled. After marrying in their early twenties Pat and Bill had gone to live in Ohio (or Ohi-a, as she pronounced it). She had become a planner, employed mostly by the State authorities, and Bill was an architectural consultant. They worked hard, and – like many American professionals – believed in God and Republicanism. Two children were born – a boy and a girl – and Bill designed and built them all a house in the woods.

By the mid-90s the kids had gone to college, but Mom and Dad had not let up working. Both of them would rise from their beds in their Le Corbusier-style home at 5 a.m., and then drive for two hours in opposite directions, to be at the office on time. It was rare for either of them to get home before eight or nine in the evening.

'It was in the fall of 1996,' said Patricia, 'that Bill began to say that he didn't feel right. He was tired all the time, and he had a pain in his back, and it just wouldn't shift. We went to a number of doctors, but they all said pretty much the same thing: that he was over-exerting himself, and should cut down on the hours and on the driving.'

She paused, and gazed out of the window and over the canal. 'Well, finally, we'd had enough of this. We could see that something was wrong, even if they couldn't. Bill went to a new guy in town. This one did what none of the others had done, and insisted on a blood test.' She sighed. 'It was lung cancer. Three months later, Bill was dead.'

Her voice was steady and there were no tears, but there was a desolation about her story all the same.

'It's funny,' she said, 'but I never considered for a moment that he would die before me. I always thought it would be me to go first. I was so accident-prone. I broke my foot in King's College Chapel in Cambridge once, just looking around the place. Another time, when we were canoeing in Ohia, I fell on some rocks and broke my shoulder. It still doesn't work properly. I was the clumsy one, Bill was the capable one, you know? I could easily imagine life for him without me, but I never once thought about life for me without him.'

With thirty-five years of mutual dependency now gone, Patricia laid some of the blame on those doctors. 'I think they just didn't care quite enough,' she said, very carefully. 'You know, they were mostly Catholics, and I guess that they just thought it was fate. People have gotta die. When they do, it's God's will.'

Patricia was not a Catholic. She and John had been very white, very Anglo and very Protestant. As we talked into the evening, and as it went dark over the water, it became clear that she had little time for immigrants with their different moral values, or for angry blacks with their affirmative action. There was a small-town Utopia that Patricia and Bill had managed to create, one of gentility, restraint, politeness, conformity and toil. And now it had been lowered, with Bill, into a deep hole in an Ohioan churchyard, and was lost to Patricia for ever.

'Bill and I would plan big expeditions,' Patricia smiled. 'Like yours, I guess, but not so long. We'd take the kids camping in open canoes when they were small. Then all that got a little strenuous for us old folks, so one year we came over to England, hired ourselves a canal boat. And we loved it, you know? Bill adored all that messing about with engines and stuff, and I liked the scenery and the history. So we began to come back year after year. Then Bill said that we might as well buy a boat here, and let it out for the weeks when we were in the States. So we did, and we moored it at Warwick. No, we used to spend the evenings planning out the next route. Now I have nothing to plan for.'

After Bill's death, the house in the woods became too much for Patricia. The money had stopped coming in, and everything started to break down. The old four-wheel drive car that Bill used to service himself conked out and had to be abandoned; the Heath-Robinson-style central heating system that Bill alone had known how to operate had given up the ghost, and repairs had been estimated at over $10,000. Patricia decided to sell up, and look for something smaller in Ohio, where her son lived. But complex zoning laws made it impossible to find a house small enough. She had found a place next door to her daughter and her son-in-law and their small children in Washington DC.

'But when I told Kathy about it, her face went all kinda closed. And I knew she didn't want it. She said that she'd talked to her husband Joel, and that he'd said that every time they had pizza delivered, I'd be thinking about how they wasted money, and that that would make him uncomfortable. So I didn't go ahead.'

Given Patricia's puritanical tendencies, Joel was probably right. But it was an irony that this woman, with her emphasis on family and duty, should find that her daughter didn't want her as a neighbour, even after the death of someone so close to them both.

Six months after the funeral she'd paid a visit to England, and taken the boat from Gayton to Warwick. As they'd passed through the Gap, she'd spotted the bungalow, still being built by the side of the canal. It had barely taken a week to complete the sale. Now she lived here, 3,000 miles away from her children and grandchildren. Did they think of her, these days, when they ordered pizza?

'I have the minimum of belongings,' she told me, explaining the sparseness. 'I don't believe in things, in goods, any more. They clutter the place up, and they'll just complicate matters for the children when I die.'

Patricia here and Kenny on the *Bella* offered quite a contrast. They had both been bereaved. Perhaps it was class or it might have been nationality, but where one was fatalistic and downbeat about loss, the other was angry and unreconciled. To Kenny death had been a thing that had happened; for Patricia it was the beginning of a pain that would never go away.

That night, under the clean duvet in the dustless spare bedroom, I dreamed about my dad. I was outside the door of a strange, but familiar house. A voice – a woman's voice – said, 'Your father's in there, you should knock.' I knew he couldn't be, but I knocked all the same. He opened the door, his hair fluffy white, wearing a striped shirt, and a shy smile on his face. My dad put his thin arms out to me, and we hugged each other and kissed each other on both cheeks. And I thought to myself that his face was bristly and that this was something that we had never done while he was alive. I felt good.

The day ended as it began: in a long tunnel, with invisible boats passing in the dark.

CHAPTER 11

Towards the Great River

I set off from Patricia's house slightly bruised and low from my dream and the previous day's brushes with death. But I consoled myself with the thought that if I was going to die soon, it was not likely to be on a canal. Canals are rarely more than twenty feet wide or four and a half feet deep; that's why narrowboats have such shallow draughts and are, as a consequence, so unstable.

But my first great river was coming up soon. And rivers – as autistic Bob from Canoeright had reminded me – are very different beasts. Rivers are natural, elemental, unpredictable things. Because they flow, rather than just are, they are full of tricksy currents, eddies and undertows. They were there, cutting valleys through the chalk and clay, a hundred thousand years before the first man-made waterway. We humans have been successfully drowning in them for millennia. Where a canal surface looks calm because the water in it is calm, a river surface can appear still and inviting while concealing sudden drops or rocks. After nine days and 110 miles I had turned northwards on to the Leicester arm of the Grand Union, and in three more days would arrive at its junction, near Nottingham, with the Trent, England's longest navigable river.

I had no idea what to expect. The Avon had been a disaster for me, and – thanks to Jim – I had ended up drinking quite a large amount of it. I had mastered a section of the Thames well enough, but only after dunking myself in it. On both occasions I had had people with me to guide me to shore, and to make certain that I survived. But there was no Jim, or even a Wo Chung on hand now. The chances were that, if I capsized, there would be no one around to hear or to help. I was getting increasingly scared; the Trent was keeping me awake at nights, and rousing me early in the mornings.

A couple of days after leaving the widow, I walked away from the canal, leaving the *Knife* basking in the early sun, until I came to the village of Naseby in Leicestershire.

Near the top of a sloping field of corn, enclosed by a low railing, I found what I was looking for: an obelisk-shaped grey monument, about twelve feet high. Here, also on a June day, 355 years earlier, the black-ringleted and moustachioed Sir Thomas Fairfax had stood and watched as the Cavaliers of Prince Rupert had charged up at the Parliamentary cavalry to Fairfax's left. By the time the battle was over, Fairfax, Cromwell and the New Model Army had won the decisive victory of the first English Civil War.

Beneath the obelisk was a fresh posy of flowers, and a card, inscribed, 'In remembrance of those who died for their beliefs'. Spread out Gulliver-like a yard or so away were the two huge shapes of the people who had obviously left the card and were now sunbathing, mountainously, with their hands shading their eyes.

One was a man in a red shirt. The shirt was quarrelling with the waistband of his tan trousers, and disclosing the pale flesh of a belly as full as that of a pregnant woman reaching term. The other form was that of a lady in a voluminous white dress, cut low enough to reveal a bosom the size of Norfolk. She sat up as I approached, and smiled a toothy smile.

'We laid that wreath, Johnny and me,' she said, proudly, indicating the belly. 'It's in memory of the Parliament side, our side. We're members of the Sealed Knot, Colonel Cloudesley's regiment.'

The Sealed Knot is another of those things that I love about England. The men and women who belong to it re-create the battles of the English Civil War, spending their weekends dressed up as pikemen, musketeers, cavalry or, in the case of the gals, camp followers. And they care about the politics of it, too. The Parliamentarians know what they fight for, and – in the words of Cromwell – love what they know: democracy, equality, freedom. The Cavaliers are all tradition and heritage. Their battles embody the two great moving spirits of second-millennial England.

'Yeah, well I started whorin' for the Parliamentary cause in about 1988,' Ms Norfolk told me. 'It was just an occasional thing at first, but I met a lot of good people, and started to take it a bit more serious. I've fought all over England. Done Naseby three times. And then Johnny and me, we met at the siege of Nantwich. I was selling me wares on a street corner, and there he was.'

'Yep,' confirmed Johnny, sitting up, 'and my first words to 'er were "How bloody much?"' And they both laughed.

''Cos my bosoms,' she said, indicating most of the space between us, ''ave been much admired by many of the men of the regiment.'

'Not Puritans, then,' I observed.

East (and West) Anglia wobbled happily. 'Men are men, aren't they, when all's said and done, Roundhead or Cavalier?'

Johnny grunted in agreement.

Beyond Leicester the valley filled up with vistas of huge power stations, their chimneys announcing the approach to the Trent. Every now and again I would pass a special project boat, hired out to a youth group or a community organisation, full of youngsters in regulation red sue-proof life-jackets.

Before hitting the main length of the Trent, I stopped in the late afternoon at a marina on the Beeston canal, which runs through the heart of Nottingham. It was a Sunday, and a grubby-faced boy in an old Nottingham Forest replica football shirt, astride a battered BMX bike, watched me with a disconcerting, unblinking stare, as I stowed my gear beside a beached cruiser. He was obviously the son of a grimy couple in a dingy boat, moored in oily perpetuity in the shadow of the concrete road bridge. Taken together, they were like something out of the stricken Appalachians.

Where to leave the poor old *Knife* overnight was one of my recurring problems. It was impossible to trundle her more than a few hundred yards at a time without becoming exhausted or a severe hazard to traffic. She would not fit in the porter's cubby-hole at a hotel, nor could she travel in a lift and share my room with me. She was far too long for the hallway of a

B&B, nor could she be safely left on a towpath while I looked for somewhere to camp in an adjoining field. She was beautiful enough for vandals to want to defile her, valuable enough for thieves to consider stealing her, and her hatches were all eminently available for little fingers to open and remove my belongings.

Most nights I negotiated a safe berth for her in the corner of a locked marina or garage, while I packed what I could in the knapsack and went off for the night. When I camped, it was only where I could have her lying safe beside my tent, a length of line snaking out from her stern, through the tent flap and under my pillow. Her security took precedence over all else.

Worried for her, I tried to curry favour with the hillbilly father.

'Nice boat,' I said to the shabby, weedy man, who wore a dirty boiler suit and spectacles held together by Selotape.

'No it en't,' he contradicted me, without rancour. 'But I'll keep an eye on yer stuff for yer.'

All along the banks of the canal, as I walked into Nottingham central, there were new buildings. Ten years ago the whole area had been covered in disused factories, corrugated iron and broken fences. But now the towpath was a promenade for the young and fit, its length lined with new eateries, housing estates, the local offices of the Magnanimous and Providential.

On a bluff above the water was Nottingham castle. Opposite this place from which, according to legend, the marauding Norman tax-raisers had once ventured forth, by magnificent irony, a new castle had arisen. The lower fortress, a vision in red brick and white stone, with rounded glassed towers, declared itself to be nothing less than the regional HQ of the Inland Revenue.

I crossed a bridge, and climbed the hill into Nottingham town. My route took me past two ghastly monolithic 60s shopping areas, complete with multi-storey carparks and blank walls. Some day soon these desolations of past planning errors will be resurrected as marvellous examples of a more optimistic age. For the time being I was glad to see them gradually give way to areas of bars, pubs and decent shops, set in older rows of houses. Here, garrulous gaggles of early-evening drinkers, mostly boys and young men, were gathering. It was still too early for fighting.

In the windows of the hotels and clubs, posters proclaimed Nottingham not to be, whatever else it was, the spelling capital of England. 'Take the Fitness Challange', suggested one. 'Capachino: £1', boasted another.

At the Stakis Hotel, Nottingham ('Book now for Father's Day'), I switched on the TV. 'Songs Of Praise with a cricketing theme, brought to you by Christopher Martin-Jenkins', was followed by Prince Edward and his bride-to-be being interviewed for forty minutes by a simpering BBC sycophantette, while sitting, hand-in-hand, in the sunlit garden of their vast new house. Outside my window a fantastic dusk reddened the skies, silhouetting a dozen church spires against the gold.

I drifted off to sleep feeling virtuous. It had taken two attempts, but I had conquered the Grand Union canal. And it had been all my own work . . .

CHAPTER 12

Middle Englanders

I woke at six in a state of complete panic. Today was the day. By eight I was back at the marina (where the grimy family was still abed), changed into my paddling togs, and minutes later was in the narrow, lager-can-flecked canal, heading for the T-junction confluence with the mighty Trent. Three miles on, I came to the Meadow Lane lock, beyond which was the river itself. But first I had to get to it.

My problem was that the water level at the canal side of the lock was much higher than that in the river below. So the lock itself was a modest affair from one side, but huge, compared to most on the canals, on the other. With no one in sight to help me, I struggled out at a high bank, pulled the canoe up out of the water, and slid her on to her wheels. Then I pulled the five and a quarter yards of blue plastic up to the lock-gate arms. These had no room behind them round which to wheel the *Knife*, so she had to be lifted four feet into the air and let down on the other side.

But I now had to get down to the river's edge. To do that I dragged and pushed the canoe up a small rise, then threaded her through a railing. A balustraded walkway now turned a sharp corner to the left, and I found myself on a high metal balcony overlooking the Trent, more than thirty feet below.

To negotiate these obstacles I had to manhandle the *Knife* at about shoulder level, slipping her slowly along the railing above the brown waters, always with the feeling that she was about to slide out of my grasp and tumble into the river below – and that would be the end of it. So I clung on with all my strength, my shoulder blades popping out of my back with the effort, my fingers elongating like something in a cartoon. Until, finally, I emerged on to a narrow, sharply descending ramp, where the boat, now back on her wheels, threatened to run away from me again.

Holding on as hard as I could, so that she and I went at roughly the same measured speed, I made my way, stumbling and cursing, down to a metal and rubber pontoon two feet above the river. There, under the astonished gaze of a couple on a cruiser, I sat, exhausted and emotional, drank some water, took my mobile phone out of its waterproof sheath, and warded off the scary moment by calling everyone who was at home: Jane, Sarah, my mum – even my editor, Andy. But it was still only eleven o'clock, and he was out at lunch.

Only then, impatience defeating fear, did I flop in, push off, and head for the right bank opposite, where the stadium of Nottingham Forest football club towered above the water. Here the river was more than five times as wide as the widest canal, and I waited for the dreadful moment when an unexpected cross-current would pull me, irresistibly, towards some maelstrom or submerged obstacle.

It didn't happen. The water was sweet and predictable. Nothing tugged or pushed unexpectedly at my poor old boat, there were no giant vessels creating terrifying wash; just a sailing dinghy, and the odd narrowboat chugging down-river. Within ten minutes I had left the city behind.

But not my problems. Rivers have locks on them too. These are not the little windy locks of the canal system, but big, hunky locks, with high granite walls like ship docks, great electrically operated gates, and dedicated lock-keepers in little huts that look like signal boxes. These locks sit across one part of the river. Then there is a man-made island, and across the other part there will invariably be a loudly rushing weir, waiting to circulate any canoeist who is fool enough to try to shoot it, in a violent water rotation at its foot, known to canoeists and hydrologists as a 'stopper'.

Canoes are theoretically even less welcome in river locks than in their canal baby brothers. The British Waterways canon is set resolutely against unpowered craft using its locks, for safety reasons. Yet there were six more for me to pass through on my way up the Trent. It would be far better if I could hitch lifts with other, powered, journeyers down the great river.

About two miles beyond the confluence I came to Holme lock. On the left orange buoys marked the approach to the weir, whose din I could now hear. To my right some slimy stone steps came down from a high dock to water level. With difficulty I landed at these, getting my backside wet as I did so, and pulled the canoe precariously up the eight or so feet to the top.

Below me there was a shiny green narrowboat tied up close-by, waiting to go through the lock. And here I met Derek and Lesley Flinders and their bull mastiff, Chloe – the embodiment of what this country is becoming; the true apotheosis of Middle England.

Derek had just leapt off the roof of the green boat and was wrapping a rope round a bollard. He looked at me – 6 foot 1, burly, blue baseball cap, shorts, sodden plimsolls, life-jacket – the very picture of adventurous late manhood, and asked me how far I was going.

'Burnley,' I told him, adding hopefully, 'what about you?'

'Oh, nothing like as far as that, just up to the next lock and then back. Otherwise I'd offer you a lift. You look a bit bushed.'

I assured him that just getting me through this one would be wonderful. So we tied *The Subtle Knife* on the roof of the green boat, and I went below to meet Lesley and to have a cup of tea.

As we ploughed gently down the Trent, past old wharves constructed from scaffolding, ancient rusting conveyor belts that had once fed gravel into the holds of river-going barges, I learned some more about my hosts.

Derek was fifty-eight, he told me, and had got early retirement and a big pay-off four years earlier when the vehicle inspectorate had been privatised.

'I was a skilled engineer,' he said, 'but they needed to lose posts, and I was over fifty, so they let me go.'

'Was that a bit rough for you?' I asked.

He laughed. 'It was the best thing that ever happened to me. When our Lesley was offered early retirement this year, I told her to take it. Who wants to work till sixty, when you can stop and still live well? Lesley's fifty-two, and she retired a fortnight ago, and now we've got the whole summer to look forward to.'

Lesley also looked good. A petite woman with brown hair, and hardly a trace of grey, she brought some more tea up to the stern, where Derek was steering, and offered a correction to his rosy picture.

'Mind you, Derek, you were getting a bit housebound at first.' She turned to me. 'He was. Didn't really know what to do with himself. That's why we bought Chloe,' she indicated the muscular heap lying on the roof, 'to get Derek out of the house. And it worked. The only trouble is that you have to keep on eye on her when we're on the boat, 'cos she has this habit of jumping into the water when you're not looking.'

Derek and Lesley had bought the *Charmaine* in 1996, and he had spent the last three years doing it up himself. He'd reconditioned the engine, and decorated the interior, lining it in a discreet, Scandinavian-style light pine. There were no fussy decorations or polished brass geegaws and certainly no formica. But having just finished it, he was, of course, about to start all over again. He was going to lengthen it, cutting the whole boat in half, adding a middle section, and then joining it all together again. When it was finished there would be an extra cabin, and friends could join them on their trips.

The pair now lived in a semi, on the banks of the Erewash canal, west of Nottingham, with the boat moored at the end of their garden. They had become part of a new generation of English retirees, part settled, part nomadic, like the trailer pensioners of America who follow the sun from one caravan park to another.

They'd recently been to an exhibition of narrowboats at Braunston, near Birmingham, where they'd met many couples like themselves.

'One lot,' said Derek. 'They'd sold their 'ouse, and they spent six months in Benidorm in hotels, and six months on the canals in their boat.'

'And there were a pair,' added Lesley, 'who have a mobile home in Florida and a boat here. It's not uncommon now.'

This is not a world that gets written about much in the British press. The retired are not sexy. Almost no advertising is directed at them, unless it's life assurance or funeral insurance being sold by a former star of 'Z–Cars'. They're never talked about on TV, except as poverty-stricken oldies (which most of them are not). But as I'd travelled around England on a week day when everyone else was at work or in school, I soon realised the numbers, financial clout and potential political power of the over-fifties. It was one of the big surprises and it constitutes one of the country's great secrets from itself.

At Braunston, Lesley had been particularly taken with an 80-foot craft, which they were shown round by a bikini-wearing bimbo. 'It had an office,' said Lesley, 'right in the middle with a desk and computers, and those Armalite floors, or whatever you call 'em.'

But what chiefly marked the couple out as New Middle Englanders was not their retirement, but what had happened to their children, Danny and Gemma.

'Our Danny was the first in our family ever to go to uni,' said Derek proudly. 'And after he'd got his engineering degree, he stayed on to do his Masters. It cost me, mind. Five thousand pounds a year I worked it out.' Then it was Gemma's turn. Her degree was in business administration. And she too had stayed on to do a Masters. 'Over four years it's set me back forty thousand pounds,' Derek said. He smiled. 'But it's got to be worth it, hasn't it?'

Derek himself had left school at sixteen, and served an apprenticeship. He and Lesley had belonged to what sociologists usually call the skilled working class – their parents would have lived in two-up, two-downs near a factory or pit – but their children were, without doubt, middle class. It was another feature of the quiet English revolution of the past decade. Where once one in ten of teenagers went on to Higher Education, by that last summer of the millennium, it was heading for four out of every ten. Soon it will be half. And with education came changes in attitude. Unprompted, Derek began to reflect on race.

'I think I have been prejudiced,' he admitted. 'But I'm changing me mind. I used to work with West Indians, and I thought they were lazy. You know, couldn't be bothered. Then my daughter brought back a Mauritian boy from college.'

'Nice boy, very handsome,' smiled Lesley.

'Yes, a decent boy. A bit fly, maybe. And I thought to myself that I could soon have a coloured son-in-law, and that the grandkids could be brown. That was a little uncomfortable, but then I thought, would that be so dreadful? I'm still not completely sure about it, mind you.

'Anyway, I was driving through Leighton Buzzard last week, and there's a bit of argy-bargy getting into one lane and out of another, and this coloured driver hoots me, you know? And I find myself saying back to him, "Get out of it, you bloody wog!" Only I didn't say "Get out of it". And then I thought to myself, "Why are you saying this, Derek, what does it matter what colour he is? That could be our Gemma's bloke." So I don't think I'll do that again.'

In fact, the only people he and Lesley didn't like were the New Age boaters, with their unseaworthy boats, their rats-tails hair and, especially, their untethered dogs.

'One just leaped off the boat and had a go at our Chloe. I had words!' Lesley said.

All this time Nottinghamshire had been rolling by, with the remnants of Sherwood Forest off to the left. I realised that we had not passed under a single bridge since leaving Nottingham, the Trent still presenting a formidable barrier to movement by road or rail. By now it had come on to rain gently, and the pair insisted on taking me on to Gunthorpe, my resting place for the night. There, a half a mile upstream from another great lock, we unloaded the canoe, and said our farewells. We were reluctant to leave each other, these curious and intelligent denizens of Middle England and I. 'Send us your book!' shouted Derek as he cast off. 'We could do with a laugh!'

Soon I had other things on my mind. Up till now I had always managed to stay in a B&B, an inn or – as in Milton Keynes and Nottingham – a swanky city centre hotel. But this was to be my first night under canvas. I had phoned ahead to The Anchor public house, where a campsite was advertised. Could I just turn up? 'Aye,' replied a sullen man, 'well, you'd better book, because you never know how many others might be coming. We're only allowed so many tents, you know.'

Gunthorpe has three pubs, two restaurants and no shops, its one post office opening from nine till one on three weekdays. Beyond the carpark of one of these pubs was the large flat field of the campsite. On which there was not one other tent visible. Like the B&Bs of Harefield, these other tent-pitchers were just another figment of the English provincial mercantile imagination. I trundled the canoe into a corner away from the carpark, and began to unload.

The only other occupant of this drizzle-sodden expanse was a sinister, dirty, brown camper van, which sat, brooding, in the far corner. Through its grimy windows I could just see two heads – one blonde the other dark – bobbing in inaudible conversation.

It took me fifteen minutes to pitch my bright yellow tent in the rain. I laid out the sleeping bag, and then changed, lying down, struggling into clean, dry clothes. But within half an hour both the heat and the stink were overpowering. Sweat mingled with the chemical used to line the fly-sheet to produce (I swear, unaccountably) something very like the scent of stale semen. I had forgotten, in my yearning for the outdoor life, that, in summer, modern tents quickly get to smell as though five gorillas have been holding a wanking contest inside.

I emerged into the rain. The brown camper van was still there, the two heads still bobbing. I took *Middlemarch* (p.53) and went into the pub. There were still five hours to go before it would be dark enough to sleep. I made a pint last an hour.

At seven o'clock I presented myself at the swish restaurant that tucked itself between the two big pubs. They eat early in the provinces, and the first customers were already on to the entrées. I was found a seat in the large back room of the restaurant, on my own on a raised dais. The menu and mineral water were brought by the sedate, unsmiling staff, and I settled down to a tedious and lonely supper. But things soon picked up.

After twenty minutes I was joined on my level by a party of four: ultra-respectable Mum, Dad, son and daughter-in-law, all dolled up and on agonising best behaviour. Next to the window a young, flabby businessman and a desiccated, spidery German with a pipe sat down and began to discuss their business. When the menu came the topic shifted to what the German might find to eat. He ran a thin finger down the list.

And asked, in a loud voice, 'Und vot is zis hake?'

'Hake? It's a white fish. Flaky. Not as heavy as cod. But I'm no expert.'

'Und monk's fisch?'

'Monkfish. White, heavier flesh. Thicker. Not making a very good job of this, am I?'

'Und scallops?'

'Scallops. Um, white flesh. Yellow inside. Seafood. You know, like oysters.'

'Have they, perhaps, any Smildehildefisch?'

'Smildehildefisch? Dark flesh? Plump? Fattish fish? Might that be turbot? Yes? Do you want turbot?'

'No, thank you. I vill have votever you have.'

To make this terrible conversation even vaguely bearable, I tried to construct hinterlands for these two – a bit like creating prehistoric monsters from tiny deposits of DNA. They were, I decided, in the chair-lift business, and millions were riding on this one encounter. Otherwise, surely, the flabby one would have reached out with both hands and gripped Herr Schtick round his scrawny throat.

This pleasing thought was interrupted by a commotion just below. The table beside the dais had been occupied, a few minutes earlier, by a couple on some kind of tryst. The man was about fifty, with a close-clipped pepper-and-salt beard, a striking black-and-white checked jacket, black polo shirt, and one of those boyish faces that tell you that his name, too, is Nick, and that he's never really grown up. Nick had been knocking it back, and been speaking in low but expressive tones to a woman of much the same age. Let us call her Nadine.

Time was not being kind to Nadine, despite her considerable efforts. Sensibly, she had chosen black for her evening out, but had made the mistake of going for tight, rather than slightly looser. Her nut-brown arms were hung with heavy gold jewellery, her raven hair hung down on either side of her deeply tanned face. She was a proud woman, I thought, and she deserved full marks for trying.

And maybe that's what he told her. Because, just after he had made a particularly emphatic comment in his low voice, his mouth setting in a self-satisfied little smile, she stood up, leaned over the table and – with cracks that shattered the polite conversation in one corner and the endless discourse about fish in the other – landed two great slaps, first with the flat and then with the back of her right hand, *whack*, *whack*, one on either cheek of the smug face in front of her.

Nadine then gathered up her handbag, and began to walk off. However, she'd barely got a yard before she seemed to recall that she had further business to transact. Returning to the table she took her large glass, already filled to the brim with red wine, lifted it high, and poured it slowly and deliberately over the man's head. Now satisfied, she walked out.

The bearded man just sat there, unmoving, the wine coursing in purple streamlets over his face and discolouring the white in his jacket, looking down at the tablecloth. Then, nonchalantly, he lit a long cigarette, and puffed on it.

Only now did I look around at my fellow diners. They were transfixed. The respectable matron, especially, was round-eyed with almost unspeakable pleasure. She caught my glance, and smiled a conspiratorial smile. The chair-lift man gave me a wink. The waiters too were obviously delighted, gathering at the door to the kitchens, nudging each other and exchanging gay little grimaces, until, at last, one of them approached the wine-soaked diner and asked if he was all right.

'Yes,' said the man, fatalistically, 'but I don't think I'll bother with the main course.'

I decided to dispense with a hinterland; it was already the most enjoyable meal I'd had so far. Like my fellow diners, I left the restaurant happy and fulfilled.

It was still only 9.15 p.m. I passed the campsite on my way back to the pub. The brown camper van had not moved, and nor had its occupants. But outside the empty field the whole waterfront area was now crawling with bikers, who must have assembled outside the two pubs while I was eating. Now they watched each other rev up uninteresting motor-bikes, or swagger around in polished leathers. Some were very young, some were wizened and grey. They were, I thought, sitting with my pint and *Middlemarch* open at page 61, the least threatening bikers that I had ever seen.

At 10.30 I made my way back across the damp field. The brown camper van was still there, a dim light now illuminating the two heads. But now it had been joined by a rusty red Transit in the other corner of the field. And I wondered what kind of distorted citizens decided to camp out next to a Nottinghamshire pub carpark on a wet Monday night in mid-June. And what they liked to do at midnight.

I cleaned my teeth against the hedge, peed nervously in the same place, struggled into the tent, into the sleeping bag, made a pillow of my clothes, zipped myself in. And waited for sleep.

One by one, at intervals of three minutes, as regularly as labour contractions, the bikers revved their engines and zoomed off back to their homes in West Bridgford and Rushcliffe. By midnight they'd all gone. Fitful sleep came over me.

From 2 a.m. I awoke about every half hour, as my bones were dragged down by gravity through my flesh, and pinned the delicate nerves of my shoulders, pelvis and back against hard, flinty things in the ground – things I hadn't seen when pitching the tent.

Another thing I'd forgotten since I'd last done this: the impossibility of actually sleeping in a tent without the aid of alcohol or other substances. I would change positions, or stuff clothes beneath me at the tenderest point, only to become aware of

the strange and unanticipated truth that Gunthorpe had somehow positioned itself under one of the great international night
flightpaths of the world, and that 747s liked to show off what their
engines could do, 33,000 feet above my little bit of canvas.

At 4 a.m. I remembered what a big day it was tomorrow, how
epic my journey was to be, and how vital it was that I was properly
rested and refreshed. And I nearly wept.

CHAPTER 13

Deliverance

By 7 a.m. the sun was high enough to turn the tent into an Indian sweat-lodge. I felt awful. I rolled out on to the dew-wet grass and, breathing deeply, dazed by the early morning sharpness of it all, peed into the hedge again. The camper van was still silent; the Transit had gone some time during the night.

Gunthorpe had little to offer the hungry traveller. The last of the commuters were opening their garage doors, or driving out towards Nottingham. The parish noticeboard ('St Nicholas's services, including Kidzone!') advertised the services of a peripatetic aromatherapist, and practically nothing else. Three pubs, two restaurants and an aromatherapist! The inhabitants of Gunthorpe would be nothing if not well-oiled. After walking a mile or so down the road I came to a garage that sold sandwiches and water. I wondered where those who could neither drive nor walk long distances did their shopping.

When I got back, the couple from the camper van had now, at last, emerged. They were not dope fiends, itinerant alcoholics or psychos on wheels.

'We're over here looking for mobile homes,' the man explained. 'You get much more choice in the East Midlands than you do near Brum.'

And here was my next lesson: the ever-present gap between my expectations of people, and what they were really like.

Four great river locks stood between me and my destination, which was the legendary lock at Cromwell, where – after a weir the size of Niagara – the Trent turns tidal.

The first was right in front of me, and I could now walk round it; it was flat and hard all the way. The third and fourth were at the town of Newark, and the chances were that I could port those as well.

The second, at a place called Hazelford, however, looked dodgy even on the map. I called up the lock-keeper and asked him how I might approach his high gates. He wasn't sure, and he didn't much care. For a fair distance up-stream of his box, the banks were very high, he said, and there were no pontoons for me to use at the lock itself. Of course, if it were left to him, he'd let me through the lock, but regulations is regulations. Still, there had once been a ferry at Hazelford Ferry, nearly a mile away, so perhaps I could get out there, and pull the canoe the rest of the way.

A mile overland would make it easily the longest port I'd done so far. And if the path along the Trent (part of the Trent Way) were uneven or difficult, then I could be in a lot of trouble. I determined to hitch another ride, if I could.

It was easy paddling that morning, as I overtook hale old ladies walking their dogs for several miles beyond Gunthorpe. The west bank was low, and cows came down to drink at muddy beaches along the way. To the east trees with dark-green foliage lined steep hills. Beyond those, lying on the plateau, were some of the airfields of southern Lincolnshire, from which Lancasters of the RAF and Fortresses of the American Air Force, had set out to bomb Berlin and the Ruhr. But I was the only soul on the river.

Then, sure enough, with Hazelford a couple of miles away, the west bank became high and overgrown, so that I could no longer discern a path, and only treacherous-looking mudflats offered themselves as potential alighting points. The current was strong enough to make me worried about passing the last possible low bank or jetty. It would be a hellish job to paddle back to it, and I could find myself hard under the high walls of the lock itself. So I began, rather desperately, to look for somewhere to get out.

At a break in the trees, a dirty, steep, concrete slipway emerged from the water. A chipped notice proclaimed this to be the domain of the Trent Waterski club, and invited non-members to stay away. Despite this, and the fact that I couldn't even see the lock, I scrambled out, and hauled *The Subtle Knife* up the flinty surface, between two railings, and on to a narrow, but even, dirt path.

Within fifty yards it was plain that I was in big trouble. Spiky hawthorn bushes now lined the barely defined way, which began to rise and fall, becoming pot-holed and rutted, twisting between beds of tall nettles and brambles. Soon pulling became almost impossible. Every yard the wheels would run askew and have to be reset, forcing me to scramble back along the boat to yank the harness back into place.

Foot by foot I dragged, tugged and lifted the *Knife*, my legs stung in a thousand places from ankle to thigh, my hands blistered from the rope. And every five yards mysterious little paths of flattened undergrowth would lead down to the river bank, each one with a small wooden marker by it. I conjectured that these unexplained memorials marked the graves of dozens of dead canoeists who had been fool enough to try and negotiate England's waterways. I half expected to find – Tomb-of-the-Mummy-style – skeletons lining the route, paddles in hands.

Once, near a clump of mauve cranebills, I sat down in the nettles and seriously contemplated giving up again. I'd leave this bloody thing behind the hawthorn, go back to the Ferry and phone for a cab. In a flash of chrome and a screech of wheels, all this would be history. But Jane's face flashed through my head. I got up and struggled on.

After nearly an hour of stumbling torture, the river entirely obscured by noxious growth of one kind or another, I practically collided with the first, huge metal sign telling those lucky enough to be on the water, that the weir was 400 yards ahead. Fifteen minutes later it was 300 yards.

Now at last, through the leaves, I could see the lock, like a concrete aircraft carrier far away on the other side of the water. Squinting I made out a little figure in green and I hurled abuse at him, abuse carried away by the roar of the weir.

'Oh, don't bloody help me!' I yelled as loudly as I possibly could. 'No, you just open the gates for all those lazy, bloody boaters, with their formica kitchenettes. Don't you give a second bloody thought for silly bloody canoeists trying to use your sodding river, and ending up like Fawcett in the Amazon jungle. Now, go back to your hut, why don't you, and have a lovely, bloody cup of tea!'

And so saying I suddenly emerged from the clawing under-brush, and stood at last on a gravel plateau, high above the rushing weir. Regarding me with obvious pleasure were two figures out of my nightmares.

Anyone contemplating a long river trip will know the film *Deliverance*. In this movie, four city types embark on a canoe journey down a river in the Deep South, and discover just how thinly the varnish of modern civilisation is spread over the elements and over man. They are taught this lesson by a clutch of snaggle-toothed, dungaree-hung, baseball cap-toting, obscenity-drawling, sister-shagging hillbillies. One of the slickers is – and it sticks in the memory of all who've seen the movie – violated while being told to squeal like a pig.

My pair weren't wearing dungarees, and their sisters were evidently at home bringing up the kids, but everything else fitted. They were both scrawny and ill-shaven, the faded bruises of old tattoos climbing up from under their Newcastle United shirts, circling their throats. Their teeth were just about their own. Behind them a battered and rusty pick-up sat beside an old chain-link fence.

'Ow do,' said the one in the blue baseball cap. Maybe he'd go first, while the other one waited his turn.

'Hi,' I said in a confident, bold voice. 'How's it going?'

'We're after barbel,' rasped the man in the red baseball cap.

Barbel? Was this, perhaps, the local badlands word for squeal-piggery? I noticed that the walkway over the weir had a locked metal door halfway along, preventing me from running over to the distant lock-keeper.

'Aye,' added the second, ominously, 'and chub.'

Barbel *and* chub? Dear God.

'Right,' I rejoined nervously, keeping them in front of me, while I looked for an escape route, 'and where do you get that?'

'Down 'ere,' blue answered, and, hunkering down on his wiry haunches, peered over into the calmer waters below the churning weir. There a dozen large fish could be seen flashing to the sunlit surface, whipping round and disappearing again. Barbel and chub.

'Coarse fishin' season starts at midnight,' red told me, adding: 'We've bagged t'best pitch, just theer.'

He pointed down the bank. The marker sticks and flattened paths made sense at last. From tonight onwards the anglers of old England would take up residence, one to a stick, and cast their flies into the water, in search of chub and barbel. These guys, utterly villainous to look at, were no threat to anything without scales.

I wished them good luck, these two coarse fishermen, and tipped the boat down the long bank, setting off north-eastwards. The next stop was Newark.

Four miles on, and where the Great North Road meets the ancient Fosse Way, stands the city of Newark-on-Trent. It announces itself from the river by its two great monuments: the sugar factory, a Romanesque cathedral in aluminium; and the spire of St Mary Magdalene. I left the *Knife* by the lock-keeper's office, and walked into town. There I had a rather disconcerting couple of hours.

The first signs were good. Newark had the best marketplace I had ever been to in this country or abroad. On its sea of cobbles floated a flotilla of garish stalls, selling fruits, cheap underwear and water pistols. Surrounding this area on all sides, like the terraces of the Colosseum, were buildings dating from the great periods of England's architectural history. There was the seventeenth-century Saracen's Head Hotel, the former coaching inn where Jeanie Deans stops in Walter Scott's novel *Heart of Midlothian* (no, of course I didn't know that; it told all on a plaque), but now a fabulous W.H. Smith's; the fourteenth century Ye Olde White Hart, with bulging wattle and wooden beams, restored, I think, by the Magnanimous and Providential; the Moot Hall, of 1708, 'rebuilt by Curry's Ltd'. And thus also saved for a grateful populace by the forces of enlightened commerce.

Inside the elegant Perpendicular church, the *Blue Guide to England* dates the oak rood-screen stalls to 1505, and the two Flemish painted panels showing the Dance of Death to 1506.

It does not, however, give the provenance of the fitted kitchen, complete with built-in hob and double drainer, that is fixed, incongruously, in one medieval corner.

But then, I gradually realised, Newark is a misleading place.

Back down by the Trent a new riverside park had been carved out on the west bank. Opposite, an Irish theme pub, Kelly's Bar, complete with shamrocks and wiggly gold, Gaelic writing, boasted that it had replaced the Swan and Salmon, which had stood there for 250 years.

Kelly's Bar! I immediately contemplated taking revenge by buying up traditional Dublin drinking holes, the kinds patronised by the James Joyce, Sean O'Casey and assorted Behans, and turning them into Cockney theme pubs, complete with jellied eels, stout and names like Doolittle's Dive, Arfur's or the Pearly King. Chas and Dave records would be played on the juke box, and the bar staff would greet customers with a cheery, 'Wotcha, cock?' Or how about a Jewish theme pub – Booze Schmooze – with kosher crisps and vodka and orange sold by the pint.

And there was something strange about Newark's youth. From the moment I had arrived in the town, towing the boat along the bank by the Town Lock, I had clocked the peculiar demented quality of the adolescents round here. In a partially deserted waterworks beside the canal, several youths of between twelve and fifteen, one of them completely naked, slid down a minor weir or lounged in the sun on ledges of crumbled masonry, while maintaining a hoarse cacophony of the worst curses.

A hundred yards further on, by the riverside park, two more boys, aged around thirteen, were idly releasing a narrowboat from its moorings, only to be chased off by its two elderly occupants returning just in time from a trip to Sainsburys. Under Newark's ancient bridge, a lad of sixteen was standing on one of the piers, a piece of rope taut in his hands. On the other end of the rope, in the fastish water, was yet another boy, screaming at the top of his voice for help. 'No, Dave! Dave, stop! Oh, help me! Fuuuuuck! Dave!' Along the bank anxious Newarkers were now standing, wondering what kind of escapade this was.

All over town it was the same. This was a Tuesday, early

afternoon in term time, but on every corner were little knots of abstracted youngsters, swearing and looking for mischief. Perhaps they had all been let off school early by a socially unaware head-teacher, and perhaps all their pranks and plans were innocent. Grown-ups over twenty-five or so are fearful of teenage boys, only half-remembering the lack of real malice of that age, but recalling all too well the maddening effect of those hormones coursing through the limbs and brain.

Six weeks after I had left Newark, a reclusive Norfolk farmer surprised two burglars in his orchard at dead of night. He shot both of them. One, a man in his thirties, was wounded. The other, a sixteen-year-old boy, was killed, bleeding to death among the apple trees. He was over forty miles away from his home. In Newark.

One possible answer to this conundrum of the beautiful town and the mad kids was drugs. That's what the neat little lady in the Tourist Information Office thought. I'd gone in to find the loos, and discovered her surrounded by a colourful exhibition of the town's past, a display of Newark key-rings, notepads and similar ephemera, and closed-circuit TV cameras.

'It's since they moved the toilets in here,' the neat lady sighed. 'Now we get the addicts coming inside, looking for somewhere to shoot up. They all need money, and a lot of them can turn quite nasty. We had a few incidents, and then decided to put those in. It's sad, really.'

Not sad by historical standards, though. In the triangle between the bridge where Dave was drowning his friend, the Tourist Office full of security cameras and Kelly's Bar, stood the last surviving walls of Newark castle, like a tooth that has been filled and refilled, until only the shell of the enamel is left. Seven hundred and eighty-three years earlier, on a wild October night, in the days when this had been a castle belonging to the Bishop of Lincoln, King John of England had died here.

CHAPTER 14

John

John haunts England. He may have died at Newark, but his shade is to be found everywhere from the Welsh Marches to the Fens, and from Exeter to the wall of Hadrian. Wherever I had already been on my journey, there – at some time or other in his seventeen-year reign – John had been too. And wherever I was going, it turned out that he had ridden that way before me. No figure from our history has left his mark on the English countryside in the way that Lackland has.

The way the story gets told, that October John is travelling about in East Anglia and south Lincolnshire, with his gold and his jewels following some miles behind in a line of four-wheeled baggage carts. One dreary night this clumsy cavalcade takes a wrong turning, and finds itself negotiating a narrow, muddy road on the fringes of the Wash. The tide comes in, or they stray into quicksand; whatever happens, by morning jewels, carts and guards are all gone.

When he hears the news, John, who has stopped for the night at an abbey some miles away, comforts himself by gorging on out-of-season peaches and old cider. He feels unwell, makes it to his carriage, and gets as far as the castle at Newark where he takes to his bed, makes out his will and – as lightning flashes illuminate the Trent – passes away, unlamented. The cause of death is given out by chroniclers as a 'surfeit'.

I don't believe it. No one dies of a surfeit today. The dictionary defines it as 'overfeeding', and there's no reason I can think of why it might have been more dangerous to overfeed then than it is now. And yet, Elvis aside, you never read or hear an obituary in which the famous film-star, politician or comedian died of eating too much at dinner one night. That is because, ladies and gentlemen of the jury, I would humbly submit to you that there is no such thing as a 'surfeit' and there never was. King John had a heart attack, or food poisoning, or was dispatched by a toxic draught given him by treacherous nuns; the surfeit thing was put down on his historical death certificate simply to make him look bad.

Few of our kings look worse. Most Englishmen and -women know of John only through the legend of Robin Hood, and because of Magna Carta. Robin may spend most of his time fighting the sheriff of Nottingham and his assorted mates (Guy of Gisborne, Brian de Bois Guilbert, and the magnificent Front de Boeuf), but behind them is the malevolent, rapacious figure of Prince John, ever plotting to prevent his heroic, crusading brother Richard from returning to his realm.

When, eventually, this effete, thin-lipped rascal does succeed to the throne, he's so wicked that the barons have to twist his arm behind his back, and make him go to Runnymede and sign a document, effectively promising that kings will behave better in the future. The chapter on him in that spoof history *1066 and All That* is simply titled, 'John: An Awful King'. Even in *The Lion in Winter*, the teenaged John is depicted as weak, slightly retarded, vicious, treacherous and egotistical.

But was he?

John was born on Christmas Eve, 1166 – a hundred years and two months after the battle of Hastings – into a badly dysfunctional medieval family. Dad was Henry II, Mum was the extraordinary Eleanor of Aquitaine, previously married to the King of France. There were several brothers (Henry, Geoffrey and, of course, Richard) and a couple of sisters, one of whom married the King of Sicily. But what really marks this family out is that almost all of its members were chronic over-achievers.

Henry himself was never still; he was in a state of perpetual motion around his lands (which, in his case, meant most of France too), fighting, hawking, battling, judging, legislating and wenching. His temper would oscillate wildly between fits of dangerous anger and moments of incredible warmth and decent behaviour. Mr Storm and Mr Sunny, if you like. Except, in his case, when Mr Storm was giving it out about what an awkward sod the Archbishop of Canterbury was being, four knights took him literally and butchered Thomas à Becket over his own altar. Henry then donned sackcloth, smeared himself in ashes and did penance. John was three years old at the time.

If nowadays Henry might be diagnosed as manic-depressive, Eleanor may have been a murderess. She was widely believed to have arranged the poisoning of the king's mistress, Rosamund Clifford (known to history as 'Fair Rosamund'), when the latter was abbess of Godstow on the Thames. Eleanor's second son, Richard, later the Lionheart, was clearly a sociopath, who had thousands of civilians beheaded after the siege of Acre in the Holy Land while he watched. He later died from a crossbow bolt in the shoulder, his own fault since he had besieged an insignificant castle in France simply because he was peeved with its lord.

It must have been hell just living next door to this lot, let alone being the youngest child of such a family. So it's hardly surprising that, according to the historian W. L. Warren, young John was a suspicious lad, always worried about what was going to happen next, and never really trusting anyone.

After his accession, most of John's reign was taken up losing bits of France. Although he won one big battle, he lost a couple of others, and that kind of thing got you a bad reputation in those macho days. Richard hardly set foot in England, and has become the misty hero of legend, turning back the cowl of his monk's hood to reveal the noble countenance of the king returned. John spent more time in Lincoln alone than his brother had in the whole kingdom, and has been written up as a cowardly, bone-idle, licentious tyrant who could have taught Caligula a thing or two.

Just like the surfeit, this characterisation doesn't survive much scrutiny. For one thing, John was clearly not lazy. Rarely stopping for more than a few nights at one of his nice, warm castles, he was always on the move. And unlike many English monarchs and not a few prime ministers, he visited the north often, turning up with a few days' notice at royal estates, hearing a few dozen law suits, being petitioned, and then departing again. A royal visit was the equivalent of a modern school inspection, and middens suddenly got cleansed, crumbling walls rebuilt and orchards pruned. Then the king would sit in judgment, on small cases as well as large ones. Had Wat the Witless made off with a cow belonging to a neighbour? Must scutage be enfeoffed to the heir of the ward of the Abbey of Arblaster? The meticulous documents kept during John's reign suggest a rather wise king, not the demented rush-eater of popular tradition.

Like my own journey, it was a big number, all this royal travelling. While the king and his entourage went on ahead, the trundling wagons of the king's train, doing just over half the pace of a fast-walking human, lumbered up behind. In them would be the king's featherbed, his bedroom furnishings (a nice tapestry or two, his chamber pot, blankets and a couple of wenches), his jewels, silver pennies packed in barrels, and all the documents of state.

On a good day the court might be moved by up to thirty miles, but if the rivers were in flux, the absence of bridges could bring the whole progression to a soggy halt, waiting for the waters to subside. It was not at all like a royal tour today, where all the powerless monarch does is shake hands, and all she needs is a couple of hats, the prince consort and the corgis; John's peregrinations were much more like an incredibly slow Air Force One. The whole government was on the move.

So John got about. And he also was the real father of the English navy. When France was lost he set up a system that allowed him to supplement a small standing squadron with ships pressed into service at various English ports. On the last day of May, 1213, the English fleet surprised a French transport armada off the coast of Holland, and set fire to or cut adrift 300 ships. The booty was substantial. But you never get to hear about this one in Robin Hood, do you?

It's true that John fathered five bastards by different women, but it should be remembered that, in those days, kings married for dynastic reasons, and not because they had met someone they fancied at a disco. Given the absence of any form of contraception, barring the unreliable dried half-pomegranate method, it is only surprising that the bastards were kept in single figures. Anyway, there is some evidence that, most nights, John liked nothing more than to go to bed with a good illuminated manuscript, since records exist of him swapping tomes with various bishops, including St Augustine's *City of God* – a bodice-ripper by the standards of the times.

So why, when John achieved so much, has he become a byword for bad government?

The boy was just unlucky. Wars are always expensive, and he had plenty of those to fight. But unlike dad and big brother, John also had to contend with inflation. Take the cost of an ordinary household item, such as a mercenary. In Henry II's time a decent mercenary, with good cross-bowing skills and a nice line in lancing, would set you back eight pence a day. But by 1210 that figure had risen to two shillings, three times as much. So John could either fight battles with far fewer people in them, or he had to get his hands on more money. And that, as ever, was where his problems really began.

His predecessors had managed to earn a considerable fortune by granting Crown lands to the highest bidders, but, after a century of this, most of the best bits had gone. John was compelled to order his justices to get back through the courts what he needed to do his fighting and maintain his government.

Slap bang in the middle of all this difficulty, John fell out with the Pope. This was not difficult to do; it was happening all the time to kings and queens all over Europe. For your medieval sovereign the pontiff was a pain. The most powerful non-royal institution in your realm would be the Church, and the ability to appoint bishops and archbishops was a useful bit of patronage to have available to you. Yet, from time to time, the Pope in Rome might take it into his head to put some enemy of yours in a key post, just to remind you who held the keys to heaven. It would be a bit like having the Commissioner of the European Union tell the prime minister who his home secretary will be.

So Pope Innocent III (who was anything but) over-rode John's choice of Archbishop of Canterbury, and installed his own. To which John replied that the papal appointee, Stephen Langton, would have to shout loudly, because he wasn't going to be allowed to land in England. Miffed, Innocent then proclaimed an interdict on the whole realm. Essentially, this was a general strike of the clergy, in which they refused to marry anyone, bury anyone, bless anyone or sell pardons to anyone. The National Union of Bishops and Allied Preachers locked the gates of their churches, and mounted a spiritual picket line.

Fine, said John, no preaching, no money. He began to seize church property and sell it, on the basis that the clergy clearly didn't need it. John's reputation was damaged throughout Christendom (pretty much the only -dom there was, outside China and the undiscovered Americas), but Innocent wasn't getting anywhere either, so eventually there was a compromise. John recognised the authority of the Pope over England, and kept the cash. Besides, he now needed the support of Rome in his battles with the barons. It's a feature of history teaching that the barons are supposed to have been good in 1215 when they took on John and asserted their independence, and bad after 1485, when they were rightly whipped into shape by the centralising Henry VII.

As ever in English history, it's a matter of who was seen to be on the side of the little guy, and in 1215 it was the barons. This was because the king could be as arbitrary towards the magnates as he was to any merchant; more so, in fact. Local lords involved in court cases could find themselves being fined for tiny and unheard of transgressions, such as bad pleading in court. 'That wasn't a very good argument,' the justice might say, 'so that'll be a thousand groats.'

Sometimes the king was not above a spot of blackmail. In 1210 a Robert de Vaux was told to pay the king five good horses, so that John would 'keep quiet about the wife of Henry Pinel'. If you were going to have to pay the king half a dozen horses every time you had a bit of baronial fornication, then clearly something was badly amiss.

The barons revolted, forced the king to go to Runnymede, and the rest is history. Well, it's all history really.

And there's the point. Who got to write the history? In the 1200s it was the Church. One man in particular, a chap called Roger of Wendover, writing a few years after the event in the abbey at St Albans, is responsible for most of the things we think we know about John. But Roger – like many churchmen, as we've seen – cannot see a lily without feeling the need to gild it. He throws miracles and witchcraft into his chronicles, as though he had witnessed them himself. Today, Roger, with his love of the supernatural, would find a job with the *National Enquirer*, reporting alien abductions. Yet he is the chief source of the stories about John's alleged idleness, lechery and cruelty. The Robin Hood sagas came much, much later. Bad King John is the creation of Roger of Wendover.

As John lay dying on that October night, with the wind howling round the battlements of Newark castle, tended to by the abbot of Croxton, how much louder he might have howled had he known how his name would linger on down the centuries.

I made a date to meet him again, a month later in Worcester, and passed on.

CHAPTER 15

Fook and Vina

It was late afternoon, and warm, when – a long way off – I spotted the pontoon at Cromwell. Behind it reared the 20-foot walls of the lock island, connected to the high bank by two huge gates. I'd had a long day.

The lock-keepers on the Trent like to know about every craft on their patch, so that if anyone doesn't show up they can sound the alert. They'll phone ahead to each other to warn that, say, a barmy forty-year-old in a sky-blue canoe left Newark Nether Lock at three o'clock, heading north very slowly, talking to ducks and complaining about his back. If no one answering that description washes up by six, they'll send a dozen motor-powered rubber dinghies out looking for an upturned boat, a floating baseball cap and a shifty-looking swan.

On the bank side of the deep chasm of the lock itself were a small, neat house surrounded by a white picket fence, a shower and loo building and a small road leading off towards the deep interior of Sherwood. Under some trees I pitched my tent. Over on the island stood a signal box on stilts, from which the duty lock-keeper could see approaching craft both up- and down-stream of the lock. The rest of this tiny isle was taken up by round flowerbeds – full of the oranges and yellows of marigolds and pansies – pushing up at regular intervals through a spotless sward of green. At the far edge of the lawn, a huge, bearded Viking was mowing the grass with a small electric grass-cutter.

Standing on the lock gates, between the lock-keeper and me, was another man. This one was in his late forties, wearing a bad haircut, dark glasses, a shit-coloured shirt, tan trousers with a mobile phone clipped to the belt, and an expression of considered hostility.

'Am I allowed to come over?' I asked mildly.

'Depends what you fookin' want,' he said surlily. I quickly decided not to be offended by his language. It wasn't for my benefit, I thought. This was just how he spoke. Mentally, I named this man Fook.

'Just want to tell the lock-keeper I'm here,' I told Fook.

Fook regarded me through his shades. 'Aye, well, that's him theer.'

By now the Viking was striding towards us. His eyes crinkling in the sunlight, the lock-keeper looked down on me, smiling through his blond beard.

I'm tall, but he was 6 foot 3 at least, and powerfully constructed. His chest was broad, and brown thighs like beech trunks emerged from absurdly short shorts. All of a sudden I felt like Robin Hood confronted on the tree-bridge over the nearby forest burn by Little John, whose local DNA was doubtless shared by this impressive man. Or, rather, two men stuffed into the clothing of one – full of physical self-assurance and brimming over with easy masculinity.

I'm not gay – at least, not very – but from my early boyhood there has always a certain sort of man who has appealed to me. A man like the gamekeeper, Mellors, in *Lady Chatterley*, with that brazenness – muscular and potent. When I was thirteen, I first saw Oliver Reed and Alan Bates wrestle naked in the movie *Women in Love* (set not far from here), and it was a moment, though I didn't realise it then, of homo-erotic pleasure. Unfortunately, Oliver Reed is no more, so there's another ambition that will have to remain unfulfilled.

Mellors was expecting me. He'd watched me put up the tent, and it had tekken me long enough (it wouldn't have surprised me if his tents, animated by testosterone, erected themselves). The route that I was taking (in his opinion) missed out some of the best waterways in England, including those in East Anglia and the West Country. Had Mellors been canoeing round England, you felt, it would only have taken him an hour or two. With just a stop to drink a lake and eat a bull.

As we talked, however, he relaxed a bit, his natural competitiveness easing. I was all right, after all. Hadn't I arrived there under my own steam, and wasn't my boat there under the trees to prove it?

So when the three of us went and sat in his neat office, it was like being allowed to sit in the driver's cab of a train. From up there I could see the massive, but strangely quiet, fall of the weir into the tidal Trent. We drank strong tea from brown-stained china, stirring the sugar in with the blade of Mellors' large jack-knife. Interrupted by only the occasional 'Fook!' from Fook, Mellors began to talk about the thing he loved most: the river.

This was the longest navigable river in Britain, Mellors told me, only deprived of that title by the fact that the very last section had been called — for no good reason — the Humber. Its course had changed many times in recent history, the water cutting new channels and curves through the famous gravel of the valley — now appearing between these two villages, now leaving them on the same bank. Down it and over it had come the Norsemen, the Romans had forded it here at Cromwell, Harold had crossed it a few miles down-stream, when hurrying desperately from defeating Hardrada at Stamford Bridge, to meet the new menace from Normandy, that was then close to the port of Hastings. Barges laden with goods, with coal, with iron, with gravel had used the river, from the North Sea to the heart of the Midlands. And to tame that flow, the huge locks and weirs had been built; the weir at Cromwell passing 93 million gallons every hour.

'Birmingham, Coventry, Leicester, Nottingham; they all drain into the Trent,' said Mellors, finishing his peroration.

'Sheffield drains into t'fookin' Trent n'all,' said Fook.

'Doesn't,' Mellors replied.

'Fookin' does,' said Fook.

'No, it doesn't,' said Mellors, firmly.

'It fookin' does, I've fookin' bin there.'

'It doesn't, you know,' Mellors said again, gently.

'Oh,' said Fook, and was quiet. Then he went out to peer into the lock.

I waved at Fook. 'Is he anything to do with British Waterways?'

'Nay,' said Mellors. 'He just comes up here every week or so. He wanders up the Trent Way, all along from Nottingham, sometimes reet up to Doncaster. And often he ends up here at night, and we give him a lift home to Sutton-on-Trent, where he lives, at the end of our shift. I think he was made redundant, and this is what he does to fill the time.'

Fook had now gone hunting mushrooms among the trees, armed with Mellors' jack-knife. Since the barrel-chested Viking and I were getting along so well, I decided to test our relationship by telling him what was on my mind.

'Today,' I said, 'I passed three boats on the river, all the way from Gunthorpe to here. Since I arrived two hours ago, no boats have gone through this lock either way. How can British Waterways get away with spending millions on maintaining a waterway that nearly no one seems to use? Don't the managers come down here and look for cuts, or try and lengthen your shifts, or sell off the lock-keeper's cottage or something like that?'

'It's true,' he said, stirring yet another villainous-looking cup of tea. 'But you either have waterways, or you decide not to. If you have 'em, you've got to maintain 'em. If you don't dredge the mud and crap out, if you don't shore up the banks, if you don't open and shut the locks or look after the weirs, then within months no boat will be able to use the rivers or canals. So we've got to be here. And if we're here, we might as well have the place looking good and working well.'

He put the cup down.

'Do you know what a lengthsman is?' he asked me.

I didn't.

'You used to have them on the railways, and on the roads too. And I'm one. A lengthsman is a man who looks after his length of whatever: road, rail, river, canal. That's his job. He keeps it neat and clean, spots repairs that need doing, patrols it like. If nothing's happening, he plants flowers and mows the lawn. If someone's in trouble, he's the man on the spot. But he costs, and that's why he's disappearing. I don't think life's any better for his going, do you?'

I didn't. I liked the idea of lengthsmen. I could see that they were expensive and inefficient and often, I suppose, bossy and officious. But a world with more lengthsmen in it appealed to me in the same way that a world with beat bobbies, lollipop ladies, corner-shop grocers and playground attendants did. It seemed a slightly more reassuring world, as I suspect it does to many English people. The trouble was that this world sat uneasily with my usual assumption that modern is best.

While we'd been talking, there'd been a steady movement over on the other bank, near the weir. In ones and twos small figures with long rods and large bags had been taking up positions at intervals on either side of the great waterfall. Here, in the absolute middle of nowhere, a little, all-male population had sprung up, encamping itself by the water, erecting shelters and unscrewing Thermoses. Down the line of coarse fishers marched a man in brown, stopping at each position.

'There's the Lord Blister's bailiff,' said Mellors, 'collecting his dues. It'd be cheaper for them to buy their fish in town.' Then he added, 'They used to fish directly off the lock, but that was stopped after the disaster in '75. Here, come with me.'

I was torn. I'd had nothing to eat since early morning and from 100 yards away and the boats at the invisible pontoon came the smell of sausages that could, possibly, be cadged. A long squeal of anguish made its way from my stomach and out into the pleasant warmth of the evening. But, sensing the sort of story I'd come on this journey to discover, I instead followed the bronzed thighs along the bank until we came to a white stone surrounded by purple orchids. It simply recorded the fact that, on 28 September 1975, ten members of 131 independent parachute squadron of the Royal Engineers were killed here at Cromwell, while on exercises.

It had happened before Mellors' time, but the previous lock-keeper had told him all about it. The armed forces had often used the Trent at Cromwell for night-time exercises. Usually they'd warn the lock-keeper that they were coming – but not invariably. And in the autumn of '75 they wanted to conduct an operation in as realistic circumstances as possible. On that night, a quarter of a century earlier, the exercise had involved coming down the Trent, unobserved from the bank, in three pontoon boats, each carrying ten men. When they came to the low bank just before the weir, they were to get out, and silently port around the fall, re-entering the water fifty or so yards down-stream.

'The trouble was, they'd picked the wrong night,' explained Mellors, shaking his head rather theatrically. 'That evening there was a power cut, and none of the lights along the lock were working. Normally you'd be able to pick out the gates and the line of the lock, but it just so happened that that night, you couldn't. And the lock-keeper didn't know there was an exercise, so he didn't know to warn anyone either.'

We looked over to the tumbling weir, now cordoned off from the up-stream flow by the line of large orange buoys: buoys that hadn't been there in 1975.

'Also, we had fishermen casting on either side – off the lock and off the bank by the weir. And they mostly had little lights with them, as they do. So it could of looked as though the lock was the weir and the weir was the lock. And of course,' Mellors added, 'this may be a great bugger of a weir,. but you can't hardly hear it from up-stream. It's an acoustic trick. From below it shatters yer bloody ears.'

The first two boats hadn't had a problem. 'Mebbe,' Mellors theorised, 'they'd had squaddies in them that had done the Trent before. They stopped in the right place and went round. But the third just carried on going – straight over.'

I pictured that night, dark with feebly-lit fishermen on both banks, and the sudden shape of the boat in the wrong place, hurtling over the angle of the weir, ten soldiers mingling with the millions of gallons of water, and then fetching up in the blackness, unrescuable.

'Most of 'em were found by the weir stopper, but they got one chap a week later, three miles down-stream.' Once again I was struck by how death stalks the river.

At nine Mellors packed Fook into a car that looked too small for them, and sped off down the small road and away. The closed and silent lock belonged to me and to a fat family on the pontoon. There were now, on the far bank, a string of little lights, as the anglers sat and waited for midnight when, at last, they could cast.

I sidled down towards where the meal had been, but there was nothing left. All I had with me was a five-day-old sliced rye loaf that had now broken up into pieces no larger than your thumbnail, some fish paste and coffee. That was it for supper, and for breakfast the next day. I turned on the late news, made myself some coffee, and tried to spread greyish fish paste on to the remnants of the bread.

I called Jane and she said that having no supper would do me the power of good. Back home the children were in bed asleep, talking to their pillows in soft snores. One floor below them, where Sarah was ironing their clothes, was a whole new kitchen, full of food.

If anything was caught during the night, its capture had been unattended by any celebrations loud enough to disturb me. Besides I hadn't much to wake up for. There was no breakfast, and the tide wouldn't let me leave Cromwell till nearly midday. Under the shade of the trees, and cushioned by the peaty bank, I slept late. It wasn't till just after nine that – awake – I decided to walk the mile or so, across the Great North Road, to Cromwell village, just on the off-chance that there was a shop there.

There was, and it was a good one with newspapers, elderly fruit and sliced white bread. The large woman behind the counter was very amused to hear that I'd come by river to Cromwell. I went out into the sunlight to eat my food.

It was there, by the church, that I noticed a sign, pointing down a short, shrub-bordered driveway. THE MUSEUM OF DOLLS AND BYGONE CHILDHOOD, PROP: VINA COOKE said the sign.

Once the A1, the main road linking London, the Midlands and the North, had run through the middle of this village. But that had been long ago. Since then the Great North Road had been put on a bypass round the village, and then the M1 had drawn much of its traffic away in turn. Now, no cars or lorries whatsoever passed this way. Yet here, out of sight of any passing travellers and far from the tourist trails, was a museum. I walked up the gravel path.

The museum had once been the Rectory, Georgian by the look

of it, sitting elegantly – if in need of paint – at the end of the drive. The windows were shuttered, but at the top of three broad steps was a printed notice that admission would cost 80p, and an invitation to ring the bell. Fully expecting the mad staring eyes of Bette Davis or Anthony Perkins, I rang.

No one knew where I was, and as I rang the bell the familiar fantasy bubbled up in my mind. If I were to be kidnapped, and turned into a sex-slave or sausages (or both) by an insane curator with a monstrous doll alter ego, it would be days before Mellors, with Fook by his side, would come looking for the owner of the abandoned canoe.

'Ah, yes,' the shop-keeping woman would have said, 'he was here that morning. Went off in that direction.'

Would they have called house to house? How long would it have taken them to get to the Rectory? Suspicious, might they break in later that night, to find me dead, embalmed and sewn into the body of a huge mannequin in the 'Dolls of our Time' room? More to the point, what did it say about me that I kept fantasising about being kidnapped and held prisoner?

Before I could analyse myself too closely, a wide vision in green velvet, with braided hair coiled on top of a broad, smiling face opened the door to me. Vina Cooke, a young-looking fifty-odd, resembled nothing so much as a happy Miss Havisham; a woman whose life had stood still at a moment of great contentment, and who had changed nothing since.

'Hello, dear,' said Vina melodiously. 'Have you come to look round our little museum? I'm afraid we have to charge, because we're not subsidised like the other museums. That'll be 80p dear.'

I paid; she escorted me. The hall was crammed with small dolls in display cases.

'I made most of them myself, dear. A few have been collected, but that's been my passion, dear, making the dolls. And where have you come from? The river? From London? Good heavens, dear; what was that for?'

On the walls were testimonials to Vina's place in doll history. There was a large photograph of a younger Vina, still in the green velvet dress, showing four male dolls to a fur-stoled lady in pearls. A typed caption read: VINA COOKE WITH THE BEATLES AND THE DUCHESS OF RUTLAND.

A little further along was an even younger Vina in an early TV studio, handing another male doll to a strangely familiar young man with a beautiful chiselled face, pouty lips and a gelled cowslick hanging over his smooth forehead. VINA WITH CLIFF, 1959, read the inscription.

In each room of the lovely rectory, from wall to wall and door to bay, dolls of all sexes and periods fixed my eyes with their own dead orbs. The six wives of Henry VIII ('As shown on BBC TV') pirouetted next to the sombre bride from the 'Wedding of Princess Anne'. In a Who's Who of regional telly circa 1962, the heroes and heroines of post-war Britain, Pussy Cat Willum, Christopher Trace, Ena Sharples and Brigitte Bardot all rubbed fabric shoulders.

'You know who that is, dear,' said Vina, pointing out a boy doll in tights and a green cap. 'That's Richard Greene as Robin Hood.' Not Robin Hood, mark you, but Richard Greene as Robin Hood.

After having admired a room full of black dollies, like a soft version of a New York ghetto, I went downstairs again. Mr Vina Cooke, a gentle-looking man with long hair and a goatee, like a Cavalier of the Civil War, smiled pleasantly at me.

'Have you enjoyed it, dear?' Vina asked me. I said that I had indeed.

'Well then, dear, would you mind awfully signing my little visitors' book?' I did, putting my signature behind those of a couple from Loughborough who'd been the week before and thought that it was all 'v. interesting'.

On the next outward tide I left Cromwell and headed north once again, making Torksey, 11 miles from Lincoln, by late afternoon.

This was easy because the *Knife* was safely stowed on the roof of a narrowboat hired by a pair of retired New Zealanders who had come up to Cromwell that morning. Together we chugged Humberwards, while Sid and Norma told me tales of the Coromandel peninsula.

On our way the river coiled in great loops between venerable villages with church spires and huge, smoking power stations. Cormorants and fishermen populated the banks, not caring about the view, the former sitting, curved like seahorses on the pinnacles of flood poles, and the latter – discoloured to a man by unwise tattooing – bursting out of and over foldaway camping chairs.

Sid and Norma had emigrated to New Zealand from Leeds in 1973. They had three observations to make about the people they'd left behind: that they didn't seem to have much to say for themselves; that the old ones were much richer than they'd expected; and that the English were getting very fat. 'I blame elasticated waists,' Norma explained. 'They give you lot the impression that you can eat what you like.'

I should have been so lucky.

CHAPTER 16

Sky

Much as I longed for kitchen, fridge and contents, I was missing my family more. As I travelled around I found myself envying the dads cuddling their toddlers and the mums coo-ing at their babies. But, as far as I could tell, my family's life seemed unchanged without me. On the other end of my mobile the children did not plead with me to come home, or sound distressed. I was the one missing out, not them. From Torksey on the Trent I still had five weeks and 700 miles to go.

In the winter of 872-3, Guthrum and his Danes whiled away the coldest months round wood fires at Torksey. The choice was a good one. Halfway down the Trent between the mouth of the Humber and Nottingham, Torksey sat (and sits still) on the junction with the Fossdyke, the canal built by the Roman legions 750 years earlier. From here York and the north were a few days' arson and rapine distant, or there was the south. When spring came, the host made off down the valley of the Trent to fight battles in Wessex.

By the Middle Ages Torksey, 30 miles from the sea, was one of England's biggest ports. Merchandise from across the North Sea was shipped and sold here, and English wool taken back in exchange. The town that sprang up in the angle between river and canal was wealthy enough to support three parish churches, two monasteries and a castle.

Most villages in England are bigger than they were, their centres surrounded by accreted rings or offshoots of low-rise housing, thrown out in various bursts of population over the centuries since the Black Death. Growth seems to be the natural order of things. But where most of Torksey once used to be, where the churches, nunneries, shops, markets and houses stood, there are now not even ruins. Empty fields run from the castle to the lock

on the Fossdyke. This shrinking had happened by the time that
the Tudor traveller John Leland visited, some time around 1540.
And the unexpected void makes Torksey a slightly spooky place.
It's a village where the inhabitants see UFOs, and strange lights
glimmer on the water.

Leaving my New Zealand pals moored by the lock, with the
Knife safely quartered on their deck, I walked the half-mile into
the village. Opposite the old church, with its weathered gargoyles,
stood a large inn, its roadside aspect dominated by Berni Inn-style
windows, its walls coated in lime-green-painted pebbledash.

I'd booked ahead, told 'em I was coming, I was expected, but
the place looked abandoned. I went up to the windows and
peered in. All was dark within, chintzy banquettes, faux-rustic
dining furniture, napkins and cruets all unused. I found a door
with the licensees' name over it, and knocked. No one answered.
I called the number on my mobile. There wasn't a reply, not even
an answerphone.

I circled the inn. On one side was a small, paved seating area,
with umbrellas and – disconcertingly – a large, mansize plastic
chef, with a ghastly smile. The door to the garden was locked.
Behind the building was a carpark the size of the Millennium
Dome, which extended way beyond the pub, and towards some
scrubland in the far distance. Part of the unspoiled beauty of rural
England, I thought. There was one old, battered jalopy parked
there, and that was it. The back of the lime inn was the usual
ugly confection of chimneys, ducts and wheelie bins. I orbited
the *Marie Celeste* of one-star hotels again.

On my fourth circuit, a middle-aged woman and a small girl
turned up to claim their car.

'You lookin' to get in?' the woman asked me. I agreed that
I was.

''E often goes to sleep in the afternoons,' she said. 'If you want
to wake him, you have to use the door round the back.' She
pointed in the direction of the duct area. There, between two
huge bins, and up a small flight of stairs, was a door that I had
overlooked. I thanked her and rang the bell.

After three rings I heard a shuffling sound. A young man in

shorts and T-shirt, with a scrubby beard and bleary eyes, regarded me with surprise. I told him that I had booked in for the night, and asked where I should go.

'Follow me,' he said, in a French accent.

After two showers and the Thai bar food (the inn came alive about an hour after I arrived, and business was so brisk that the carpark was eventually almost one-hundredth full), I settled down in an old nun's bed, and once again (like an old nun) grappled with *Middlemarch*.

Roman roads are straight, but not as straight as Roman canals. The Fossdyke between Torksey and Lincoln is 11 miles long, and consists of two straights and one loop. Almost nothing was visible above the reeds on either bank. So it was a surprise to discover that behind each large bush was hidden an angler connected to a long, hardly visible rod, each of which sent me on a sudden flurry of diversionary paddling to avoid becoming entangled in their infernal lines. Along the placid canal I even came across the occasional sedate lady angler, each managing without the assistance of the small mountain of colourful equipment that the men all seemed to need.

Then, a small moment of revelation. Three miles down the Fossdyke I suddenly – for the first time since I had left London – saw the sky. I mean, properly saw it. I had started off from Camden Town only really being aware of what was under me (water, which I might fall in), and immediately to each side (banks, which I might not be able to climb). I might just as well have been boating inside a gigantic stadium or conservatory, because I had no sense of being outside.

Now, however, half the world was sky, with great stripes of cloud and colour passing across the void. The journey was no longer a strange and uncomfortable extension of being at home or in the office; it was something utterly different. Something big. I was having this substantial, metaphysical thought, when I almost collided with a dead deer, whose ruddy furred carcase was floating about three feet from the reeds. A hundred yards further on, there was another. And a third lay hard against the bank a few feet beyond that.

This deer problem now replaced the sky moment in my skittish brain. What could account for this highly localised watery holocaust? No dead deer for 160 miles and now three? Did the inhabitants of the marshy land between the Trent and Lincoln indulge in the arcane sport of fawn-dunking? I constructed a past time in which men in flippers, wielding long poles and yelling 'Doe canal! Doe canal!', chased the terrified animals over the wet meadows and into the Fossdyke.

An hour later I entered Lincoln, paddling into Brayford Pool, the small lake that sits at the base of the hill. High above me stood the great cathedral and castle of Lincoln, a sight almost unchanged in seven hundred years, save for the cathedral spire, which had collapsed in1547, the year of Henry VIII's accession.

Down here, on two sides of the water where once were factories, now sparkled the spanking new buildings – all ruddy brick and glass – of the University of Lincolnshire and Humberside. An establishment that hadn't even existed twenty years earlier, the new varsity now boasted over 10,000 students, almost as many as Oxford. Behind me the highly coloured boxes of the halls of residence marched off to the south, cheap but optimistic testimony to the belated spread of higher education in England.

Not that all this impressed Simon, beside whose beached boat I sought to leave the *Knife* for the weekend. In his mid-thirties, with a small-boy grin and quickness to take offence, Simon told me – as the unspoken price of his hospitality – about life, boats and women.

Simon had escaped from Hampshire in a different vessel a few months previously. He was getting divorced and didn't want his wife's lawyers to find him. His story was an odd one.

'Two days after we were married she told me she was a lesbian,' he confided. 'Two days! Well, I was buggered if she was getting my money, so I skipped, and came up here.'

That was rough, I agreed (while wondering whether the lesbianism had pre- or ante-dated their marriage), but had he not, since then, felt tempted to marry for a second time?

'She *was* my second wife,' he snorted. 'My first wife two-timed with me a super-grass. You know, he was informing on accomplices in organised crime.' He paused and gave me a movie-style meaningful look. 'They found him, you can be sure of that. Not nice.'

I was beginning to wonder about Simon. He could simply be a liar. But what if what he said were true? Was it possible that women, initially attracted to his essential Simonness, found that he did not improve on close acquaintance? His next sentence gave me a clue.

'Now my motto,' he laughed, humourlessly, 'is "woo 'em, fuck 'em and dump 'em", simple as that.' I wished him luck with the wooing, the fucking and the dumping, commended the poor old *Knife* into his care and went on my way.

Into a city which amazed me and made me glad that I had come.

The old part of Lincoln is reached by an ancient lane (Steep Hill) the gradient of which is so ridiculously severe that cars can't be trusted on it, and your calf muscles begin to stretch alarmingly after the first ten paces. I had never heard of it before, or of the twelfth-century stone houses jutting at right-angles from the hill, or of the profusion of delicatessens, art shops, second-hand bookshops, coffee houses and everything that could attract the eye, the nose and the palate. Mollusc fossils were offered for sale next to tattered documents; old wines beside older cheeses. It was wonderful, and – unlike Newark – apparently unplagued by delinquents.

Not everyone likes Lincoln. Daniel Defoe, when he visited the city as the king's spy in the 1720s, moaned about it. 'Lincoln', he wrote, 'is an ancient, ragged, decayed and still decaying city; it is so full of ruins . . . that the very hog-sties were built church-fashion; that is to say, with stone walls and arched windows and doors.' Defoe hated disorder and muddle, both of which he associated with hills. 'Nothing', he complained about the Steep Hill, 'is more troublesome than the communication of the upper and lower town, the street is so steep and straight.'

~ The Trent ~

In 1934, travelling for a book he was to write about England, the left-inclined writer and playwright, J.B. Priestley also passed this way, arriving by train on a foggy day. Priestley, trying to get to the tank factory close to Brayford Pool (now the scene of a thousand student trysts and a million snores), walked down Steep Hill as ice formed, and saw men with zinc baths strapped to their backs, sanding the impossible slopes.

At the top of the hill, between the spiritual and temporal monuments of the Middle Ages – the castle and the cathedral – I had booked, as a treat to compensate for all that time under canvas, a room for two nights at the White Hart, the most expensive and oldest hotel in the city. Each of the chambers in the creaking, low-ceilinged corridors was named after a bishop of Lincoln. I passed John Thomas (1744), with regret, feeling that sleeping there might have fostered exotic dreams concerning Lady Jane (I was due an exotic dream). But I settled for Edward King (1885), especially when I saw that, from the window of my small living-room, the entire cathedral rose to greet me over the chimney tops of a small intervening terrace. I opened the windows on to the warm rose- and car-perfumed air of early evening. Close enough to hit with a stone were the deep recesses of the great doors, the intricate carving of the saints and monarchs, the twin towers.

And then the bells started to ring, first singly, then building to a great carillon, sounding out from the towers and filling the sky over the upper town. It was a moment of such unexpected joy that, at first, I had to search myself to think how I ought to respond. Should I sit down? Should I shut my eyes? Should I look at the towers where the bells were swinging? I did all three, and more; a man of the age of the Internet touched by the technology, the sounds and sights of the twelfth century.

The only thing that could have made it better would have been the presence of four people, who were still in London, 160 water miles and three weeks away.

CHAPTER 17

The Jews of Lincoln

Not long before he died, my dad and I got to talking about anti-Semitism. For some reason, perhaps because he was so unreligious and secular himself, we had never touched on the subject before. I had been wondering how it was, in the 1930s, that the fascists and those who hated Jews could tell, at a glance, who was Jewish and who wasn't. With black and Asian people it was obvious, but Jews came in many colours: I'd been at school with several blond ones.

'Oh, they know, all right,' Dad shook his head. 'They know.' He obviously considered my question to be naïve.

From a man as unmystical and rationalist as he was, this came as a shock. Here in England, apart from the occasional schoolboy joke – as offensive as those about Scots and considerably less than those concerning the Irish – I had never felt in any way noticeable. I wasn't circumcised, true, but the name was a giveaway. No one I had ever met seemed to care. The English were all right about Jews.

So what had he meant?

Looking around Lincoln I found out. For here, if you searched, was the evidence that life in England had not always been so comfortable for those of the diaspora – like the tomb of Little Saint Hugh.

Inside the soaring cross of the cathedral, half-way down the aisle of the south choir, and inset into the light, soft stone of the choir screen, is what looks like a low, wet, dark bench. But it's not a bench. Hewed 200 years earlier than the screen from a shinier rock, this is what remains of a thirteenth-century shrine. Once a small statue stood here, and offerings of money and lit candles were left on the slippery ledge. In supplication to, and memory of Little Hugh, the small boy of Lincoln, who was killed, so they said, by the Jews.

It was in 1255, writes the medieval chronicler Matthew Paris, that, 'about the feast of the apostles Peter and Paul, the Jews of Lincoln stole a boy called Hugh, who was about eight years old'. He was kept in the house of a local Jew for ten days, Paris claimed, and during that time he was horribly tortured.

'They scourged him till the blood flowed, they crowned him with thorns, mocked him and spat upon him, each of them also pierced him with a knife.' Finally the Jews put the innocent Hugh out of his misery. 'After tormenting him in divers ways,' Paris continues, 'they crucified him, and pierced him to the heart with a spear. When the boy was dead, they took the body down from the cross, and for some reason disembowelled it; it is said for the purpose of their magic arts.'

The murder was discovered when Hugh's mother, who had been looking for the boy for several days, was informed by one of her neighbours that he had been seen going into the house of a Jew. She entered and soon came across the remains of her son at the bottom of a shallow well in one of the rooms. The bailiffs were called, and the body was recovered.

This set some of the more interventionist citizens of Lincoln on to questioning the owner of the house, a man called Copin (or Jacob) about the murder.

Copin was urged by one of the Gentiles present, a John of Lexington, to confess to the crime. Said Lexington (according to Paris): 'I will tell thee how thou canst save thy life and limb from destruction. Both these will I save thee, if without fear or falsehood, thou wilt expose to me all that has been done in this matter.'

Copin confessed immediately to the murder. 'What the Christians say is true,' he said, adding that, 'almost every year the Jews crucify one boy in injury and insult to Jesus.'

He was taken away in chains, and his confession did him no good. When the king – John's son, Henry III – heard about the case, he was suitably enraged and would not countenance (said Paris) the promised leniency. Copin was sentenced to die.

On the eve of his execution the desperate Copin elaborated even further on his admission. This time, though, he implicated the entire Jewish community. 'Nearly all the Jews in England', he is recorded as having claimed, 'agreed to the death of this boy, and from nearly every English city where Jews live, some were chosen to be present at this sacrifice as a Passover offering.'

The next day Copin was tied to a horse's tail, dragged to the gallows and hanged. Now there remained the question of what to do with all the other Jews, whom the unhappy Copin had fingered. Paris reports that 994 Jews were taken to London and imprisoned there, though he claims that most were set free the following spring. Other sources state that eighteen Jews were hanged in London, and there are local records suggesting that a number of Lincoln Jews were indeed executed, and their property disposed of to local Gentiles for knock-down prices.

While the Jews were being put to death or dispossessed, the body of the child himself was taken up by the clergy and buried, with honours, in Lincoln Cathedral. There he became known as Little Saint Hugh, distinguishing him from the original Saint Hugh – the legendary bishop of Lincoln in King John's time.

Little Saint Hugh's saint's day was 27 August, and his shrine soon became one of the most popular in the cathedral. One hundred and fifty years later, Geoffrey Chaucer, creating his own story of Jewish ritual murder in 'The Prioress's Tale, referred to the canonized infant:

> O yonge Hugh of Lincoln, sleyn also
> With cursed Jews, as it is notable
> For it nis but a little while ago.

In the eighteenth century a tomb in the cathedral was excavated, and the skeleton of a boy discovered. It was about 3 feet 3 inches in length, and preserved in some kind of pickling fluid – into which the head of the local antiquarian society, in line with the enquiring Spirit of the Age, dipped a finger and tasted the brew. Also in the tomb was a 20-inch statue of a boy, with the marks of the stigmata and fingers raised in benediction.

But by now, Little Saint Hugh's shrine was disused. As one local historian commented, 'The popularity of the tomb declined as the Jews became a memory.' For four hundred years or so, beginning shortly after the death of Hugh of Lincoln, there were no more Jews here, or anywhere else in England, to blame for Little Saint Hugh's death.

They'd been there for only just under two centuries. The first Jewish communities had been established in England after 1066, arriving in the Conqueror's wake, a continental innovation. Usually banned from carrying on a trade, or from joining craft guilds, Jews were allowed to do just one thing: lend money at interest, something Christians were not permitted to do. This made them very useful. Any kind of investment or economic change will require loans. So the Jews became the medieval equivalent of Lloyds or Barclays. If you wanted to start a new sheep-rearing venture, or add a wing to your abbey, or buy a title from the king, you could go to your local branch of Jews International, sit down with your own personal banking adviser, and negotiate a loan.

From the king's point of view, though, it was even better than that. Because every Jew was deemed to be the king's own property and under his protection, he inherited everything – including the debts that were owed to them – when they died. In modern terms it would be like the Chancellor of the Exchequer getting all the branch assets every single time a bank manager retires. And imagine a situation where a customer borrows money to pay off the Inland Revenue, only to discover that the debt has now reverted to the Treasury, and that the taxman is after him again. That is exactly what many barons and merchants found happening to them.

When Aaron of Lincoln, supposedly the richest Jew in England, died in 1185, details of who owed him what were written down by the king's scribes, because the debt all now belonged to the throne. Nine Cistercian abbeys were into Aaron for considerable sums (which some of their chronicling monks resented bitterly). The Archbishop of Canterbury was also a debtor, as were half the nobility and some of the royal family. And, crucially, many of the ordinary, lynch-happy citizens of Lincoln. On some debts the interest charged had been at the rate of 43 per cent.

So the king valued the Jews, the economy required them, and the people indebted to them variously saw them as a necessity or as a plague.

And there was also every incentive among the more un-scrupulous debtors to find excuses for murdering a Jew or two, and burning the records of their debts. From the late 1100s onwards, this is exactly what happened. In Norwich, in 1144, a massacre was occasioned by the first allegation of a ritual murder of a Christian boy by the local Jews. This 'blood libel' was to be repeated in cities all over Europe until well into the Renaissance. The last recorded occasion was in Damascus, in the mid-nineteenth century.

Nasty though all this was, as long as the king broadly favoured the Jews staying alive, then – give or take a pogrom or two – they could exist. In 1223, when the Archbishop of Canterbury and the bishop of Lincoln both ordered that no Christians in their dioceses should sell food or other necessities to the Jews, the king intervened, and told his subjects to take no notice.

But, bit by bit, as other sources of finance became available, it was more tempting for the king to steal the Jews' money, than it was to leave them be. As a consequence, the Jews became poorer, and less valuable. In 1278 the entire Jewish community of England, now down from 4,000 to just over 2,000, was accused of coin clipping – a capital offence. Many – men and women – were hanged.

Then, twelve years later, in 1290, England became the first European country to expel the now friendless Jews altogether. Never mind William Wallace and Braveheart; this expulsion was the most shameful episode of Edward I's reign. France followed suit in 1306, and Germany in 1348.

In Lincoln, outside the cathedral there were still some reminders of the Jewish community that, for a century and a half, had lived close by the castle. Like Jews Court, one of the oldest houses still standing in England today, with its Norman double-arched windows and decorated door pillars.

A brochure about this house was produced in 1911. *Jews Court and the Legend of Little St Hugh of Lincoln* was written by one Thomas R. Howitt, a sanitary inspector with the rural district council. In one room of this house, claimed Howitt, there 'was the veritable well into which the body of little St Hugh was thrown after his crucifixion'.

Visitors came to see the well, clutching copies of this publication. In 1928 the corporation began to discuss means of preserving the infamous hole to help boost the tourist industry. It was only then that, on hearing this, an old workman admitted that, years earlier, he had been employed to build the well in the first place. The thing was a fake. Shortly afterwards the liberal anti-fascist J. B. Priestley was in town, and saw Jews Court on the way to his hotel. It started a revealing chain of thought:

> I enquired for the proprietor, to congratulate him on his hotel . . . He is, it seems, a Jew, and I was told that this was not his only hotel in the city. A very smart man, they all said. I could not help reflecting on the odd prominence of Jews in the history of Lincoln. In the Middle Ages the Jews of Lincoln were notorious for their supposedly gruesome pastimes. And now, in the twentieth century, it is a Jew who controls the hotel business there.

Substitute 'Scot' for 'Jew' in that sentence, and Priestley's comments seem very peculiar. Especially in his use of that word, 'control'. Could it really be said of this Jewish hotel owner that he 'controlled' the hotel business? Were there no other hoteliers operating independently in 1934?

That was also, as it happens, the year that my dad, then aged fifteen, was recuperating in St Mary's hospital, in Sidcup. While hiking from the Jewish East End of London to the Rhondda Valley, he'd contracted rheumatic fever which had weakened his heart. So he was sent to the sanatorium in the heart of Kent.

In one ward, he told me later, were the TB sufferers, all coughing together; in another those with St Vitus dance jigged and capered endlessly; and in his ward all the cardiac cases were made to lie down for twenty-four hours a day, complete rest being needed to take any potential strain off the heart. They were all young men, and they all flouted such obviously absurd rules; and since it was soon obvious to them that my dad was a Jew, one of their preferred forms of exercise took the form of fighting him, or just beating him up.

Though the short-term reason for his presence was his heart, my dad was really in Sidcup because of Oliver Cromwell. Three hundred and seventy-four years had passed since the expulsion. Shakespeare, writing *The Merchant of Venice* half a century before the Lord Protector's reign, probably never actually met a Jew.

There were plenty of Puritans in Cromwell's day who didn't want to meet Jews. The reason? A pamphlet of 1656 argued against readmission on the basis that, when they were last in England, 'the Jews used every year to steal a young boy, and to circumcise him . . . and crucify him to death . . . 18 Jews were drawn and hanged for thus crucifying one Hugh Lincoln.'

Still, England was a different place by the late 1600s. Bit by bit, in that incremental English way, restrictive laws against Jewish liberties were eased or fell into disuse. Besides, at the time of Dickens, say, the Jewish community was still small and unthreatening. Then, in 1881, Czar Alexander II of Russia was blown up in his carriage. The resulting chaos unleashed anti-Jewish riots and massacres, which in turn led to measures to discriminate against the huge Jewish population in Russia. One of the great migrations of history began.

Hundreds of thousands of Jews, mainly those who were ill-educated and rural, took ship to America, South Africa, South America and Britain. Between Alexander's death and the First World War, 100,000 Jews came to live on these shores; and my young grandparents, Moishe and Gittel, were two of them. In

1899, a century before my journey, they arrived in the Port of London, unskilled, illiterate and speaking only Yiddish.

My dad, the youngest of three, was born in Cable Street, in Stepney, on Boxing Day 1919. His father was a second-hand clothes repairer, the lowest of the low in the tailoring business. They were all there when, in 1936, Mosley's Blackshirts were prevented from marching through the area by a huge demonstration composed of Jews and Gentiles alike; an event that proved – for those who doubted it – that England was no Germany, no Poland, no Russia. It's the England of Cable Street and of the Second World War that liberal English folk want to recall. The rest they'd like to forget.

By the shrine of the Little Saint Hugh, in the gloom of the central cathedral, an apologetic notice, put there by some dean or canon, tells the visitor about the blood libel, and deplores it. It ends: 'Such stories do not redound to the credit of Christendom, and so we pray: Remember not, Lord, our offences nor the offences of our forefathers.'

Other things may, however, be remembered. On my way out of the cathedral and into the sunlight, I picked up a copy of a crisply printed newsletter, the *Cathedral Community Quarterly*. Inside, the Bishop of Lincoln, whose predecessor once forbade Christians to sell food to the Jews, reflected on the spread of his religion by its early followers. 'Yet on the day of Pentecost,' he wrote, 'these small-timers took over history: they began to supersede Jewry and to challenge the Roman Empire.'

Oh, yes, I thought. They superseded Jewry all right! On Jews Court in Steep Hill an explanatory plaque with gold letters says only that the building was, 'Owned by a member of the Jewish community in 1290'. It doesn't say why it wasn't owned by a Jew in 1291.

On 10 July 1958, a travelling salesman from Missouri, Max Hunter, driving through the Ozarks, took his reel-to-reel recorder into the house of Mrs Allie Long Parker of Eureka Springs, Arkansas. There, the old lady sang him a song in her reedy voice. It was called 'The Jews' Garden', and part of it went like this:

Th' Jew's daughter came walking out
Dressed up in silk, so gay
Saying, come in, come in, my pretty little boy
And get your ball away, way, way
And get your ball away.

She took him by the lily white hand
An' led him 'cross th' hall
An' with a broad sword cut off his head
An' kicked it against th' wall, wall, wall
An' kicked it against th' wall

She threw him in a new drawn well
Jest fifty-five feet deep
With a catechism at his head
An' a Bible at his feet, feet, feet
An' a Bible at his feet

CHAPTER 18

Responding to Change

You can get too much history. It was Friday morning, and modern England lay all around me. One floor down from Edward King, and close enough to John Thomas to overhear any nocturnal activities that the room name might have brought on, the Black Prince room was about to host an all-day event.

On one of the double doors someone had Blutacked a large white notice which read: 'Welcome to responding to/rejecting (crossed out)/resisting (crossed out) change! Run by DMT.' Inside, some twelve chairs had been set out in an ominous circle, and little pads and pencils placed on each seat. Already, at nine in the morning, hot sunlight filled the room, promising a dozen middle managers a stifling and sweaty day in the company of a teenaged trainer called Ranjit or Paul, learning to embrace constant upheaval. It was not to be resisted, this change; nor might it be rejected. One might only respond to it.

At a guess DMT stood for Dynamic Management Trainers, and this had to be DMT's dynamo, a well-scrubbed man in his early thirties, with slightly over-long hair, and a horribly enthusiastic manner, bustling along the corridor with a large flip-chart, and a badge with 'Jerry' written on it in blue fibre-tip. 'Ter-pom, ter-pom, pom, pom,' sang Jerry, incongruously.

I had met Jerry, or, rather, those like him, several times before. He was a more affable, slicker, distant cousin of Jim from Canoeright.

'Good morning!' he'd say. 'Welcome to "Responding to Change", my name – as it says here on this badge – is Jerry. It's written down just in case I forget it! I have some badges here for you, if you wouldn't mind putting them on, just for my benefit. Now, if we could go round the room, and each of you could tell us all – in your own words – what you're looking to get out of today. I hope you get what you want.'

That would be their day, these personnel managers from brewery chains, marketing executives from electronics retailers, or call centre staff from the Magnanimous and Providential: a sealed room, a bottle of mineral water and Jerry beside them. I, on the other hand, was free.

My intention had been to go to the lower town and mingle with the shoppers, but the castle entrance gaped too wide, and I thought I'd stand on top of a tower and survey Lincolnshire first. I found that the past and present co-existed within the castle walls in a strange and appropriate way. A square Georgian building held – illuminated and air-conditioned – one of the four surviving copies of Magna Carta (John again). Fifty feet away, in a piece of decorated Victoriana, a process was going on, however, that was very much in the now.

A gaggle of people whom, from a distance, I had taken to be tourists, or yet another school party, became coalescing and dividing groups of bewigged lawyers, clerks and – judging by appearances – clients. They were sunning themselves and chatting in the periods before and between the proceedings of their business within. For the Victorian pile was evidently a courthouse, operating here, within yards of the document that first established habeas corpus.

Two particular corpuses, however, took my eye; reclining on a low wall, still, like fabulous lizards. The first was a gorgeous blonde girl in her late teens, wearing rings through her eyebrows, cycling shorts and a boob-tube through which her nipples winked impudently at the pin-striped men of law.

Almost as irresistible was her companion, a shaven-headed youth of sixteen or so, bare from the waist up, legs encased in scarlet track-suit bottoms. His was the torso of a Praxiteles sculpture, the waist narrowing from the perfect chest; on his *linea alba* a downy fuzz, catching the sunlight, plunged in a straight golden thread, down towards his groin. His face was also beautiful, prevented from being perfect by the blemish marks of old spots. On this countenance he wore an expression in which boredom alternated, when he was spoken to, with an innocent malevolence. He was a sprite, but one that could do you damage: a violent Ariel, a fucked Puck.

Inside the courtroom, into which I strolled completely unchallenged, as though in a democratic country, a bewigged judge was presiding – all jowls and scowls – from atop a carved dais, surrounded by carved angels. Around him his attendants and slaves, acolytes at the Temple of the Legal Mysteries, read out charges, shuffled papers, gave the five or six people in the public gallery the once-over. On the second of four rows of banked seats, I sat next to two stripy uniformed schoolboys, obviously there from their minor public school, taking a lesson in practical civics, 'How the Other Half Lives'.

Sentence, held over from a previous appearance, was being passed on a meagre, rat-faced Irishman called Keane. The judge reminded the court that Keane had been paid £500 to drive £250,000 worth of cocaine, cannabis and ecstasy. 'Drugs', said his honour, sonorously, 'that might have been supplied to the young, and made their lives even more miserable than they otherwise might be.'

Not on that lot, they wouldn't be. Had the man in the wig been talking about heroin or crack, he might have had a point; but, as it was, there was a huge, ridiculous gulf between the solemn words and the social reality. Keane was as welcome a visitor to the recreational drug-takers of Lincoln, as the wreck of the SS *Statesman* had been to the deprived wartime drinkers of the Hebrides in *Whisky Galore*. At any rate, the gulf cost the rodentine Irishman three and a half years in the clink. He didn't complain, just went down without a murmur.

Next up was the Adonis of the inner bailey, his classical breast now covered in a canary Nike T-shirt. 'Are you Gary Wayne Bridges?' asked the clerk. 'Yeah.' His barrister, whom I had seen earlier stroke the boy's head affectionately, rolled his eyes slightly. But it didn't matter, this was merely a committal for trial, on the charge of possession of an offensive weapon. Within seconds Gary had disappeared again, into the bosoms of his gum-chewing Aphrodite.

I needed to be on my way. The route out took me past two benches where defendants sat, and exchanged stories of porridge done and porridge still to do. They looked at me expectantly, as I passed, thinking from clothes and trainers that I had just been up before the beak myself.

One of them, a man in his early forties, his head more bald now than shaved, had the word SKINS tattooed across his forehead. His skin, once smooth, now corrugated around the blue letters, making it look like very old graffiti on aging concrete. This tattoo had been a bad idea when it was done, back in the late 1970s. Now, it was a catastrophe; he might just as well have had the words, 'Send straight to prison', added, to run down his broken nose.

Outside the castle it was now hot and somnolent. The middle management in the Black Prince room would be done to a turn now, happy to sack themselves in the name of progress. There was no one hanging around the entrance to the Cobb Hall centre, an arcade offering the unusual combination of 'Crafts, gifts, antiques, ladies' sportswear'. Perhaps there was a traditional cottage industry in old Lincoln, where wizened old men with deft fingers and disappearing skills would stitch together cycling gussets and sports-bras.

Back, for a last time, at the Jews Court I was accosted by the one woman in the street. No more than twenty years old, she was a Jehovah's Witness, and I was her only possible target. Perspiring, she approached me, proffering a copy of the *Watchtower* and eternal salvation.

'I'm Jewish,' I lied, defiantly.

She was slightly taken aback, but not for long. They are nothing if not crafty, these missionaries, as generations of Africans can testify.

'So you too believe in Jehovah?' she shot back.

'Look here, my dear,' I said to her, making myself sound like Alec Guinness as Fagin, 'what are the chances – nought to ten – of our having a conversation in which I convert you to Judaism?'

'Zero,' she conceded. 'And it's the same for you?'

I nodded. And, oh sweet victory, she walked away first! Try it, it works.

At the bottom of the hill, near the water, there was a happy thronging. A pavement artist had nearly completed the Grand Canal of Venice in chalks, the British Legion were selling their flags, a juggler tossed balls above the heads of gently grazing shoppers. 'Prosperous' was the word that came to mind. I was sorry to leave Lincoln; it had been my favourite stop so far. I wondered whether life would seem so gentle and pleasant where I was now headed: the North.

CHAPTER 19

Scuddin' the Puss

From Torksey the tide carries the Trent due north, through the pretty town of Gainsborough. Two miles further on is the village of West Stockwith – in late Victorian times a town of over 5,000 souls, its prosperity based on ship-building, but now a small village of 200 or so. On the left, as you head towards the Humber, is the great flat area bounded by waterways known as the Isle of Axholme, once marshland but drained by a great Dutch engineer, Cornelius Vermuyden, in the 1600s, the days when we still had things to learn from Europe.

Twelve miles on and the tricky junction with the Stainforth and Keadby canal appears, linking the great Trent with the Don and the Aire. On this straight and featureless stretch, little breaks up the skyline save for the occasional power station or pylon, and flat farmland borders the water as far as the eye can see. When people say that England is 'full', they do not have these parts of Yorkshire and Lincolnshire in mind.

The Don itself marches briefly beside the man-made waterway, departing eastwards after four miles as the canal branches off and north again, meeting the imposing Aire and Calder navigation two hours' paddling later. Now it is west by north-west, between steel-piled banks, passing barges laden with coal. The surrounding land is bleak with few trees, though squat power station chimneys grow well here.

The canalised Aire flows the wrong way for paddlers, not at a rush but strongly enough to force the weedy kayaker – a month and nearly 300 miles from the soft comforts of his southern home – on to the charity of passing powered craft. This is a better, higher way to watch Knottingley and Castleford slip by. After eight more miles the first outcrops of the city of Leeds edge the increasingly busy banks. Two more and you're at its heart.

★   ★   ★

The first true northerners that I ever really mixed with were Black Tom, Big Angus and Goggle-eyed Dick.

In the gap year between school and university I worked for a time on the electrification of the east coast railway – or, at least, a southern spur between King's Cross and Hertford. On weekends and overnight we would be taken by vans from the industrial wasteland of the King's Cross goods yard to a works train located somewhere on the dusty track. At the front of the train was an augur, with a drill bit about four feet in diameter, which would create seven-feet-deep holes at regular intervals, about two yards away from the tracks. As a college boy, I got the supposedly skilled job of dropping a polystyrene 'core former' into the centre of each hole. Concrete would then be poured around it.

The safety standards observed by BICC, the contractors on this operation, to be honest, were utterly scandalous. Hard hats were almost never worn, and we clambered over the trains while they were still in motion. Twice, I fell into the deep holes, and had to shout loudly into the night to be pulled out. I remember when a drunken, toothless Scot called Lachie, who lived in a grim hostel near King's Cross, once fell asleep in the sand-hopper at night, and nearly donated his right leg to a concrete plinth just outside Southgate.

The aristocracy of the work-force were the men of the North, who lived for months at a time in caravans at King's Cross, and who had been the boys who had electrified the west coast railway from London to Glasgow. What these guys wanted was to make as much money as possible in as short a time as they could, working day and night, and then go back to Carnforth in Cumbria, and piss it away on dogs and boozing. Too much scruple about safety would slow things up, and lose them money. They were prototypical unregulated free marketeers. They loathed unions and thought of themselves as free spirits. In reality, they were conveniently cheap labour.

Oh, and they were terrifying. Angus and Dick, in particular, were pure bastard. Angus, who was built like Siamese twin prop forwards, and whose perpetually scowling face was topped with an incongruous pageboy haircut, liked fighting. On one afternoon shift, where the railway ran behind a supermarket, I saw him head-butt the Glaswegian petty criminal who served us as a look-out. Blood went everywhere, and the little, sallow man lay on the ballast, his warning whistle and pork-pie hat framing his head, apologising profusely for whatever he had said that had provoked the assault.

Dick was more a man for hitting the defenceless. He boasted one morning about how he'd been home that week, and beaten his missus up, because she hadn't taken proper care of his whippets. And it wasn't a joke.

Anyway, one night, near the end of the shift, we were all in the brake van drinking hot, sweet tea out of milk-bottles (there were no cups). And the thing that I had long feared, now happened; Angus and Dick's satirical attention turned to me: eighteen, long-haired and about to go to university.

'Hey, Brenda!' said Angus, leering. 'Does tha 'ave a girl-friend?'

'Yes,' I answered, full of dread.

'Is tha pokin' her, then?'

'Sure,' I mumbled.

'So thee says,' Angus went on, remorselessly. 'But,' and he winked at Dick, 'the question is: art tha scuddin' the puss?'

Dick laughed. I was flummoxed. Scuddin' the puss? What the hell was that?

Whatever it was, I clearly couldn't win. If I said no, then I was a nancy boy, too southern and poofy to do the things, like puss scuddin', real men did. If I said yes, then I would doubtless have inadvertently confessed to something for which I could expect to be ribbed, violently, for as long as I stayed on the railways. I hesitated.

'I asked thee,' Angus demanded again, thrusting his face forward, 'art tha scuddin' the puss, college boy?'

'Yes,' I said at last, desperately. 'I am. In fact, I'm scuddin' as much puss as I can lay my hands on.'

There was a pause, and then Black Tom, who wasn't so bad

and who often acted as interpreter between Dick, Angus and civilisation, clapped me on the shoulder.

'Ee, tha dirty little bastard!' said Angus approvingly, and offered me a Woodbine.

For the benefit of southern readers, scuddin' the puss is a term meaning cunnilingus. And I can't remember now whether I was or not.

This incident didn't cause my apprehension of the North, but it did represent it. By the time that I met the three Cumbrians in the mid-70s, the positive images of the North – independence, lack of deference, red-brick modernity, economic success, political radicalism – were all being supplanted by the negative.

The Mersey Sound and the modernising sagas of David Storey and Alan Sillitoe were being replaced as images by factory closures and problem estates. The companies that had symbolised the white heat of technology were beginning to shut down. The great urban plans of the 1960s Labour administrations, so pure and graceful on the drawing-board, were now realised in alienating city-centre motorways and concrete ghettoes. The virtues of the North had come to be seen as being its vices.

Sometime – perhaps in the winter of 1980 – I came to Leeds to a meeting at the university. The great Thatcher recession was already biting, and the bulletins were full of announcements of job losses in the North, as some of the most famous industrial names went out of business.

Worse even than that, though, was the effect on the people of Leeds, Bradford and the surrounding area of a capricious but somehow representative scourge. It was wet, and getting dark by three in the afternoon when I arrived, and the Yorkshire Ripper, unfound after twelve murders, had just killed a student from the university.

I have never experienced such an atmosphere of distrust, hatred and fear. Mini-buses took female undergraduates the half-mile from the Union to their halls of residence. Every man in every car and on every corner could be Him, especially if he had a northern accent. Three people turned up to my meeting, all men.

Listening to the flat vowels of the hoaxer who convinced the police that he was the Ripper, I associated the whole phenomenon with Angus and Dick and their hatred of women. Thus are prejudices born.

Nearly twenty years later this felt crass; an internal libel which had gone on too long. People are more complicated than that. My frayed tapestry visions of sink estates, industrial desolation, racial prejudice, teenagers who – unlike us southerners – couldn't take their drugs, and social conservatism, needed a makeover. For a start, sculptures like Antony Gormley's triumphant Angel of the North, and reports of the Manchester renaissance, now suggested a region unsilted by working-men's clubs, homophobia and chronic pessimism. A place where you wouldn't be stopped in the street and asked, roughly, whether tha scudded the puss.

The Leeds and Liverpool canal starts at River Lock, in the middle of Leeds. I arrived there on a breezy, grey day in late June. A few boats were moored by the dockside, and a banner over the old warehouses announced that Granary Wharf, 'a unique shopping experience', had reopened. 'A Millennium Facelift', we were told, and 'Business as usual'. I never could resist a millennium facelift, so I went in.

From the city side, you reach Granary Wharf by walking towards Leeds Central station, and then ducking down on to a dank, long stretch of smelly road that passes under the roaring railway lines. This stretch is, with northern candour, called Dark Arches (the same principle applied elsewhere would furnish England with any number of Polluted Roads, Chintzy Gardens and Twee Avenues).

Beyond Dark Arches you turn sharp left through a large unpromising arch, like the entrance to Newgate gaol, and find yourself crossing rushing water on a subterranean walkway over the captive Aire. Another yard or two, and in the vaults you come across an indoor New Age Covent Garden, filled with everything that the stressed professional could possibly want. It was my kind of place.

Set into every Victorian arch was a second-Elizabethan glass-fronted shop, and in the passageways between stood a couple of dozen stalls and little pylonned kiosks. There were bookshops presided over by middle-aged women with large bosoms and large glasses. Jewellery stalls with suitably rustic and unfussy ear-rings, and necklaces the size of coral reefs, were tended by men with ponytails. There were stalls with lamps, stalls with nothing but mirrors, stalls all dolphins and crystals. One table boasted a variegated army of New Age statuettes, including dragons, wizards, Buddhas, many-armed Hindu gods, and native Americans – one of them a foot-high figure of a rather unspiritual squaw with red lips, snake-hips and pneumatic breasts.

But for every sexy squaw, every book of *Make Your Own Japanese Water Garden*, every bottle of room fragrance oil, there were ten candles on sale. I don't know whether you've noticed, but England is in the middle of a pointless-candle epidemic. Here there were tiddly fat ones, long etiolated scented ones, candles shaped as little fat Chinese men, candles shaped as the Eiffel Tower, penis candles, bum candles, candles as big as a child, candles as small as mice, candles smelling of jasmine, candles with the whiff of rhubarb. Above all, candles that would be pretty useless for the purpose of lighting anything.

True, most middle-class houses will have a candle or two hanging about. But there must be millions, trillions of candles, given as presents or bought in a dull whimsy, stuck in boxes in cellars and attics. Inspiration failed at Christmas time, or a romance needed something, and you just happened to be passing one of England's ten million candle stalls, and someone wound up with yet another coloured stick of wax with a wick in it. Just what they'd never really wanted.

But wait! Beginning to edge out even the candles are the -opathies and -erapies. There in Granary Wharf, they were (as one stall-holder claimed), 'Taking the best from the East to improve life in the West'. So you could purchase the quick way to balance your chi with Feng Shui, to locate your chakras with Reiki, to find your bladder just behind your big toe with Reflexology, to be greased up with the pleasurable stink of aromatherapy oils, to make a naturopathic compress with gunk from 'the comfrey range'.

What could be more English, as the millennium changed, than to buy your furniture from a Scandinavian warehouse, place it according to a far-Eastern semi-mystical philosophy, and then invite someone in to prod your feet? While listening, of course, to the music of Sumatran dolphins, or songs from Ghana and Zimbabwe.

And then, like a smack on the back of the head when you're dreaming, or a face full of cold water when you're in the bath, you come up once again with the deep England, the ur-England of Hogarth, rudeness and the Inter-City firm. After deep inhalations and establishing contact between body and spirit – thus achieving deep calm and relaxation – how about subjecting your children to twenty minutes of terrifying violence?

Performing at hourly intervals through the day, from behind his candy-striped awning, was the invisible Professor Robantio with his traditional Punch and Judy show. As Punch bounced into his window, the parents took up their places at the back, shuffling their kids into the front. Punch, for our entertainment, threw the baby down the stairs, hit his wife with a stick, killed a policeman, killed the hangman and loved only his dog. If I had wanted to find the prototype for Big Angus and Goggle-eyed Dick, here he was, the great grand-daddy of every soccer hooligan, wife-beater and child abuser.

That dreadful, vicious, high-pitched squeal carried its cargo of malevolence to the far end of the arches, and out to the canal. I looked around, and realised that most of us were watching out of duty. This was part of our heritage, like Princess Margaret and dirty pubs.

I turned to go. Next to me a young man bent down, and tenderly kissed his baby son on the cheek. It wasn't the first, and wouldn't be the last time that I saw this happen. At that moment I longed once again for my own babies, growing up so quickly down South. I didn't buy a candle.

★　　★　　★

I wasn't surprised that almost the first building I came to as I walked along Leeds' new river front, down from Granary Wharf to the Royal Armouries museum, was the red-brick local HQ of the Magnanimous and Providential. Its walls bore the legend that this was, 'Near the site of the first Quaker House – Leeds 1699'.

The conjunction was apt; by 1999 Leeds had become the third largest financial centre in England, and now the eager young execs and office workers, single or gay – people with money and without children – could live beside the Aire, in converted five-storey brick wharves, with crimson sash windows, the detritus of the Industrial Revolution turned into living heritage.

This was mostly good. Areas that had been full of dreary, decaying, dangerous rubbish were now well-planned housing developments. I came across a pound full of water – an old dock – swimming with waterlilies. Crossing the pool was a picturesque nineteenth-century swing bridge over which carts, and then lorries full of machinery and coal, once used to pass, and which had now been put to use as the centrepiece of the water feature. Over this bridge, at eye height, a notice had been posted. 'Private Property No Access Residents Only', it read, evincing a breathless exclusion.

With the Aire on my left, I strolled past the museum devoted to the history and manufacture of Tetley's beer (right up there for excitement with the Chateauroux Tyre-making Museum), under a road, and found myself beneath the the Royal Armouries, a high, towering silvery building set on an isthmus surrounded on three sides by canal and river.

A few years earlier – as one of those exercises in moving things from London so that people in other parts of the country could have a go at culture and art – the suits of armour, flintlocks and halberds had been moved from their dusty cases in the Tower of London and into this purpose-built museum on the reclaimed Leeds river front. There had been fanfares and pzazz, and, after a while, disturbing reports that not enough people were actually going to the Armouries to keep it solvent. Prices were dropped, and special rates for Leeds citizens were introduced.

I wish that the Armouries had existed when I was a boy.

Over four floors, airy and well-lit, there was everything that a history-obsessive could possibly want.

Some of the armour I recognised from the Tower, especially King Henry VIII's jousting armour with its protruberant metal cod-pieces, a piece of vanity that had made me worry (when I was a child) just how large that bit would get when I grew up.

Most of the common-or-garden flintlocks, wheel-locks, cross-bows, pikes and rapiers were to be found hanging on the vast walls of Yorkshire Electricity's Hall of Steel (the Magnanimous and Providential would doubtless want to find something more single-female to sponsor). Elsewhere the uniforms and weapons of countless wars faced each other belligerently across the rooms. Small film displays showed the stations of the musket and the cuts and parrys of the duelling rapier. This was glorified maleness, with epaulettes and buttons, shouted orders and courage. And then, suddenly, I came across images of the Basra road; that anonymous, incinerated Iraqi, his face charcoaled, as he looked over the visor of his jeep.

The big innovation, though, was the actors. Every half-hour a young man or woman, trawled from the pages of a theatrical agency, would get up on a small stage in the corner of a hall and, dressed as a Greek hoplite, or a soldier of the American Revolution, begin to read from Xenophon or Thomas Paine. Small children and parents looked on as three of the museum staff dressed one of their number in the elaborate costume of a sixteenth-century Japanese samurai. In the basement, at the heart of an exhibition which told the visitor everything about Buffalo Bill that he or she could possibly want to know, four actors re-enacted melodramas of the Old West as they were once performed in the rough saloons and music halls of Arizona and South Dakota.

Then, at three in the afternoon, there was a tournament. Down by the Aire, separated from the boats and any daft passing canoeist by a green fence, knights in full armour thundered towards each other, their plumes nodding, the hooves of their horses raising flying clods as lance smote shield. Ten years old again, I applauded these heroes and their skill.

But where was everyone else? It was a bright weekend on the cusp of July, and, had this been taking place in London, I would have had to queue for Buffalo Bill, stand in line for the tournament, squint over a shoulder at the hoplite.

I would hazard a guess that approximately half the people that they had expected were actually turning up for this magnificent museum. Why? Leeds is easy to reach by every means except, perhaps, canoe. A few miles north, in York, the Viking museum – where the curators are so conscientious that even the distinctive odour of berserker poo has been sprinkled on the ride – is always heaving. But not very far south, the Sheffield Centre for Popular Music was also facing a visitor crisis, jobs were being lost, and metropolitan critics who resented anything not being in London were all saying 'We told you so', and totting up the subsidy that had gone north.

Were the citizens of West Yorkshire not proud of the Armouries? Was it possible that they thought of them as some kind of alien outpost, as an extension of London? Certainly there wasn't quite the same feeling of ownership that the inhabitants of York display for Jorvik.

I checked into a vast hotel just beside the station and a short walk from the aromatic pleasures of Granary Wharf. This establishment, a 1930s battleship in light stone, took up one entire side of Leeds City Square. The equestrian statue of the Black Prince and other monuments donated by wealthy citizens in the Edwardian era were corralled into one corner of the square by the four lanes of traffic which dominated everything.

At the mile-long reception, unadorned by picture, map or photograph, I asked for information about Leeds. They had none, said the receptionist, but if I cared to walk to the railway station the Tourist Information Office would tell me all I needed to know, she was sure. I was amazed. There were 300 bedrooms in this place; thousands of visitors to Leeds must stay here every week, and yet there was not a brochure, not a pamphlet, not a timetable, not a flyer, not a map, in the whole damn place. Like the tourists, it seemed that the people of Leeds themselves hadn't cottoned on to what was going on in their city. Here was a place being transformed, and yet its inhabitants, its hoteliers, didn't seem to know about it. It was the Armouries writ large.

Maybe they'd got too used to the idea of decline. Leeds City Hall is magnificent but moth-eaten. The faces of the lions have been eaten away by pollution, and the ceiling of the vast, classical portico is hung with chicken-wire to stop the pigeons roosting. Once Leeds had been the Silicon Valley of England, the place where the pushy, quick-witted innovators had come to make their money and fund their arts. Even as late as the 1960s a notion of progress had gripped the area, flinging three-lane one-way systems to carve metallic swathes through the city's heart, thanks to Professor Buchanan and his idea of walkways in the sky soaring above the car-flow below. Then came slump, depression, Dark Arches and the Ripper. It's a difficult mind-set to alter, even with a Harvey Nicks.

I escaped the traffic for a few moments in the Municipal Art Gallery, where nearly every painting has long been available as a jigsaw. Here were the reminders of Empire: Lady Butler's 'Scotland Forever', depicting the Royal Scots Greys at Waterloo, painted over seventy years later; the painting of 'General Gordon's Last Stand', showing the eccentric adventurer at the top of the stairs in his fez, waiting to be kebabbed by a dozen fuzzy-wuzzies. Here, too, the underestimated English painters of this nearly past century: Walter Sickert, Gwen John, and – most interesting for me – Stanley Spencer, in the shape of 'Christ's Entry into Jerusalem'.

Leeds was livable. More than livable. Perhaps its main enemies were a slight pessimism, too much modesty and an over-regard for the past. The people were gentle, considerate, self-deprecating even; as far removed from Dick and Angus as they were from the conventional stereotype of the bluff, arrogant Yorkshireman. They had a lot going for them.

Later that evening, on the bridge of the hotel battleship, as the last light was chased away from the far moors, I watched the minorest of princes, now – absurdly – dubbed Earl of

Wessex (the name stolen, surely, from a theme pub), being married to a woman in Public Relations. It was the top item on the news.

Time to move on.

CHAPTER 20

The Beautiful North

The half-way point of my journey approached and it was time to cross the Pennines by canoe. It put me in mind of that man who dragged a paddle steamer from one huge South American river to another, killing dozens of innocent peons on the way.

The canal had the reputation of being both beautiful and lonely, which was a problem because, in about 50 miles time, I would have to hitch another lift through the unappetisingly named Foulridge tunnel, a half day north of Burnley in Lancashire. The Foulridge is 1640 feet long, with no towpath, and a failure to negotiate it would leave me completely stuck. During the next three days I had to look out for any kind boaters going my way, who might take pity and let me live on their roof.

Out of Leeds proper, and past the ruins of Kirkstall Abbey, the canal followed the line of the River Aire through Airedale. Very soon the water seemed a long way from the lapping encroachments of Leeds and Bradford, in fact hardly a few hundred yards to the south. The towpath wound alongside me, kept from the light by steep hills and dark woods, quite still and almost completely empty of walkers. Once, with a suddenness that almost made me start, a bright yellow pipe arced across the canal from dark stands of trees on either side, as though it had just been thrown.

There was a new hazard now. To locks and swans could be added swing bridges. These are heavy old bits of road, crossing the canal about four or five feet above water level. They rotate about a pivot at one end, swinging out to allow boats to pass, while dropping barriers to prevent cars and lorries from plunging into the temporarily unbridged canal.

Boaters deal with them by tying up to the bank, one of the crew getting out, operating an opening mechanism using a British

Waterways key, while the captain takes the boat through. The crew then closes the bridge again.

Since Newark I had possessed such a key, costing £3.60. But how was I to use it? There was no advantage in getting out of the *Knife*, opening and swinging the bridge, getting back in again, going past it, getting back out again, closing the bridge and getting in for a third time.

So, arriving at my first swing bridge, by a lovely old mill miles from anywhere, I looked around for someone else to give my key to. Just then an old woman came by, bent with age.

'Old woman! Old woman! Old woman!' cried I.

This is nonsense, of course.

'Excuse me!' I said. 'Do you think you could help me by . . .'

Taken by surprise by this emanation from below, the old woman nevertheless cut my sentence off promptly.

'I'm afraid', she said, querulously, 'that I've just had a triple heart bypass, and I'm not allowed to do anything.'

'Oh, not to worry, then!' I called back breezily to this woman who was holding on to life by her whitened fingertips. She looked at me as though I were mad. I got out and dragged the poor old *Knife* round.

The next swing bridge arrived at a place where uncommunicative men in blue smocks wandered in twos and threes along the towpath, taking tea breaks from adjacent factories. The least taciturn of these men was, of course, a wag. When he saw me stopping a few yards from the bridge, he called out to me. 'What's the matter? Can't you do the limbo?' This was just my second swing bridge and the first of dozens of limbo jokes.

At my third, a nice young man with his pretty wife and gurgling baby gave me a hand. This being Yorkshire he was, inevitably, a vet.

Number four I decided to go under. I reckoned that the canoe had about two foot clearance below the highest point of the bridge – just where it pivoted. All I had to do was lean back or forward enough to reduce my own height to less than two feet, and it should be easy.

I sidled towards the bridge on the mechanism side, holding on to the rusty, cobwebbed underneath with one hand, and guiding myself along the concrete bank with the other. Half-way under I nearly tipped, a slight movement being enough to fill the canoe with water, soaking my arse and causing me to curse loudly. I imagined some pedestrian crossing the bridge at that point, and being taken aback by the sound of demonic swearing coming from beneath their very feet.

Still, I made it. And I managed seven out of every ten bridges after that. I soon learned that it was no use hoping to find boats at the bridges, and slipping through with them. Only three boats had passed me going the other way all morning. It was not a good omen.

Near Shipley I came across a Miserable Man. He had been a canoeist. He had been a boater. He had seen the world. And he could tell me that this stretch was Las Vegas compared to the run-up to Foulridge. 'You've got no chance,' he told me, relishing every word, when I asked him about my chances of a lift. 'No chance at all.'

I was now passing through Saltaire, the model industrial community built by the Victorian industrialist and philanthropist, Sir Titus Salt. On either side, great honey-coloured buildings rose above me; warehouses, a classical church with pillars.

Just beyond the church I found myself paddling alongside a young woman, by her dress probably a worker at the nearby Hockney gallery. Looking over her shoulder, she began to quicken her pace. I realised that she was worried that, from my vulnerable position four feet below her, and perched on a two-foot-wide bit of plastic, I was following her, a waterborne flasher.

She wasn't the only woman who seemed put out by me that day. Occasionally, coming down beside a Barratt's estate, with houses whose pocket-handkerchief gardens stepped down to the water's edge, I would catch a housewife looking at me edgily, as though wondering whether I mightn't suddenly make land on her patio and − Viking style − carry off her washing, the pewter heron and her vainly struggling self. I'd take her to a marina full of fellow Norse kayakers where we would sing naughty songs and drink Ribena till late in the evening. Hmmm. I was now fantasising about abducting rather than being abducted. Was this progress?

I was approaching the famous locks at Bingley. Here there is a rise of three consecutive locks, a break, and then another rise of five. The whole effect of this watery staircase is rather as one imagines the Hanging Gardens of Babylon to have been, just before the garden designers put the plants in. From the bottom, they are quite beautiful in their own way, forming a step temple of gates and black-and-white lock paddles, looking like an industrial pagoda.

They were a bugger to pull a canoe up, though, and I was already tired. As I contemplated the climb, the *Knife* resting beside me, I fell into talking to a man of about my own age, who was out walking his Scottie dog. I was beginning to discover that the cliché about people in London being so unfriendly was true. It was indeed much easier to have conversations with strange northerners than with my fellows of the South-East. Nice conversations, and the other sort.

We walked together. No. He walked and I struggled. Half-way up the long incline, and after I'd changed my pulling hand a dozen times because the rope was cutting into my palms, he observed that it looked like hard work. Perhaps he'd like to swap for a moment, I suggested, adding that I could just fancy a go on a Scottie.

'Ooh, do you know, I would,' he replied, seriously, rotating each shoulder in turn, as though in discomfort. 'But I had two rounds of golf yesterday, and unfortunately I've really stiffened up.' As if by magic his posture had become that of a much older man. I let it go.

It began to rain gently. We parted, I crossed the canal, bedded the *Knife* down at a local boatyard, and walked in the drizzle towards the comforts of the Five Rise Hotel.

There are lots of different sorts of hotel in Britain, and most of them are bad. There are salesman and anonymous stopover hotels, like the Ibis, which manage to be expensive, unfriendly and supply the bare minimum. If they say it's the least they can do, that's because it is. In many luxury hotels, with pools and porn on the telly, the rooms are carpeted boxes with no atmosphere, all identical and dark. Many B&Bs are damp, with strange rules and smelly toilets.

But there is another sort, like the Five Rise, which is family run, slightly chaotic and where everything is a bit quirky. You'll find odd reminders of the children everywhere in the shape of photos or sharp toys left in the beds. Questions about the area will turn into real discussions. Invariably, in your room in the Quirkhotel, you will find a brochure, with a little history of the place's owners. 'It's four years', the brochure, all copperplate and drawings, will begin, 'since Jancis and Toby set out from Birmingham for Little Dollop, leaving behind them the world of PR and marketing, and determined to lead the good life as hoteliers in this idyllic spot.' Then comes the bit about the family. 'Bringing with them Adeline, aged 11, Noah, aged five, and Mr Fernypants, the Siamese (age unknown), Jancis and Toby had always planned for a special kind of hotel.'

There follows a long description of building works, restorations, plans for extra bedrooms and conservatories. There will be potted biogs of the chef and the gardener and a not uninteresting – if exhaustive – history of the house itself, from its early life as a muddy field in Tudor times, to its purchase – semi-derelict and with the original wainscoting – from ninety-year-old Ada Gruggins just a short time ago. And it will all be written in that intimate, self-mocking style that educated English people affect.

As he showed me to my room and my brochure, I told Toby, the owner, about my worries concerning the Foulridge tunnel and cadging a lift. I shouldn't get too concerned, he said, they'd had some Americans staying. They'd left two days earlier, and I might be able to catch them up. I doubted it. It was all getting a bit like crossing bits of the Pacific by tramp steamer; they might come along this month, they might not. Till then I could stay in port and enjoy the native dancing.

At dinner in a light room overlooking Bingley, Jancis served the lamb and pointed out that the locks, built in 1774, had been there when the Brontës lived in Haworth, just over the way. How different, I mused, the course of English literature might have been if the sisters and Branwell had actually gone on canal holidays. Linton could have converted Heathcliff to the gentle pleasures of phutting along at 4 mph (a great speed in those days), while Cathy cut the sandwiches in the galley. Meanwhile, Mr Rochester's mad wife would have been locked in the combined shower and toilet, where even she could have done no harm, except get herself wet.

Over a home-made chocolate mousse I got to talking to the woman dining alone at the neighbouring table. She was a slightly diffident southerner, who now lived in Pangbourne on the Thames; I'd pass her house in a few weeks' time. She worked, she told me, for a housing association, and she found what was happening to the country, in terms of North and South, fascinating. For example, her association was having to close its Reading office, because it simply couldn't get any staff. 'Unemployment down there is zero, or as near as makes no difference,' she said. 'It isn't the same up here.'

After a quick visit to Bingley proper, the only interesting feature of which was a restaurant called the Kebab Ranch (sister, perhaps, to the Curry Hacienda?), I set off again.

As I paddled along I saw occasionally-pretty turn to sometimes-beautiful. It was still Airedale and there were still swing bridges, but now there were long vistas across to castles on hills far away. The villages I passed through were smart and flowery. At Silsden the stone-clad Barratt's houses tried to outdo one another in floral displays, showing off to the occasional canal traveller and to each other.

I'd now been away for over four weeks. Although such sights made a pleasant change from 6-foot bankside nettlebeds and the backs of factories, I was still lonely and a little grudging and prone to self-pity. When a man hailed me from a garden with a friendly, 'That looks like fun!' I wanted to shout back, 'Oh, does it. Well you come and do it, then, with your nether regions in permanent Weil's Dip, and I'll sit in your warm living-room with your warm children, toasting crumpets and watching "Coronation Street".' Not my proudest moment.

And then, at a place called Kildwick I stopped by a bridge and looked down from the raised canal on to a perfect scene below. Right beneath me, in a long, sloping field below a dry-stone wall, forty or fifty primary school children chased and played and sat and talked, watched over by two women teachers. They were gay and unburdened, and, yet again, I felt the physical pain of separation from my own children. Then from a small, grey church, across a lane from the children's field, the sound of bells added to the calls and laughs, and didn't stop for a full half hour, as they rang out whole peals or tolls or anything that took the ringers' fancies. The campanologists were practising.

Walkers took their ease on a bench. Far in the distance I could see a busy road and a gigantic Homebase. But that was there. Here, where I was now, I could live, among the yellow iris, the mayweed, the red valerian and the sheep's bit. This was why I had come.

At the end of Airedale is the town of Skipton, through which runs the meridian line of England. Here the canal plays a river's part, passing through the town's centre. And here, too, the first thing that the tired boater notices, as he or she steps on to the towpath, is the local obsession with dog-shit.

You can't blame them. In this part of Yorkshire even the dogs have dogs, as though making up for the lack of human beings. There's lots of empty countryside, of course, but dog-owners like to walk where everyone else walks, and so their dogs go with them. The result seems to have been a major shit crisis.

Down south there are notices on lamp-posts advising dog-owners of fines should their excreting pooches, by some miracle, be spotted by anyone willing to act. Up here I had already come across larger, more aggrieved signs, such as the hand-painted notice which read: 'We don't want any more crap. Scoop if you poop.'

On the path at Skipton they had taken to naming and shaming. In a large glass-fronted parish noticeboard, were photocopied clippings from the local paper. Under the headline 'Local Woman Fined', one detailed the trial of 'Mrs Violet Higgs of Farnhill, accused of not clearing up dog faeces on the towpath at Silsden', a crime which had cost her £50. She was joined in ignominy by an Elsie Rogers, who had been seen to kick her poodle's poo into the canal, as the turd inspectors approached her. At this rate it wouldn't be long before the townsfolk of Skipton shaved these women's heads and paraded them round the market cross.

Trundling my 17-foot canoe down the main street, taking care to keep its wheels out of the poo, I found lodgings in a pub called The Woolly Sheep, quartering *The Subtle Knife* in a stables over which – in copperplate – was the legend 'Thos. Irving. Post horses and gigs for hire'. I was shown my room by the landlord's daughter, blonde, bespectacled and high-breasted, and – in the traveller's tradition – lusted after her. My early fantasies, fuelled by my lack of confidence in my own journey, were indeed now being replaced by day-dreams of chance seduction and wayside encounters.

Her physical qualities were shared by many of the ladies of Skipton. Everywhere my restless and deprived eye looked, there was another lovely young woman. Serving in shops, chatting by the war memorial, sitting in cafés, the place was full of nubility. Walking became a pleasure, as I discreetly studied each profile. And there were many here, walking with confidence, talking with animation and intelligence, so many . . .

Luckily, the fair maidens of Skipton were outnumbered ten to one by their ubiquitous grannies. For Skipton was also Oldladyville. Boats drew up at the canal quay full of them, coaches arrived in the main street stuffed to the gills with them, restaurants and tea-rooms heaved with perms and spectacles. Their comfortable twittering rose above them, as they moved in slow groups across the town.

I liked them. They expressed an unself-conscious sociability; all worry done, no mobile phones or pagers. Those on sticks hobbled along cheerfully uncomplaining. If you smiled at them, they smiled back. I was largely invisible to the young, as once middle-aged men with well-developed shoulder muscles and an air of intelligence were for me; but to the old I was of some interest. But then, everything is of some interest to the old.

Onwards. The *Knife* was trundled back to the water and the first swing bridge negotiated. But, yet again, all next morning I met no one heading out west. No boats were upping mooring spikes, no salty canal-dogs thrumming their engines. The water was oily, though the canal's course was more eccentric and pretty.

Five miles on, and – after 350 miles of travelling – I reached the exact half-way point in my journey. A watery milestone! It was all downstream from here!

Unfortunately I was no longer on the water, having been forced out of the canoe by the most aggressive and obviously disturbed swan I had so far encountered. From 200 yards I had seen him displaying to dog-walkers on the bank, standing five feet up in the water, beating his wings and hissing. I disembarked and towed the boat by its rope, the appalling bird following me for nearly half a mile. Now long-haired Highland cattle, cranebills and daisies crowded down to the waterside, and I was alone.

Then at a place called Skegneck, a deserted lock tucked between hills in the middle of nowhere, I once again came across death. A bouquet had been placed on an old, disused water tank, where it had withered. The mildewed card, just visible through the plastic wrapping, read: 'For Peter, from his Mum and Dad. Much missed.'

Peter had died like this. The previous August a narrowboat called the *Drum Major*, carrying some men and women with learning difficulties and their helpers, had, unnoticed, got caught up on the sill of the lock gate. As the water drained out of the lock, the boat, one end caught, began to tilt downwards.

One helper was steering the boat, the others working the lock gates. The passengers themselves were all at the back. Suddenly the boat came free and crashed down into the water, submerging the rear section where the handicapped men and women were. Four had drowned, said the newspapers, including a Peter Burgess. The helpers escaped. A week or so before I stood by the place where the four had drowned, experts had agreed that they were not to blame, adding that this was the first time such an accident had happened on the British waterways. Death here is wily.

For several miles after Skegneck the towpath carried the

Pennine Way with it, and jolly walkers in bright shirts strode along, singing hallos. Many of them were carrying peculiar alpenstock things, which they used like bendy walking-sticks; I thought they looked silly.

At just before three, in a deep cut, woods on either side, I arrived at the hamlet of Abbott's Harbor. Here, between two bridges over the Leeds and Liverpool, was a place that had nothing to do with either. There was a café in old stone, kids' slides in the garden, a two-storey Jacobean house, and a riding stable.

Inside the café, once a hostel for monks walking to Fountains Abbey, the patroness was ill, coughing fit to bust. It had been going on for some time, she said, pulling on her third cigarette in ten minutes, but she couldn't get rid of it. She'd go and see her homoeopath and get it sorted. But, yes, she did have a room for me.

I eviscerated the canoe, and then walked along the canal and back up past the isolated church. Here were new detached houses carved from the land surrounding the church, with landscaped gardens and 4WDs in the yard, and names like St Peter's Barn and St Peter's Cloister.

Up the hill the large old pub, the Cross Keys, had just opened, and I interrupted two fortyish barmaids who were exchanging stories about their bras.

'Well, I found with that one, that if I reached right up, then everything'd suddenly tumble out!' said one.

'I know,' said the other. 'They've never found the happy medium between support and comfort, have they? Yes, sir, what can I get you?'

I sat with my notebook and a pint in the corner, and watched life, in this wealthy part of Yorkshire, pass by. Three women, two young and one older, came in, took a seat by the window, and began to discuss further education teaching. I wanted to join their conversation, but I feared that I smelled ever so slightly, of sweat and canals.

Five minutes later four rock-faced old Yorkshiremen, with craggy trousers and big shoes, sat themselves down with large grunts. Here, at least, I thought, I'd be able to connect with the old North Country. This foursome would be bound to sink pint after pint, offering the travelling eavesdropper story after story about farming the high Dales.

Not here. The granite quartet didn't sink as much as a half between them. Instead they ordered four coffees, one with cream (Barmaid, make mine a latte, with a vanilla chaser, it's bin a 'ard day!). Here I was in rural Yorkshire and I might as well have been sitting in a cappuccino bar in Notting Hill. Pub coffee, mewses, college and homoeopaths. I felt depressingly at home.

It was still early when I got back to my damp room in the Jacobean house. On the wall, over a hideous white chipboard vanity unit, was the date 1682, picked out in black lettering on ancient, chunky plaster decoration.

I couldn't really face any more misunderstandings between Dorothea and Mr Casaubon. On the bedside table were stacked three brown-leaved paperbacks – books, it transpired, from the golden period of English historical fiction. I lay on the lumpy bed and began to read.

I didn't go for Georgette Heyer's 1938 masterpiece on the escape of Charles II after the battle of Worcester. There was too much of the witty, young king stuff for my republican sensibilities. Georgette's Charlie, travelling in disguise as a valet, is constantly being insulted by commoners, and his trusty sidekick is perpetually at the point of running varlets through for their impudence. 'Nay, Grosvenor!' Charles tells him. 'The fellow but speaks his mind. 'Tis good for kings to learn from their subjects!'

The second book, *Cry God for Glendower!* was by Martha Rofheart, authoress, the jacket revealed, of *Cry God for Harry!* *Cry God for Glendower!* was published in 1973, and I wondered how many more of the *Cry God for!* series had been penned. Did Martha get as far as *Cry God for the Cardinal Bishop of Ely!* before she left off? Or did she manage the even more democratic, *Cry God for Wiggin the Carter!*?

I opted instead for the third, a novel concerning Anne of Cleves, Henry VIII's fourth wife; the one he married on the basis of a flattering miniature, and later unchivalrously dubbed the Flanders Mare. The cover illustration showed a pretty, large woman in the period clobber, with a hands-on-hips Henry in the background. Inside I found nearly the perfect historical fiction sentence. 'Soon, she would be Queen of England, Queen of the most advanced and enlightened nation in Europe. She pulled her mantle more tightly around her, and shivered.' I pulled my mantle around me, and laughed.

The next morning I got up early and was given the biggest breakfast I have ever had: five rashers of bacon, five sausages, three eggs, a toasted loaf, a forest full of mushrooms, ten tomatoes, three gallons of orange juice and an urn full of tea. I waddled off to the canal, and plumped myself into my poor canoe. The water level rose slightly. I had 12 miles to do by 11.30, if I was to have any chance of getting that lift.

There was still no one out there. The canal was as deserted and lovely as ever, following a winding course between hunched hills. Just me, the wild-flowers, the cattle, the sheep and the miles slowly ticking down.

In the middle of this landscape I came to a series of locks – the Greenberfield locks – that seemed far from any building. As I pulled into the bank an old Land Rover drove down the path to the lock and stopped. From it a matching farmer, old and khaki himself, emerged. He saw me, walked over and, without being asked, bent and held the *Knife* while I got out.

After a few pleasantries the farmer pointed over to a small hump among larger hills, a half mile or so away.

'Do you see that hill theer?' he asked me. I leant on my paddle and said I did.

'Well, there was this woman come up 'ere every year for 'er 'olidays. Long time back. 1800s or so, this was. Well, she wrote poems, 'ymns and religious music. An' she wrote one about that hill. She called it "There is a Green Hill Far Away". Do you know it?'

I said that I used to sing it at primary school. 'Well that's it theer,' he went on. 'That's the green hill. Except it ent far away, is it?'

It wasn't. Two hundred miles of Yorkshire, and now – as I was about to leave it – I'd encountered my first bluff Yorkshireman.

By midday I had officially entered Lancashire and was passing moored boats on the approach to the Foulridge tunnel. I had not seen a moving boat all day. 'You've just missed one,' said a man on the towpath. 'There won't be another for an hour. If then.' Oh, for God's sake . . .

Just before the tunnel, beside the canal, were an antique shop and a café with a garden. From this latter establishment a plump, bearded café-keeper would come out from behind the counter from time to time, and stand among the chairs talking to customers and towpath walkers, or feeding a large family of ducks. I bought some tea inside and walked back into the sunny garden.

There he told me the story of the Foulridge cow. In 1912 a large cow, chewing cud in a field beside the canal at the south end of the tunnel, had lost her footing and slipped into the water. For some bovine reason, instead of staying where she was, she turned north and into the tunnel. There she struggled through the mile or more of pitch-blackness until she arrived, exhausted, at the other end, where the astonished drinkers from the local pub pulled her ashore and revived her with ale.

And if she could do it without a canoe, the proprietor implied, then what was I making such a fuss about?

Just then – happily – salvation appeared in the shape of the local British Waterways man, who came along in his shirt and pick-up. If I hadn't found a lift by two, he said, then he'd drive me around the tunnel, no worry.

Lunch came and went, the man with the beard and I discussed bypasses and conservation, and still no boats appeared. At 2.30 the BW man returned. I admitted defeat, and – with guilty pleasure – tied the canoe to the top of his pick-up, and drove out of Foulridge, heading south for Burnley. I shall probably never know the essential character of the Foulridge tunnel. Never mind.

CHAPTER 21

Goodbye, Centenary Way

You didn't ask, but I'll tell you all the same. The most spectacular entrance to an English town by water must be the Leeds and Liverpool's triumphant progress into Burnley, Lancashire. From the south end of the Foulridge the canal carries along the Colne valley, yet is still 30 or so feet above the valley floor when it hits the centre of Burnley. Then, for nearly a mile, it runs dead straight on a raised embankment high above the houses and shops. To the north-west is the long, dark purple hump of Pendle mountain, home of the witches. Off, nearly due east, is Black Hameldon. Between are the high moors. In the middle distance sinuous lines of hills undulate, between the unravelling ribbons of approaching roads.

Hard by is the townscape of Burnley itself – the rough outline of which was familiar from past towns. There were the blunt needles of chimneys (many fewer than once there were) and the sharper spires of churches, the squat whiteness of civic buildings, some medium rise estates (the one high-rise had been dynamited a couple of years earlier), the ubiquitous presence of four-lane highways blasted across the middle of town, the familiar oval and stalks of the football ground and its floodlights. Then, just below the embankment, on either side, the herring-bone formations of two-ups, two-downs slope towards the spine of the canal, uniform ochre chimney pots on slate roofs.

A million quid or so, and this embankment would be one of the glories of England – the Magnanimous and Providential Burnley Sky-walk, perhaps. But the money isn't there and neither is Burnley. Instead it's overgrown, weed-covered, rubbish-strewn, and slightly menacing. What should be a promenade, is instead a run-down strip of dirty water. On the Net boaters tell each other scare stories of what they've encountered here. I saw only one boat brave enough to have moored in Burnley, and they didn't look as though they knew what they were doing.

I walked across the empty highway and into the shopping centre of a town that had lost it. A friend, a native of Burnley, had told me that the town has very high addiction rates, and holds the British record for incest. It isn't hard to believe. In the relatively empty shopping arcades (it was Thursday afternoon), the women looked normal enough. But the men; I had never seen such ugly, ill-favoured blokes. Almost every male was scrawny and pallid, tattooed from head to foot in ancient designs that had turned to the colours of intricate bruising. Poorly dressed in shabby shell-suits, they lounged or sat around on benches, the corners of their mouths turned down, their shoulders slumped. Some of the very youngest, not yet beyond hope, were pushing baby buggies around after their even younger spouses. Or, if my friend was to be believed, their sisters. This was the obvious human residue from dead industries, whose mills and lathes were now dust. Had the only men on the planet been the men of Burnley, and the only women the women of Skipton, the human race could never have survived.

I got lost, and found myself in a back-street. On either side of a low, old, crumbling street were two relics of the past. On the left the Fulledge Conservative Club offered 'Quizes! [sic] and Prizes!' Almost opposite, its equally redundant historical rival, The Burnley Miners, was also open for the downing of mild. But there are no miners in Burnley any more. Or Conservatives. The Tory candidate in 1997, the appropriately named Mrs Brenda Binge, had walked off with a mere fifth of the votes.

There was little to see in Burnley, or, rather, little worth seeing. It was still early, and I thought that I could catch an early show at the cinema. In such a compact town the local fleapit shouldn't be hard to find. I stopped a teenage girl and was directed towards a rise in the ground just beyond the town hall. When I got there, I could see nothing that resembled a cinema. I asked again, another teenage girl.

But, no matter how many teenage girls I asked, and how often I was directed, I just couldn't reach the place, or even get a glimpse of it. The roads seemed to dominate Burnley, somehow, carving it into little dusty segments that were unreachable on foot. Flyblown corners and dusty enclaves could present themselves within yards, yet be as inaccessible as if they were on the moon. I stood on Centenary Way, a high-level, high-speed road, opened in the 60s to a great fanfare by some vainglorious, modernising alderman, and gave up.

Eventually I found my way back to the embankment again, and walked along it until, on my left, I saw the entrance to a park, and went in. It was late afternoon on a hot day, and the shadows of the trees fell long across an almost perfect Victorian pleasure gardens, re-created as though by Disney. Sloping lawns framed meticulously maintained flowerbeds and fountains, the whole enclosed by newly painted iron railings. Under the gaze of the bearded Sir James Mackenzie, a GP in Burnley for thirty years in the late nineteenth century, there was a boating lake and an elegant cafeteria (both closed).

I had the garden to myself, this Thursday late afternoon; there was no one else here at all. In my mind I handed this park and the embankment over to a team of designers, gave them a lot of money and said, 'Make me something that will be the envy of the north-west!' If any town could do with it, Burnley could.

Poor places attract bad services. My hotel was not cheap, yet the room was poky, with a TV so tiny and set on a bracket so high that only a long-sighted giraffe could have watched it comfortably. There was no bath, just a shower. And on the customary brown tray there were little packets of coffee, teabags and sad, stiff sachets of sugar – but no cream. Instead, a mean notice informed guests, 'Milk portions available on request'.

I had never seen that before, but it chimed with the staff mission statement which, for some reason, had been mounted on the wall outside my room. 'The objective of all who work at the Beaverbrook Hotel', it said, 'is the maximisation of reasonable profit, which will then provide a stable basis from which to provide our customers with a first-class service.' But the most surprising notice was the one over the bed: *'We respectfully request that you do not iron anything on the carpet, as it will melt.'* Only experience can explain a notice like this. I imagined the manager standing puzzling over patches of congealed floor covering, and then gradually and furiously realising what had caused the damage.

That night I crossed the road to the cavernous Indian restaurant opposite the hotel, where they served me with a dish consisting of six tiny pieces of chicken floating in some reheated sauce, which I washed down with flat Coca-Cola, and all for London prices. In the background an Asian radio station belted out music and ads, of which the only recognisable words were 'reduced cholesterol'. Perhaps decent-sized portions were, like milk, available on request.

The next day I headed south and west. My journey was now half over in mileage, and more in time. I'd been over a month in the boat, and covered something like 400 miles. I didn't love the journey yet. I still felt sorry for myself and suffered almost unbearable pangs when phoning home and having one of the children answer. But Sarah was evidently proud of my progress, if slightly surprised, and even Jane conceded – from time to time – that she hadn't expected me to get this far.

So it was in this mood and in this way, that for the next few days the journey went on. From Burnley the Leeds and Liverpool passed between the moors down to Blackburn, beside Chorley, through one and a half miles near Wigan where twenty-one murderous locks succeeded one another, forcing another marathon walk. Here the Leigh branch headed towards Manchester, flowing by the old mines at Worsley, before skirting the city where I studied for three years.

Then into the fatlands of Cheshire on the Bridgwater canal, into various tunnels, along the edge of Shropshire. And, at last, to the Severn and the borders of my mother's country.

CHAPTER 22

One Hundred Minutes of Solitude

Some people love solitude. Explorers, that sort of person. They like to be far from any man-made artefact and a thousand miles away from the nearest flush lavatory. At the top of the Severn, as it looped away from its Welsh meeting with the Montgomery canal, I was about as far away from other people as I would be on this journey. But would this solitude suit me? My experience thus far did not augur well. Trying to get to the Foulridge on the deserted canal had been bad enough.

This river was much swifter running than the Trent and, initially, much narrower. It also did strange things. At some points it would hardly clear a mud or gravel bank, leaving me grating over stones, pushing against the bottom with the paddle, and then it would abruptly shoot me into a narrow, fast current.

So idiosyncratic was it that I had a book to help me; a little white *Canoeist's Guide to the Severn*, strapped to the outside of the cockpit. It would give guidance such as: 'River shallow left below confluence, fast water under trees right. **Caution**.' That word Caution always made me worried whenever I saw it.

The book was usually right. Sudden fast currents would run from behind half-submerged bushes. The biggest danger was of being pushed by the water under overhanging trees, which could then catch at the paddle and topple me into the water. Being on my own, and far away from any help, such an event could lead – at best – to the loss of the boat.

One late afternoon I fetched up on a dark, overhung little beach. Ominously, an old copy of the *Canoeist's Guide* lay here, abandoned among the stones. I dragged the *Knife* up a steep slope, through a field, and into a camping field behind an old pub, the Wingfield Arms, where the *Guide* claimed there was camping. Above the field a road – formerly the A5 Roman road, now a B route – ran alongside, then crossed the Severn on a bridge dating from 1792, with a toll-booth at one end.

Like that other field by the Trent, this one too was empty save for a camper van. This was no brown job, though, but a vast white and chromium Peugeot Hypermobil with TV aerial, fridge, double bed, shower and Palladian entrance with telescoping classical columns. Outside, on collapsible chairs, sat a couple in late middle age, their position designed to give them a first-class view of the pub carpark, to put them within easy earshot of the traffic on the road, and to turn their backs firmly against the river: sight-seeing English style.

A familiar pattern was emerging. The pub was not open yet. There was no telly, no one much to talk to, no privacy, no chairs, in all probability no breakfast tomorrow. By 9 p.m. it would be far too early for bed, but far too late for exploration. The only bright moment was provided by the fact that there was no paper in the loo that had obviously been set aside for the use of campsite patrons.

This would not bother the Hypermobil couple, since they almost certainly had a combined lav and bidet, which automati-cally scrubbed the vital area using expensive French detergents. And it wouldn't bother me either. For 800 miles I'd carried my own toilet roll, it had been my constant companion since Camden Town and now, at last, I got my chance to use it. Pathetic, perhaps, but out of such small triumphs is life on the water constructed.

Just outside the pub garden were two scruffy little caravans, quite obviously inhabited. The city may have its slums, but the country has caravans where the people who don't quite fit in end up. In odd corners all over rural England these dirty white boxes sit amidst buckets, old tricycles and washing lines, with electric cables snaking across gravel and into the sides.

I walked out on to the road, severing my links with the empty river, and forging new ones with the world of houses and cars. I was in Montford Bridge, a Marcher village, fast becoming a commuter suburb of Shrewsbury. The Wingfield Arms and the two or three old brick houses around it were obviously the oldest habitations here, certainly dating back to the time when the toll-booth was established and the bridge built. One or two cottages were added in the nineteenth century, dotted about the crossroads.

Then, over a hundred years later, in the 20s, a line of white-washed prosperous houses had been put up along a lane running at 90 degrees to the road. They sat, shady and contented behind their deep gardens, with names on their garden gates such as 'Bienvenu' and 'The Willows'. This end of the village had then been left alone for a few decades until, in 1999, a brand new development of six detached brick houses, each with some architectural reference to the deep past, was put up. Arched Norman windows were clearly in vogue as were gables, with the essential modern element added by the double garages.

Facing each other a few yards down the road were a 50s Post Office and shop, run by a Filipino couple, offering everything at all times: newspapers, drycleaning, videos and aromatherapy while you wait. Well, maybe not that. Opposite was an ugly house with leaded windows and a yard full of hideous constructions. 'Half-timbered birdhouses for sale,' a sign threatened. On a lamp-post nearby a yellowing notice advertised a car rally held in central Wales some two years earlier.

I ambled down the road, back past the pub and towards the south end of Montford Bridge, taking notes as I went for an essay entitled, 'Montford Bridge: the evolution of a suburb'.

Behind a gate, in a field next to a brick house, I saw a pair of beautiful old Singer cars – two-tone in light green and white, the chrome on the midline and wings gleaming. As I walked up to the gate to take a closer look, two squint-eyed men in overalls emerged from the yard, and looked at me with such overt suspicion that I had no option but to explain that I was a writer, that I was travelling around by canoe looking at things, and I was definitely not a bizarrely opportunist classic car thief. I showed them my notebook to prove it. They nodded and said nothing.

Across the way were the council houses. Clustered along a road called The Crescent, a curved row of terraced pebble-dashed houses had been erected (according to a concrete inset) by the Rural District Council in 1921. And here I found the eccentricity which tends – these days – to be the province only of the proletariat. In one garden lay a series of old fridges and electrical appliances, rotting in the early evening sun. Next to it was a house called 'Balmoral, The Eagles'. This two-storey house was covered in bright plastic and porcelain imitation birds, animals and insects. Two black eagles with yellow talons guarded the door; four butterflies, two ladybirds, a raccoon, a squirrel and a skunk climbed from the base of the front door, to the chimney pots on top. Whatever the neighbours thought, for me it was a fabulous sight.

On the other side of The Crescent was a row of equal length built in the 60s out of a lighter brick, but the whole thing had obviously been designed before poor people had cars. None of the houses possessed garages, and, with no room in the road for parking, cars littered the pavements, leaving centimetres for pedestrians to push past. After forty yards The Crescent simply petered out in scrub. A stile led over into a dry field beyond.

And that was Montford Bridge in the last year of the millennium. Given a few more years there would be more detached developments. In the meantime I observed that 'The Yews' had no yews, and that 'West Wynd' was a 60s bungalow. I walked back past the Singers, but they had gone, safely hidden by their silent owners from the dangerous author.

On Montford Bridge at 8.15 the late sun caught the wisps of smoke coming from a large, aromatic wood fire over the river. A cyclist zoomed past. By now the pub was open, and I ate beside a middle-aged Welsh couple; a pair for whom every conversational serve was an ace, with no rallies, the subject never being returned, but trickling past at snail pace, and into the long grass of their relationship. 'Shoot me,' I thought, 'if ever I get like this.'

I was up at five, absurdly sweaty and with no way of sleeping again. A car had driven in overnight and was parked perilously close to a notice tacked to a riverside tree warning, 'No vehicles

beyond this point'. Which was good advice, in view of the
20-foot drop.

At 6 a.m. the man who lived in the caravan appeared, and
walked down the field towards me. He was sixtyish, a Brummie,
with a large grapefruit-shaped goitre on his neck, trailing a large
black dog that peed everywhere, and had to be warned off
my canoe.

'I collect the money from campers and the fishermen,' Goitre
explained.

The charge was £3.50 per night, but for me (he smiled) he
would make a special reduction to three quid only; 50p was
obviously a lot of money where he came from, so I decided not
to mention the toilet paper.

As I began my daily packing ritual, Goitre eyed my sleeping
bag; a sleeping bag that would have cost the best part of £120
in a camping shop.

'I need one of those,' he said. 'Last winter I was very cold in
the caravan. Could I get a good one for ten or fifteen pounds?'
Maybe a bit more, I said, and slid the boat down to the river.

Today it was five weeks since I set out in search of myself. Where
was I? In an empty tract of river completely on my own. How
silent it was! No hum of cars, drone of planes or chug of tractors.
There was just me, the ickle birdies, the herons, the dragonflies
and the occasional splosh of my paddles. Nor were there roads, or
houses, or wharves. I scraped over stones, whizzed down channels,
and no one appeared through the rotting undergrowth of the
river bank.

Within half an hour it was sending me totally bonkers.
Unmodified nature is rarely very beautiful. The flowers were
fine (all buttercuppy things and foxgloves), but who needed all
those untidy nettles and fallen trees, the tangled brambles and
smelly mud?

I began to hold conversations with the wildlife, while longing
for any sign of human habitation, for a homo sapiens alteration to
the ragged greens and browns. I was isolated, cut-off, vulnerable

and – above all and most unforgivably – I was bored. Predictable, yes, but still bored.

I paddled away for an eternity, round bend after sharp bend. And then, after 100 minutes, just as the *Guide* promised, the tips of the spires of Shrewsbury hove into view above the intervening banks. Soon handsome houses were to be seen on bluffs above the river, and my heart – the heart of supremely unnatural man – lifted.

I emerged from the wilds into civilisation by the bridge at a place called Frankwell, where a couple of amiable teenage boys were jumping off the bank into a large inner tyre.

Then I looped the great loop that the Severn describes around the centre of Shrewsbury, the castle high above, the roofs tumbling down to the path beside the water. Elegant Georgian bridges crossed the river at intervals, interspersed with equally elegant metal footbridges. Victorian villas gave way to the hill-top expanse of Shrewsbury School; Charles Darwin's school. From this pile an excited group of public schoolboys in white singlets and blue shorts rolled, like a stream of healthy piss, down to their huge boathouse and, via boats, into the river. In a park, just opposite, the large tent and gold letters of the Moscow State Circus suggested less exclusive entertainment.

At the weir I was forced to impress an unhelpful canoeist, standing beside a dozen kayaks, into assisting me to launch the boat beyond the boiling drop. Immediately I was nearly dragged under a tree, then twice semi-grounded on shallows, with heavy currents tugging at the end of the boat. Sullen fishermen grudgingly raised their vast roach poles as I was swept past, hardly grunting in response to my hellos.

In no time I had covered the four miles between the weir and Atcham. I beached by a cow-dung-filled meadow just before a pair of bridges, and walked towards the square, Queen-Anne-style house, on whose ivy-clad wall was the legend in large gold letters, 'The Mermaid'. I pulled the *Knife* over the road and into the yard.

I entered the reception where, bright and greasy with sweat, I saluted the woman behind the desk. Someone to talk to at last!

'Hi!' I shouted, my voice loud with anticipation. 'I'm the mad canoeist!'

She looked at me with a mixture of complete bewilderment and unfeigned dismay, as though I was a nudist covered from head to foot in lobster sauce. It occurred to me that she might not be the bubbly woman that I had spoken to on the phone the previous weekend. I quickly shuffled off to my room and made myself less obnoxious.

Immediately opposite the Mermaid, across a busy road, invisible from the river, stood the great bulk of the gateway into Attingham Park, one of the jewels of the National Trust; an organisation of which nearly a tenth of adult English people are members. Including me. I found my little card, and entered under portals. The motto over the gate read QUI UTIT SCIT EI BUNA. I wondered what it meant. The honey bulk of the house was visible down a long drive through a large deer park. Above there was a china-blue sky, with lazy, puffy clouds. Below, on the ground, old gents and biddies were being ferried from the carpark up to the house itself on a stripy golf-cart.

Where they disappeared, somehow. Arriving at the main staircase, and entering, I found the entire house empty save for me, and the keen-as-mustard room minders.

I had had no conversation of longer than five minutes in over a month, but here I could have a chat in every single room. The bright-eyed guardian of West Anteroom passed me on to the enthusiastic custodian of the Inner Library, who gave me twenty minutes of her time before sending me on to the mature Diana of the Dining Room. Each was delighted to find someone wanting to talk, and they reminded me of how those teachers of unpopular subjects would brighten up if any child expressed an interest in their abstruse specialism.

Not that they were experts. I liked their cheerful philistinism, which dismissed a good-enough Sickert portrait of an Edwardian countess, while praising a series of quite dreadful copies of Italian seventeenth-century landscapes, brought back by a long-dead member of the family from a Grand Tour.

'The family.' Whenever one of these splendid ladies mentioned those two words, her voice would drop in deference to the long-dead nobs. 'This,' she would say, lowering an octave, 'was the fifth Lady Berwick.' I was shown silver salvers presented to a junior Berwick in 1898, 'on the occasion of his attaining his majority', by the grovelling 'tenants of Attingham', and another from 'the following tradesmen of Shrewsbury', all the names carefully inscribed and for ever visible. The Berwicks had been ennobled only in the 1780s, but they had been treated then – and were whispered about now – as though they had come over with the Conqueror.

I was over-heating and, after an hour and a half chatting about the balls and parties that had been held at Attingham, I made for the Trust tea-room. Here, cooling in a high-ceilinged chamber, among the large rustic tables and flap-jacks, were all the missing biddies, pouring tea. Over each chair-back there seemed to be an oakleaf and acorn carrier bag, bulked out with sweet-smelling pot-pourri, and copies of *The Recipes of Shropshire*, featuring heart and kidney pie and pigeon casserole. In the garden – the third part of the Attingham Bermuda Triangle – there was little shade but plenty of room, and I drank elderflower pressé and pushed a small fork into a huge slice of home-made coffee cake. Then I walked back through the park.

A look in the handbook had revealed that the Berwick motto translated as 'Let Wealth be His Who Knows Its Use'. What superb arrogance this was! How very *nouveau riche*. And how appropriate that back beyond the gates, on a noticeboard by the bus stop, the local police had put up a series of statistics concerning the activities of some of those modern Englishmen whose motto was very similar.

ATCHAM CRIMEWATCH NEWSLETTER
15 crimes in May 1999:
1 Theft of and from a motor vehicle
1 Burglary of houses
3 Burglaries of other buildings
3 Criminal damage
Assaults at Belton and Cross Houses

This did not feel like the rural crime-wave that we were, that summer, hearing so much about. Most London schools record more crime than that.

Beside the Mermaid a short walk took me past the old malt-house, presented by the Berwicks in 1925 as a memorial hall to commemorate the Great War. In the churchyard of St Eata's (I had just missed the 'Grande Fete and Grand Duck Race. Raffle, Bric-a-brac, Bar-B-Q'), a bench celebrated the life of Atcham's greatest animal lover and RSPCA chairman: the eighth Lord Berwick. A gravestone commemorated the life of a housekeeper to the Berwicks. This had obviously been a one-lord town.

I'd had a good day after a bad start, the current having helped me to cover over 20 miles. But this was far better. Standing on the old bridge I watched as the late evening sun, still warm at nearly nine, washed over the far Shropshire hills that circled the scene: the Long Mynd, the Wrekin, the Clee hills and Caer Caradoc. Golden light caught the edges and details of the old church and hotel, played in the river as it turned and narrowed to the south. It brushed the willows, grazed the two placid fishermen in the shallows, held a candle up for the kissing couple in the churchyard.

And once again I felt wonderfully happy. It was a scene of exquisite, minute beauty, and it was as English as Constable. I could be in no other country, and I stood on that bridge until dusk fell.

CHAPTER 23

Uriconium and Smegwort

There were no newspapers at the hotel the next morning. The woman there explained that the last local shop had closed the previous October. The nearest store now was two and a half miles away; six minutes there and back by car, over an hour on foot.

Breakfast was taken in the unnecessary gloom of a dining-room in which the heavy curtains were mostly still drawn. The strange, unnerving sound of muzak accompanied the bacon: 'Bright Eyes', 'We Are Sailing', 'Monday, Monday'. On the next table a bearded man pugnaciously bullied a clean-shaven colleague also in software.

My destination that day – a day when I'd leave the *Knife* and travel by other means – was the Roman city of Wroxeter, Viroconium, three miles to the south of Atcham.

There was a bus, but I decided to walk there, down the narrow country lanes. And though there was no warning to match those I'd received about rivers, it was probably the most dangerous and foolhardy thing I'd done since setting out. For the first mile the road had a pavement, but even so the speed of the traffic was intimidating. Buffeted, shaken in the slipstreams of cars zooming past at sixty, I looked up to find myself under a sign saying 'Atcham. Please Drive Slowly'. No one slowed down at this notice, or showed in any way that they'd even seen it. A bit further on, another sign showing a deer prancing across the road seemed only to provoke a universal acceleration. What, you couldn't help asking yourself, did these drivers think the sign meant? Free deer here? Eat all the fawns you can crush? Knock one over, stick it on the roof-rack and then throw it in the Fossdyke?

Once the pavement ran out, however, I was the target. On the narrower roads each bend became a hazard, to be approached carefully, and with an escape route in mind. Was there a gate to jump over, a culvert to fall in, a gap to jump through? Around these corners every size and colour of motor vehicle would shoot out, as though oblivious even to the possibility of a walker or a cyclist. Pretty soon I found myself shouting epithets, as speeding cars flattened me against the hedges. Drivers stared at me, as though amazed. Once again, pedestrians clearly did not have right of way.

I turned carefully down Thomas Telford's turnpike, which breasted a plateau beside the Severn, and walked through to the fenced-off excavated ruins of Wroxeter, now guarded by a little ticket office and shop run by English Heritage. A quartet of Scandinavians had arrived just before me, and were strolling round the site with translation headphones on, yelling snurdeferdets at each other at the tops of their voices. We were the only visitors, so I started at the far end of the site.

Wroxeter/Viroconium was the fourth largest Roman city in Britain, with 5,000 inhabitants. It stood just off Watling Street, connecting North Wales with the South-East, via Patricia's lonely house. Originally a huge legionary fort, the only parts still visible were the bottom brick ranges of the covered market area and part of the walls of the huge public baths.

To help one visualise life in ancient Viroconium, English Heritage had placed occasional illustrations around the ruins, depicting what the visitor might have seen in the same spot when Hadrian ruled England. So, inside the line of the colonnade I found myself face to face with a foxy brunette, her large brown eyes fixed on mine and toting a shapely amphora as she wended her way to the forum. I might have been wrong, but I got the distinct impression that she fancied me, so it was a shame that she was just an artist's impression.

The baths, though, really required an effort of imagination. In an area the size of a cathedral, the Britanno-Romans had built a large warm pool, several side pools, a cold plunge bath, and wide public vestibules in which citizens could meet. The underfloor bricks, once used to heat the water and the air, had been re-piled on top of each other, showing the scope of the building.

The inhabitants of Viroconium were early Greens, and when the water in the pools was replaced, the dirty water was used to flush out the communal loos. This was a long thin room, divided by a screen into gents and ladies, in which the inhabitants would have sat next to each other in an excreting line, all equal in this function at least. Unfortunately for my residual internal schoolboy, English Heritage had not seen fit to commission an impression of these latrines.

The baths had stood at the centre of a much larger town, which extended over much of the plateau. Here beside the Severn and overlooked by the Shropshire hills, an urban civilisation had briefly flourished and then disappeared as suddenly as it had arrived. Members of the Cornovii tribe had become assimilated into the Roman Empire, tasting the pleasures of an urban existence, before reverting to barbarism, which (properly understood) means a state of no baths.

This short span of enforced civilisation left the English with ambivalent feelings. We profess to love nature, but we do not like wilderness. The passing of the Romans somehow left us with a feeling of loss; of guilt almost. In 1913, the year before the First World War began, Wilfred Owen wrote the poem, 'Uriconium', and included this verse:

> It lieth low near merry England's heart,
> Like a long-buried sin; and Englishmen
> Forget that in its death their sires had part,
> And, like a sin, Time lays it bare again.

In 1926 another soldier of the Great War, H. V. Morton, returned from Palestine to travel around his beloved England, researching one of the biggest-selling books of the inter-war period, *In Search of England*. Here, at Wroxeter, he came across the excavations in full spate. He wrote:

> For five hundred years, the ordered life of Rome was lived within these walls; harvests sold, cattle sold, skins sold; and most men thought it was permanent perhaps, only the hills

knew differently as they brooded on the sky, only the grass
knew differently, only the wind from the north beating on
Uriconium in the wild nights may have whispered of the
death of Rome, and the coming of the wild men, who were
frightened to sleep under a roof, with fire and with sword.

English culture seems always to be torn between a love of the
rural, and a deep, social need for the urban. The former may tug
us emotionally but, in the end, the baths usually win out.

A bus appeared on the road next to the Heritage shop; the bus
to Shrewsbury. I still had an afternoon to kill, so I boarded it
and became its only passenger. Half an hour later I was at the
bus station in the shadow of the castle, preparing to explore by
foot what I had only glimpsed from the water.

Modern Shrewsbury's oddest characteristic is that its most
famous historical inhabitant, the one it brags most about now,
is not Charles Darwin, who was born here, but an entirely fictional
medieval monk called Brother Cadfael. For twenty years an old
lady called Edith Pargeter, writing under the pen-name of Ellis
Peters, churned out thriller after thriller in which Cadfael, a
worldly veteran of the Crusades, a herbologist and amateur
pathologist, uses his sagacity and open-mindedness to solve various
murders. I bought a booklet telling me how to tour Shrewsbury
in the footsteps of Brother Cadfael, offering information like,
'Rumple Hill is where Dung the Nightsoilman was found with
a chain round his neck in *Three Virgins Too Many*'.

Down the hill, in a sort of action museum called the Shrewsbury
Quest, embarrassed actors played almoners, priors and maidens,
raised and lowered their cowls and tried to judge whether now
was their moment to step forward and say, 'What ho, stranger,
crave ye some bergamot, or mayhap a poultice of smegwort?' Less
confident than their Yorkshire cousins at the Armouries, they gave
me a wide berth. Perhaps, rightly, they intuited that – desperate
for conversation – I'd talk back.

Stepping out on to the street the muscles of my legs and lower back felt sore and over-used; strangely I'd felt more pain in my lower extremities as a result of paddling than I had in my shoulders and arms. And there, right in front of me, was a little sign pointing down an alleyway offering therapeutic massage from a qualified practitioner. With two hours before the bus back to Atcham was due to leave, I decided to risk it, ducked down the narrow road, and rang a bell.

If, by any chance, you're smirking now, then stop it. For the last decade more and more ordinary Englanders have been spending their money on various therapies, as advertised at Granary Wharf, ranging from the daft (including crystals therapy and reflexology) to the more sensible which actually do things that you can feel. Of these, the most real, in my opinion, is massage by someone who is qualified, and knows your gluteus maximus from your ulna.

Iris did, because she had the charts up on the walls. She was in her late fifties, with a granny haircut and sensible specs, a white blouse and track-suit trousers. Originally from Essex, she had come to Shrewsbury a few years before, but was now thinking of going to Bishop's Castle, just below the Long Mynd, a town that was fast becoming the New Age capital of England. The problem, she told me, as she unfolded the massage couch in her minuscule room, was that too many people in Shropshire still regarded massage as disreputable, involving the rubbing of body parts by someone other than one's wife.

The afternoon was stifling, the room was small, and it was all like a Tennessee Williams play, to the extent that I fell asleep. Veils must drop here, particularly across my condition when I awoke, but safe to say that it was probably the single most embarrassing moment of my life.

As I retreated to the bus stop I passed the stadium of Shrewsbury FC. In a past era it had been named Gay Meadow, and now the butch soccer stars of Shrewsbury were saddled with this fragrant title. Given that only one gay footballer had ever been identified, and that one in ten probably is gay, it seemed odd that only the stadium had come out. But, then, as I'd just discovered, out is not always the most comfortable place to be.

CHAPTER 24

Epiphany

In one sense my journey had been a huge disappointment to me. I had enjoyed some pleasant enough moments, but almost always when the paddling had stopped and I was safe on dry land. The resumption of life on the water had never stopped being a matter of daily dread, packing me into the confined space and even narrower psychology of life afloat. For six or seven hours a day I would be able to think about little more than staying upright, or about where I would be able to get out. I was prey to any ill-tempered goose or impossibly constructed lock. And, each evening, some muscle or other would rebel: trapeziuses, hip flexors, biceps, whatever.

And then came the day of epiphany, the one that all the journeyers I had spoken to had told me would surely arrive. Two miles out of Atcham, at eleven o'clock on a day of coruscating beauty, the sun throwing diamonds at the water, and it being my birthday, I suddenly – and without expecting it – laughed out loud.

I had just squirted out of a small rapids, past a surprised fisherman, and was making fast time. And I realised that this was working; that this river really would take me all the way down to Ironbridge, to Bewdley, to Worcester and Gloucester. Maybe my absurd idea was a good idea after all.

Physically I was now in very different shape to a year before. I was still a bit girthy, but my musculature had changed. A new ridge of muscle had developed, bridging my scapulae, and giving me a pleasing (I felt) Schwarzeneggerishness when flexing my shoulders. I could paddle away for two or three hours without stopping, which was allowing me to cover greater distances in a day. My only physical problem was a developing pain in my right hand that was making it increasingly difficult to curl or uncurl my fingers.

Best of all, maybe, I was noticeably less wimpish and more decisive in instigating conversations with strangers, asking for things that I needed, and pressing others into my service when necessary.

On this day it seemed to me that some change had taken place in my wind-down towards senility; I felt more vigorous, almost as though I'd had some hormone supplement, Eau d'Angleterre, injected straight into the bloodstream. No longer was I the bedraggled inferior of those on the bank; I was doing what they would have loved to do.

Some of this was down to the river. The Severn was far more varied and intriguing for me than the canals had been. It was, almost all of it, interesting. And interesting was what I needed. It amazed me that it had once been the daddy of the Industrial Revolution, plied almost its entire length by boats of significant size. Early in the day I had passed the confluence with the River Teme, which flowed back through Attingham Park. At that junction was an old lock, going back to the days when iron ore was extracted at forges in Lord Berwick's lands, and barged down the Teme, to the Severn, and on to the wharves at Ironbridge and Bewdley.

Happy under the hump of the Wrekin I ate birthday fruit by the side of a field, a tractor making lazy lanes two hundred yards away, and shoals of tiny fish flashing next to the boat in the shallow, meandering river.

And then the topography changed. The meadows closed in and disappeared, and in their place rose wooded hills as the river valley fast became a gorge. As the Severn got narrower and deeper, it also became much swifter, and the *Knife* with it.

I felt my heart rate rise. Soon I would pass under the famous iron bridge of Ironbridge. Then, within minutes, I would find myself shooting the Jackfield rapids, about which the *Guide* said, 'Grade 1 to 2 rapids at normal level. Very fast.' I suspected that Grade 1 was the easiest sort of rapid, but the shocking truth was that I didn't know. I began to conserve my energy for some of the more radical corrective strokes that I might be forced to make.

So on I go, beside the ancient abbey of Buildwas, under the

chimneys of the Ironbridge power station, past some schoolgirls sitting on the deserted steps of the boat club with no time to wave at them, and there's the feathery metal structure of the famous Ironbridge itself. I barely manage to take in the elegance of the structure, and its steep slope to the centre, when I realise that I'm nearly there. The gorge is even narrower than earlier, its sides littered with huge landslipped rocks. And bang, before I can do much about it, before I can prepare myself or plot my passage, I'm hurtling through the Jackfield rapids, paddling like hell to stay the right side of a vicious boulder and to remain in the channel. The water smacks the bows hard and lands in great waves in my lap, slopping into the cockpit, a good five inches above the floor. I can think of no good reason why I shouldn't be tipped out at any second.

But the *Knife* is a splendid boat and I'm now nearly on the other side, safe and exhilarated and still going like the clappers, and I let out a great undignified whoop, to the derision of a group of young canoeists who do this five times a day and six on Sundays. This would be a birthday that I'd remember; not just another year marker on the way to the grave, but an affirmation of still breathing.

Soaked and happy, I had an assignation to keep a few yards below the rapids. Sure enough, there on the right bank, waiting like a Hebridean wife for the fishing boats, was a peroxided woman of sixty or so with two large Alsatians.

The woman was Pauline of the Severn Trow guesthouse. She waved me down to a fortuitous bit of stony beach just next to a large, long, deserted public house, and watched me uncoil myself from the *Knife*, whom we then stowed in a neighbour's garden.

Pauline had seen me shoot the rapids, and had been alarmed. 'I expected you to be wearing a helmet,' she said, reprovingly. 'I saw a boy die in those rapids two years ago. He was thrown against one of the rocks, and couldn't get out. It was terrible, we just stood there, and had to watch him die. But I suppose you're very experienced.'

We strolled up the bank. She and her husband Jim, who'd died the previous spring, had bought the Trow fourteen years before. It had an interesting history, from the days when cargo boats – most particularly the sailed trows – used the river.

'The Trow was once a sailors' brothel, you know,' said Pauline. 'We still have one of the original brothel cubicles. But we don't do that any more. Some do ask, but I tell them to bring their own! I'm past it.'

I had the smallest moment of discomfort. This pleasant spherical old lady didn't, by any terrible chance, want me to contradict her?

Of course she didn't. The trouble was, as I'd discovered on my trip, England is full of saucy grannies; old ladies who would show their knickers at parties, embarrass even skinheads with their shameless sexual innuendo, and suggest a lifelong attachment to unrestrained carnality that must make their dead husbands rotate in their half-empty family plots. They giggled on buses (''Ere, Lill, this conductor says he's going all the way!' 'Yahahahahahaha!'), embarrassed shop assistants ('Aven't you got any of those crotchless ones? Yeeheeheeheehee!'), and made even mature canoeists feel wary. Today the saucy granny is a modern English institution. I bet they don't have them in Greece or Spain. I blame Esther Rantzen.

In fact the brothel cubicles were about as bawdy as Pauline got. She was more interested in travel, as her T-shirt, featuring a map of Russia and bought in St Petersburg, attested. Not so long ago only the professional middle classes went to places like Russia. Now the Paulines take wing for other cultures. Another way in which the English are changing.

Heading away from the bank Pauline led me along an overgrown path. As we went we stumbled over old stones, lumps of brick and shards of tile. This was the wreckage, Pauline said, of the great landslip of April 1952, when water building up in the underground clay quarries behind Jackfield caused the earth to move. A great gap was torn in the middle of the village, and sixty houses in all had slipped into the river. There was little left of the structures, but other evidence did come to light from time to time. 'We still find the odd apple and cherry tree from someone's garden among all this wilderness,' Pauline told me.

The slipping had never stopped. A tarmac ribbon, which now described a mazy series of lurches to right or left, and up and down, had been flat and straight as a Roman road when first it was built in the 70s. A few yards away, in 1960, the church had fallen down. Was that, I asked her, the source of this tile debris scattered down the hillside and into the Severn?

'Oh no,' she replied, 'that's what them Victorians did with rubbish. Any old stuff that they had lying around the big tile factory that they didn't want, they just shoved it in the river. There wasn't any Friends of the Earth then.' She laughed.

But Jackfield had had to survive more than one affliction. Here, in the gorge, the Severn – in any case a river prone to floods – would periodically mount something really special. When the great rains fell on the rocks of Plynlimon in Wales, and the mountain streams burst their banks, they would know about it in Jackfield within hours. Pauline told the story of the local publican who, just a few years earlier, had got everything ready for Christmas. It began classically.

'It was the day before Christmas Eve, and he'd bought in all the food, you know, turkeys, chipolatas, lots of champagne and spirits for the Christmas parties. That was all in the cellar, and when he went home to bed that night, it wasn't even raining. Late that night the river come up. By eight it was two foot above the cellar, and everything was ruined. The whole lot. It wasn't insured against flood damage, cos that's an act of God. So he'd lost thousands. Well, we felt sorry, all of us did round here. We chipped in and helped him get back some of the cost of his stock. So, he didn't go under. And on the day before New Year's Eve, he's done exactly the same thing; all the food, all the drink. That night, you wouldn't believe it, the river floods again, and he lost the lot again. Everything. Twice within a week. So he just packed it in and went back to Glasgow, I think it was.'

I speculated that, what with the landslips and the floods, property prices were probably not that high. That was true, said Pauline, but if you liked a place, what did it matter? Mind you, she said, some people who had bought in and then couldn't sell out again were less enchanted with the place.

We arrived at the Trow, an irregularly-shaped, interesting little house looking over towards the river. Pauline proudly installed me in a chintzy, comfortable room above the neat garden, dominated by a dark-wooded four-poster bed and full of statuettes, thimbles and silver clothes brushes. Disconcertingly, to add to the stories of brothels, floods, landslips, and to the sheer size and toothiness of the two shaggy Alsatians, there was a porcelain sampler on the wall. Its legend painted on the tile read: Prepare To Meet Thy God.

You get used to thinking of post-industrial towns and villages as being like Salford, or those old mining places, now all unsaleable houses, weed-choked ruins and depression. But I supposed that Ironbridge had had more time than most to come to terms with its change of status: from foundry town to museotopia.

Here, where the English Industrial Revolution was born and whence industry had long since fled, was a neat, cosy strip of houses and shops, rising beyond the famous bridge. In 1982, as the historian Raphael Samuel noted, there were – in Ironbridge alone – 200 work experience kids working in the heritage industry. This had been a wise investment. Now the place was doing OK; plenty of school trips, plenty of tourists.

Everything – Post Office, newsagents, cappuccino emporia – seemed to be run by entrepreneurial hippies, who also carried on lucrative sidelines in statuettes, yurt furniture and, yes, candles. At an outdoor coffee shop, off the road where once wagons pulled coke, groovy types now looked as though they'd just been snorting it. Young blokes with ponytails and gentle voices were reading books on magic, and discussing careers in the media.

On this less vulnerable bank there was, unlike in Jackfield, obviously a point in buying and selling property. Indeed, to judge by the billboards, there were two local firms of estate agents to assist with the task. Nick Tart was the name of one company, and Nock Deighton was the other. Go there, I'm telling the truth. If they went all monopolistic and merged, I speculated, then they might between them become the more respectable Nick Deighton. But

I hoped they'd be Nock Tart. I'd buy a house through Nock Tart. Especially one that had been a fishermen's brothel.

Nick and Nock had quite a lot of new stuff on their books. I passed a number of runs of smallish brand-new houses. They were not always well-named. One row of five brick cottages were identically plaqued, from left to right, Rose, Lilac, Oak, Honeysuckle and Willow. It made the rebel in me want to buy one, just so that I could rename it Pancho Villas, or Prolapse Cottage.

As the last evening light came down the gorge, I stood on the high centre point of the iron bridge and looked down-river. Two hundred years before, when the bridge was new, the whole gorge would have been lit up by the savage flames of the blast furnaces, showers of sparks; illumined, foul-smelling smoke, a steady and terrible din. Travellers, who came in their thousands from all over Europe, remarked on the weirdness of it, and its resemblance to their expectation of hell.

The revolution here, as with all revolutions, owed something to accident. In this part of Shropshire the wood, the iron, the water and the coal were all present within miles of each other, and running through it all was the navigable Severn. A catalyst had been needed. Most of this land had once belonged to the Cluniac Priory of Much Wenlock, but had been sold off to local gentry when Henry VIII dissolved the monasteries. This gentry it was that had begun the industrialisation of Shropshire, using money to attain rank in a way that was always uniquely possible – for all the talk of class – in England. In a way this was like the privatisation of state industries in the 80s. Familiar, if reviled, institutions were sold off at low prices for political reasons to men who were more ruthless and dynamic than those they supplanted.

I enjoyed a solo birthday supper at Da Vinci's, a fine Italian restaurant originally fitted out as a Montparnasse café of the 1890s, and then simply hijacked by the new owner (another Brummie) with a few pictures of la Bella Italia, and Italian music. 'Volare, who-ho,' went the record, 'Cantare, who-ho-ho-ho.' Which means, I think, that singing is even better than stealing.

★　　★　　★

At breakfast Pauline was wearing a California T-shirt, as she served me my umpteenth full English breakfast. Over the years B&B landladies have developed a culinary tyranny, presumably based on customer expectations of a decade or two ago.

Now, after five weeks, I felt I could be reconfigured as a breakfast myself. I'd have two fried eggs for eyes, a grilled tomato as a nose, my mouth would be a slice of streaky bacon, my body a fatty wedge of friend bread and my limbs four browned pork sausages. I yearned for melon, pineapple, flaky croissant, freshly squeezed juice. I wanted yams, whatever they were. But I ate the sausages all the same.

This was to be an epic day's work, with over 25 miles to cover. The river soon passed out of the gorge, and back between 6-feet high banks, along which were scattered the detritus of village water fights, old rafts with bucket seats washed high up above the waterline.

Beyond a gnarled red and black lump, called High Rock, I came in sight of the old town of Bridgnorth, one part high up on a bluff, one part low. This was the town where, just before the turn of the century, my mother's mother, the grandmother I never met, had been born.

I ate lunch by a slipway giving on to a small park in which the local pensioners had driven their cars up to the water's edge, where they now, perversely, sat behind them, giving their beloved motors the best view over the river. And there, on the slipway, for the first time since setting out from Camden Town, I slipped, and fell in arse first with a huge shout of surprise and a great splash. Rarely have I seen so many happy pensioners in one place.

I'd return to Bridgnorth later, but for now – more damply – I pressed on.

A new sub-culture materialised. Trailer parks, 'holiday chalet' villages and long caravan sites ribboned the river bank. Some of the structures were little more than shanty-town shacks, with rusting corrugated iron and broken spars, giving on to angler's perches made of old scaffolding. Others were anal summer residences in cream and strawberry, with scrubbed dads and mums listening to the radio in the sun.

I felt very surprised by the scale of it. Here was an England so deeply, impossibly unfashionable that we metropolitans had assumed that it died at the end of the 50s, when they built the airport at Palma de Mallorca. We were wrong. Hundreds of thousands of our fellow citizens have merely waited for global warming to supply them with their own little place in the sun.

Not only was this trailer country, but now it became angler territory too. For the next five miles lurking fishermen became a serious hazard. I think there must have been some kind of competition going on, for now anglers appeared round every hedge and bush, behind every tree, standing in every channel, camped on every island, their thin lines snaking across the water head-high to a canoeist, visible only at the last second, when they would be grudgingly lifted.

They never spoke to me, and they rarely spoke to each other. Claiming their territory and marking it out with folding seats, bait buckets, rod-stands, plastic sun-shelters, cool-boxes and bottles of various kinds, they remained, unmoving and taciturn. Roach poles would sometimes extend from one bank of the river to the other, exerting dominion over the entire waterway.

'Hello!' I'd say, dodging a line. 'Caught anything?'

'Are there any more behind?' would be the only response. Not once did any of them ask where I was bound, or how far had I come. There is a form of self-containment – I thought to myself – that can, sometimes, be mistaken for coma. Still, even anglers were better than solitude. And I supposed that, given the number of tattoos and shaven heads among them, there were worse things they could be doing.

And so, one epiphany down and expectant (anglers notwith-standing) of more, Mr Sunny beat on, carried by the current, borne back hopefully into the past.

CHAPTER 25

A Child Abandoned

At five o'clock one July Friday I arrived in the country where my mother was brought up. On that hot afternoon in one of the hottest summers of recent times, I turned a bend of the low, lazy river, and came under the high wharves and lined pubs of Bewdley, where once the trows had tied up. And as soon as I passed through the middle of the arches of the bridge linking the two parts of town, and looked up at the Georgian houses on the banks, I felt as though I had come to somewhere that had something to do with me.

My mother lived here, off and on, only for the five years of wartime between 1940 and 1945, between the ages of seventeen and twenty-two. Much of that time she spent away, a member of the WRAF (the Women's Royal Air Force), either on barrage balloon duty or driving lorries and ambulances around Wellington bases. But Bewdley was the only bit of ground that we kids could associate with her, in the way that Stepney and the Jewish East End were so obviously my father's. A few times, we had visited the town when I was very little, and the impression of it, the lines of houses on the wharf, were like a half-remembered photograph in an old album.

Nearly seventy years ago something terrible had brought my mother to this part of the country; an event so sad, followed by a betrayal as inevitable as it was crushing, that I am astonished she survived it without going mad. Or, at least, without carrying around an anger twice as great as the one she actually possessed, and that she – I believe – passed on, in an attenuated form, to me.

My mother, Lavender Walmsley, was born in 1923 in Rawalpindi, then part of British India. Her father, an alliterative soldier named Wyndham, originally from Preston, was serving in the sub-continent at that time. WW played his part in the First

World War, and had been one of the few to stay on in the peacetime army when it was over. Lavender was his second daughter, following her sister Eve by three years. A third girl, Gill, was born in 1928.

WW was a handsome man, in a regular way, tall, dark-haired and steady-eyed, but it was my grandmother who really captured hearts. Her name was Ida May Greatwich, and, as noted, she had come originally from the town I had just slipped through, Bridgnorth.

Not short of a post-Edwardian bob or two, Ida's family took up residence in Lickhill Manor, a square, elegant house on the Severn, just north of Stourport. There Ida developed into a beauty, with large, deep eyes, a slow smile and ringlets of auburn hair. Looking at her photographs now I see a resemblance to some of the silent movie actresses of the period, women like Norma Talmadge. And it's quite probable that others did too, for, soon after the first war had ended, Ida left home and ran away to London to the stage.

When my officer grandfather first saw Ida, she was in the chorus of one of the West End's many peacetime productions. WW turned stage-door Johnny, and met his middle-class dancer every evening with a bouquet. She succumbed, they married, had one daughter, went to India – where they had my mother and were photographed carrying her into the Himalayas – returned to England, set up home in a mansion block by Battersea Bridge and had a third daughter.

According to my mum's necessarily vague account, Ida was quite a special mother, though by no means as faithful to her soldier husband as our rather naïve view of the period would lead us to suppose. She sewed the dresses, taught songs, decorated the doll's house that WW built, and was a gay, rather fabulous parent, whom her young daughters obviously adored.

And then, in the summer of 1930, when Lavender was seven, Ida died suddenly. The cause of her death was as banal as it could possibly be. Out one day near the town of Battle in Sussex, she was stung by a wasp, the sting became infected, and within days Ida was dead of blood poisoning. The three sisters were motherless.

I can only imagine the Dickensian dreadfulness of the moment when they were told that she was not returning.

In this first year of the third millennium, there isn't much question about what would happen now to the girls. Their father would look after them, and the wider family probably rally round. But these were different times; WW was in the army, and had no obvious career outside it. So, for the time being, the girls were sent to various relatives and friends, mostly of Ida's family in Worcestershire. Lavender and Gill were packed off to live with the scion of a Stourport construction company (the firm, R. P. Vale, exists today), Robert Vale and his wife Winnie who were childless, in their forties, and old acquaintances of the Greatwiches.

In 1933, when Lavender was ten, Wyndham married again. His wife was another beauty, a warm woman called Theo. Within months Theo was pregnant and soon Wyndham had a new family. And, in a quiet betrayal, he never called for the old one. You can see the logic, perhaps even imagine the consultations between the Vales and the Walmsleys. About how unsettling it would be for the girls to leave their adoptive families to set up home with a woman they didn't know. About how hard it might prove to be for Theo to take on three daughters not her own. In Worcestershire the orphans grew up by the Severn, while their father's new family burgeoned a hundred miles away.

A year into the war the Vales moved from Upland, their house in Wilden, to a large house called Sandbourne on Bewdley's east bank, a red-brick mansion with stables, a rose garden designed by Gertrude Jekyll, and a long gravel drive for limousines to crunch along satisfyingly.

It was to this house I came when I was a small boy. Sandbourne – no architectural jewel – had large, dark rooms with dark furniture, and in its bookcases were volumes like Sylvanus Stall's *What Every Young Man Should Know*. By the time I visited, Auntie Winnie was long dead, but ancient Uncle Bob made himself popular doling out ten-bob notes the same colour as the walls of Sandbourne. Bob Vale, this house and this place were my exotic connections to the world of the aboriginal English.

While she was away from Bewdley, in the month before VE Day, Lavender had a fin-de-guerre fling with a married RAF officer, and became pregnant. Soon after my older sister, Sabrina, was born – a few weeks before Christmas in 1945 – my mother took her off to live in a small cottage on a farm in Snowdonia in North Wales. She wasn't cut off without a penny, or shunned, or anything dramatic like that. But she had rebelled; had made an almost incoherent statement about her place in the world, and her determination, from now on, to fashion it her way. She'd been a victim; now she would shift for herself.

In 1953, the year Stalin died and Everest was conquered, Lavender was living in London, in Hampstead – then a land of bed-sitters and artists occupying houses let out by well-to-do escapees of the Blitz. In someone's Bohemian flat she met a dark, thin, married man, who worked for the Communist Party. She fell in love with him. And he with her.

I holed up on the east bank, within yards of Sandbourne, in a guesthouse by the side of the Severn Valley Railroad viaduct. The landlady's name was Christine, not Pauline, and her T-shirt was from the Galapagos, not Russia. Christine had an extant husband, Tony, and shoulder-length red-mouse hair. Otherwise she was identical to Pauline, in size, shape and demeanour.

The house that Christine welcomed me into was full of trains: pictures, paintings, models, timetables, cartoons, collector's cards, brasses, plaques and whistles.

'You all right with the mentally handicapped?' she asked me, as she showed me my room, ''Cos we've got some in.' I nearly told her that I'd already eaten, but settled for an over-sincere expression of delight.

I told Christine what I was doing in Bewdley, and about the connection with my mother, and she took a moderate and undemonstrative interest. And in return she gave me the edited highlights of her life story, in particular the recent fact that her teenage daughter – mentioned in the guesthouse brochure – had left home to live with a 'homeless' young man. Actually it transpired that he wasn't really homeless at all; Christine called him that because he wore his hair in dreadlocks, and was obviously a New Age traveller. In fact, he was the vicar's son from Cleobury.

This was to be Christine and Tony's last summer in Bewdley. The place had changed, there were too many visitors (an odd and very English complaint this, coming from people running a guesthouse), and they too were off to Bishop's Castle, where they would run holidays for the learning impaired. Perhaps, I thought, they could meet up with Iris for embarrassing massages.

Bathed and sweet-smelling, I strolled over the Friday-night bridge into town. The place was humming. There were kids from all over. Free from their parents – now presumably drinking G&Ts in their summer gardens – the teenagers lined the wharves, mingling with the bikers and anglers. A fish and chip shop was doing solid business, and the rubbish bins were already overflowing. Cod and chips was the last thing I could stomach with another English breakfast hardly ten hours away, so I settled for the mediocre rural Chinese by the bridge, and rubbed shoulders with elderly solicitors in ties and courting couples out on a classy razzle.

Back in my room, full of rice and seaweed, it was a sultry evening. The open window invited in the sounds of other people having fun. Loud conversations, strange far-away calls, whoops, the screech of tyres, a distant thrum of music, all wafted past the net curtains and circled my head. At 1.30 a.m. a car parked directly outside my room, with both its lights and the radio on full beam, and didn't go away for an hour. London is quieter than most country towns on drinking night.

In the morning, still sleepy, I began my search of the mother country, taking in the centre of town, where the cottages off the roads were strangely shambolic; not prettified. Two or three times I looked through open doors to see a hallway full of mouldering books and old furniture.

Finally, in the bookshop I found one of those fashionable paperbacks ('Your town in pictures') with grainy photographs of Bewdley in the old days. There were the Free French officers swanning around the place, fags in their Gallic mouths in the way that Mum remembered them. And yes, here was a picture of Sandbourne in the 50s, with an old man in jacket and tie sitting on a bench outside. It was Uncle Bob.

At ten I walked over to the railway. Not the real, grimy, commute-to-work railway, but a fantasy, retro railway. Bewdley station and the other stops on the Severn valley line between Kidderminster and Bridgnorth were all closed in the early 60s by the notorious train murderer, Dr Beeching. But in 1970 the omnipresent English steam enthusiasts of the Midlands opened up the first halts on the Severn Valley Railway, a 16-mile stretch running alongside the river and crossing it three times. Just as in the not very good Ealing film of the amateur's defiance of the establishment, the little man against bureaucracy, *The Titfield Thunderbolt*, a regular service was maintained on the line by volunteers, using cannibalised carriages and engines.

I bought a stiff card ticket for Bridgnorth, and boarded the train, or, rather, the locomotive.

The dirty old carriage with filthy windows clacked pleasantly alongside the river, taking forty minutes to cover the 12 miles. Two coaches were full of something called Beaver Scouts, forcing all the other passengers into a closer proximity than they had planned. There was a scurrying for seats, and a fussing and a changing of minds and a moving of coats and carrier bags. It was turning into a hot, hot day. Young boys with bright eyes, sweaty lips and good manners helped their fathers, uncles and grandpas with the ticket collection. At various stops elderly male volunteers leaned on shovels and told other old men dirty stories that they would be forbidden to repeat at home.

Bridgnorth was both the terminus and the epicentre of the railroad. It was here that volunteers staying overnight would sleep in a manky-looking carriage in the sidings. As I alighted from the train into the sunlight, I found myself at once engaged in conversation by a tall, colourless man in a smart uniform, with a watch-chain and peaked cap.

He'd spotted the notebook, and wanted to tell me about the marvels of the voluntary railroad.

'I come in every weekend from Wolverhampton,' he revealed, in a Black Country accent. 'It takes me half an hour to drive here.' He outlined his route in useful detail.

I asked him if, given the magnificence of his outfit, he was the station-master. He was unembarrassed.

'Oh no,' he said. 'That's a job for a full-timer. I don't aspire to that. I just keep the platform tidy really. In fact, my main job is to pick up the cigarette ends.' And he produced, from behind his back, one of those flaps on the end of a stick, whose sole use is the retrieval of butts. He looked around. 'For some reason, though,' he said, in a puzzled voice, 'there are always more of them round the benches.' No wonder, I thought, they don't let him drive the train.

Crossing a high footbridge from the station, I joined the other passengers, all panting and thirsty, as we climbed the winding hill to the upper town.

In three hours of searching I found only two pieces of evidence that there had once been Greatwiches here. The first I discovered quickly: a board over an ironmonger's shop off the crowded High Street, reading, 'Shakespeare's. Formerly Clive Greatwich'. After that it looked as though I would discover nothing at all. The oldest church, St Leonard's (like so many others on my journey), was now a church no longer, but an arts and crafts fair. There were no gravestones marking the resting places of generations of my ancestors. The church's one prize exhibit, Colonel Billingsley's Civil War sword, which the old Cavalier had dropped, dying, in the churchyard in 1646, had been stolen six years before, and had never been recovered.

Then, just as I was about to take the slow train back to Bewdley, at the furthest tip of Castle Hill, beyond the strange funicular railway to the lower town, beyond even the crazy angle of the last remaining wall of the castle, I came across the war memorial – a fantastic bronze figure of a uniformed boy pointing out over the valley of the Severn. Near the bottom of the long, long list of the dead was inscribed the name 'H.

Greatwich. PO. RAFVR'. So Harry or Hugh or Herbert had been a pilot officer in the early Royal Air Force, and a cousin, perhaps, of Ida's.

And that was all. Two names is a small return on a day in the heat.

Back in Bewdley that evening, I took a tiny table in the Rajah Indian restaurant and planned my next day. The clientele seemed to be divided equally between northern anglers and university lecturers.

The anglers entered with a defensive swagger, as though expecting to be slighted. 'Table for five, awright?' demanded a bullet-headed fat man with a loud voice. Once it became clear, however, that fishermen were welcome in the Rajah, they relaxed. The racist insults culminating in overturned tables and a bloody nose for me (the scenario for which I prepared as I watched them) never happened.

But now a middle-class woman – obviously an academic – was asserting herself. She was one of those professional people who suffer from an acute need to leave a place other than how she found it. She was forever on the verge of sending things back, commenting on portions, colour and spices. 'Shall I ask for Indian music?' she demanded loudly at one point, as the sound system gave us a version of 'Born in the USA' played on the xylophone. When her bill arrived she queried it. She was wrong.

As I emerged the riverside was teeming. On the water itself young canoeists plied to and from the Boat Club steps, dodging the rowers in their sleek, blind, backward boats. The wharves were lined with drinkers; visitors promenaded with ice creams or hung out of the windows of the Mallards guesthouse. Anglers carelessly set up their lines by the bridge, forcing walkers to detour around their rods. Kids threw stones into the shallows, while the old fed the swans. Dogs sniffed around the legs of the shirtless bikers draped over the balustrade by the Mughouse pub, and a hot air balloon passed overhead, towards Kidderminster. It was like one of those kids' books in which you have to find a man called Wally in a crowd. I was Wally.

As it got darker, and the drinkers became louder, I headed off. At eleven or so I fell asleep, the blankets thrown back and only the cool sheet over me, and had a strange dream. I was compèring a new, live, TV show. For some reason this job required me to jump into deep water wearing a white tuxedo, and to stay below the surface for five minutes at a time. My career depended upon my performance underwater.

And while I was lost in this anxious dream, there was a double drowning down by Bewdley bridge: a couple of men who were among those drinkers outside the Mughouse that I had left an hour or so before. Some time just before midnight, these two guys, both from Kidderminster, decided to wade across the shallow, cool river. Their friends – remembering something of the Severn's reputation – urged them not to go, but the night was hot and the water looked cool.

Barry and Graham jumped down from the wharf to the rocky margin of the Severn and then walked across half the river on the stones that broke its shallow surface. The day before, when I'd paddled this way, no part of the water had looked more than a couple of feet deep. They had got half the distance over when, according to the publican of the Mughouse, they abruptly disappeared. One moment they were standing in the water, and the next they were gone. 'They must have lost their footing,' he told the local paper the next day. 'One of the wives was shouting, "He can't swim."'

By now a small crowd was watching from the quayside, every one of them thinking that it might be their job to try and rescue the men who were so obviously under the water. In the end two twenty-one-year old anglers stripped off to their underclothes and bravely waded into the middle of the river. 'It was easy to swim out,' said one of them, Peter Kerr, 'but suddenly I could feel this very strong current underneath me. We managed to get hold of one. The other one just disappeared, he went under the water and never came back up.' The rescuers were in some danger themselves. 'It was harder swimming back, but we managed to get one on to the steps. We were literally sick with the amount of water we had swallowed,' he said. But it was too late. The guy

Kerr pulled out, 43-year-old Graham Mapp, was declared dead at Kidderminster hospital half an hour later. The body of the other man, Barry Edwards, had vanished. By the next morning, when a shocked Christine told me the story of the night before, Barry's body had still not been found.

The Sunday morning was delicious, pudding warm with a sorbet breeze. Down by the bridge a few onlookers watched a yellow fire brigade rubber dinghy with outboard motor scour the banks. Two firemen with poles and rods probed the overhanging bushes and the submerged caves. A red helicopter hovered above the church. 'Thermal imaging,' someone next to me said knowledgeably. People didn't linger, not wanting to be thought of as ghouls or voyeurs, but just took one long look at the scene and moved on. I thought of my own carelessness and of Pauline's words. 'But I suppose you're very experienced,' she'd said. I recalled, with a slightly sick feeling, just how easy it is to drown, even when you don't want to.

I left the recently dead, and resumed my search for the roots of the living.

When Uncle Bob died, R. P. Vale and Co., which had owned Sandbourne, sold it to property developers. They demolished it and in its place built three closes of agreeable-looking brick semis over the land where the house, the gravel drive and Gertude Jekyll's gardens had been. These fifty little red houses, set in a landscape of lawns and mature trees, were habitable, I thought, as I walked between them and watched neighbour-women converse amiably on the path between their lawns.

The rose garden, though, had been special. A National Trust book devoted to Gertrude Jekyll's gardening splashed a plan of the Sandbourne paradise over two full pages. It had been a sad act to root that up, and I tried to concentrate on the loss as I stared at the remains of the stable block with its clock tower, now converted to a pair of cottages. But my mind was too undisciplined in the heat and I found myself speculating about whether, on certain nights, the demure green-fingered Gertrude

Jekyll had become transformed into Gertrude Hyde, a nightmare with bushy eyebrows, who roamed the crepuscular countryside chopping down pergolas and spraying prize blooms with paraquat.

Obstinately I took the high road towards Stourport, over a dusty hill, dodging traffic, and down into Lickhill, now a suburb of the former canal town, straggling comfortably along the road. A right turn brought me into an area with a park on one side, and 60s housing on the other. The Little Lords and Ladies Nursery was closed, but small children were gathered round the newsagent's, pulling the sticky paper off ice lollies. When Ida lived here, none of these buildings existed.

Lickhill Manor could be reached only by traversing a huge caravan park. Dozens of smart trailers, surrounded by their doll's house penumbra – awnings, collapsible chairs, sun-umbrellas, cool-boxes, bicycles, dads in shorts and loud shirts – shimmered in the sun, linked by yellow and blue umbilical cords to electrical boxes by the path. In such a wonderful July, the sun made even this maligned way of spending time seem tolerable. I could imagine sitting out in my checked shirt, drinking my chilled beer, with a splendid view up the chromium rear of next door's Peugeot Hypermobil.

The house itself, my grandmother's home, was a large square mansion with twenty-eight windows (yes, I counted them), fronted by a large, square gravel area. By the main door stood two women in nurse's uniforms, who looked sourly at me as I leaned on the gate. White heads in the windows told the inevitable story of how the manor had become yet another old people's home.

This isn't surprising; with the population of England getting older and older, this is where the smart money is. But, like caravan parks, aging is an unfashionable truth, like haemorrhoids or male underwear, largely hidden from view by a youth-fetishising media. Here at Lickhill we had one naff reality located in the heart of another. Perhaps the occasional hopelessly out-of-touch caravanner, when things got too much for him or her, simply made the twenty-yard transition between the trailer and the home.

There was nothing of Ida here, save to imagine her sitting in her bedroom, looking out over the river. I walked on.

I headed north, along the Staffordshire and Worcestershire canal at first, under Baldwins bridge, and then on a road running parallel to the canal and the River Stour, and away from the Severn. After twenty minutes I'd left the houses and pubs of Stourport behind, and was walking along Wilden Lane, with a long hill to my right, and the valley of the Stour on my left.

A couple of miles further on and I came to Wilden church, a Victorian affair, reputed to have some fine glass designed by the artist and friend of William Morris, Edward Burne-Jones. This was where my mother had been brought to worship but, though it was Sunday today, the church was locked. There were no Greatwiches or even Vales in the straggling graveyard that climbed the hill above the closed church, though I scanned every stone.

Next to the church was the little C of E school, a simple box-chapel affair with a small asphalt playground. By the gate a noticeboard displayed a couple of kid's drawings and a printed notice.

This told the story, on its centenary, of Thomas Jones, a farm labourer, who had been born in 1820, had lived in Wilden and died at the good age of nearly eighty in the last year of the nineteenth century. Old Mr Jones left his money, quixotically, to Mr Alfred Baldwin, the owner of the local ironworks, MP for the area, and philanthropist. His one other asset was a large field that ran down to the Stour. This he directed to be sold and the resulting annuity, valued at £15 per annum, he bequeathed to the children of Wilden school, so that they might go on pleasure trips to far-off places. There was, however, one condition attached to this gift. Every summer, on St Swithin's day, the children of the school should sing a song over Jones's grave. And this year – the following week, in fact – was the hundredth anniversary of that first song.

When it was first sung, Mr Jones's money would have paid for a whole charabanc trip for the entire school – now it just bought the sweets on the annual outing.

A turning up a steep hill, through a tumbledown gateway

marked STRICTLY PRIVATE brought me out on the wooded edge of a rabbit-infested plateau. There, with a steep red-slated roof, looking like a large Alpine chalet, was The Upland. The wire of a tennis court rose in the middle distance, and a flat area suggested possibly even a swimming pool beside the house. The rabbits were unafraid, but – intimidated by the signs and spotting movement in the distance – I lost heart and retreated back down the slope. 'My mother lived here before the war,' sounded like a good idea for a book, but a bad one for a conversation with an anxious householder.

I found a long, dry path down to the canal, crossing it where it met a thick rope of new factories in metal colours, all with large yards full of lorries.

Heading down small roads back towards Bewdley, I encountered sporty England on a Sunday. Spread out in the gap between three towns was a cricket ground, with a match in full flight; a bowling green populated by shuffling, bespectacled figures in white; and the long expanse of a golf course, with its irregular knots of brightly coloured men pretending to take exercise. Only the bowling seemed to involve women at all. So where were the wives and girlfriends of the golfers and cricketers? They couldn't all be at their aromatherapists.

I limped back to the guesthouse, exhausted. It was six o'clock, and the body of Barry Edwards had still not been found. The local news bulletins featured the yellow dinghy and the helicopters, as well as someone reminding the world to be careful in water this very warm July.

And so, another dark moment. No sooner had I begun to regard the water as my friend, shooting the rapids at Jackfield, than my confidence in my relationship with it was under assault. I'd spent ages preparing to be on it, had tried hard to enjoy having it under and around me and had nearly succeeded. But now I could feel myself anticipating the day when I wouldn't be on the water any more.

CHAPTER 26

The Politics of England

Our association with the Communist Party made my family unusual. When my little school friends went off to St Anne's church on a Sunday, dressed in green caps and shorts, to salute the flag, we attended Socialist Sunday School and learned about internationalism and the workers. Where we lived, an estate where the blue Conservative posters far outnumbered the red Labour ones at election time, our lone Vote Communist imprecation stood out like a plastic shark emerging from the roof.

But if I was a bit strange to the English, then they were, in return, a bit strange to me. My mother compounded this with baffling tales of how, as a girl, she had been forbidden by her guardians from playing with the village children. What sort of people were these? I recognised the tug of many English traditions, learned at school or passed on by Lavender, without feeling that they were mine.

Yet, ancestrally, they were. My mother was brought up a Conservative, here in Worcestershire. At election times, when she was a girl in the 30s, she was taken out canvassing at general elections in his Daimler by Uncle Bob, who was a mainstay of the local association. And for two of those elections, the local candidate for the Tories was their leader, and the epitome of Englishness, Stanley Baldwin.

There never was, and probably never will be, a better articulator of Middle England's sense of itself than Baldwin. And his England – my mother's England – had been located here, in the lanes and towns that I had been exploring. His father had been that Alfred Baldwin to whom Thomas Jones had left his small bequest, and whose family ironworks out at Wilden had had Baldwins bridge over the canal named after it. When I had gone looking for Greatwiches, I had found mostly Baldwins.

Baldwin was popular then. When the septuagenarian retired in 1937 – one of those rare PMs who chose the moment of his own going – a *Punch* cartoon entitled 'The Worcestershire Lad' depicted a satisfied John Bull taking an honest-looking old ploughman by the arm. Birds rise over a copse in the background, and the plough-horse waits. 'Well done, Stanley,' says John Bull. 'A long day and a rare straight furrow.' It was an epitaph that Baldwin would himself have chosen.

He was the Tory who had campaigned under the slogan, 'Safety First! Stanley Baldwin. The man you can trust.' With his trademark wing collar, open face, large nose and pipe, Baldwin was elected PM three times, twice with huge majorities. In an age when Europe was convulsed by -isms, Baldwin represented the phlegmatism, the calmness of the English. And then he was banished from history, as completely as those commissars who fell foul of Stalin and who were removed from photographs of the Russian Revolution. He was airbrushed out because he reminded the English all too well of what they could be as a nation. He was a mirror in which, when they looked into it after the start of war, they could see themselves all too clearly: decent, humane, undynamic and, above all, complacent.

Baldwin suffered historical cleansing because he was the Prime Minister who didn't rearm enough, who didn't support the Republicans against the fascists in the Spanish Civil War, who laid the ground for appeasement, who allowed Neville Chamberlain to succeed him as Prime Minister. All of which he did with the active support of the English themselves.

As a reward for Baldwin's faithfulness to his constituency, George Orwell said of the former Prime Minister that, 'one could not even dignify him with the name of stuffed shirt. He was simply a hole in the air.' By 1945, in the eyes of the now Churchillian British, Orwell's view represented the consensus.

Yet, twenty years before, Baldwin was the man who defined how the English felt about themselves, a definition that has never been bettered, and one that united Wilden in the 20s with my Cub chums in the mid-60s and with the spreading waterside suburbs of the new millennium.

On 6 May 1924, during a brief spell in opposition, Baldwin made a speech about England to the annual dinner of the Royal Society of St George. And, Lord, how the words can tug the Englishness in you even today:

> To me, England is the country and the country is England . . . The sounds of England, the tinkle of the hammer on the anvil in the country smithy, the corncrake on a dewy morning, the sound of the scythe against the whetstone, and the sight of a plough team coming over the brow of a hill, the sight that has been seen in England since England was a land . . . for centuries the one eternal sight of England. The wild anemones in the woods in April, the last load at night of hay being drawn down a lane as twilight comes in . . . and above all, most subtle, most penetrating and most moving, the smell of wood smoke coming up in an autumn evening . . . These things strike down into the very depths of our nature, and touch chords that go back to the beginning of time.

Baldwin was no sentimentalist. He presided over one of the most urbanised peoples in the world. He knew all too well that most children in modern England were unlikely ever to hear the smithy's tinkle and the whetted scythe; that he was conjuring up a largely vanished world. The people's desire for the original England, he asserted, lived on in other, more manageable ways. 'Nothing can be more touching,' he went on, 'than to see how the working man and woman, after generations in the towns will have their tiny bit of garden if they can, will go to gardens if they can, to look at something they have never seen as children, but which their ancestors knew and loved.'

This was an astute observation. The English live in towns, and long for the country. The Russian commentator Vitali Vitaliev once told me that the desire for a garden of one's own is a characteristic of crowded countries, whereas those who live in huge nations want nothing better than to pile on top of one another. This is true; if an English writer had penned Chekhov's *Three Sisters*, the miserable troika would have been found in Moscow, pining to get back to the bucolic boredom (or 'tranquillity') of provincial life.

In *Great Expectations*, the clerk, Wemmick, takes Pip on a long walk to his tiny castle in the outskirts, where a working drawbridge crosses a little moat, and from whose roof a gun is sounded every evening. And there's another association, that of eccentricity and individuality with the ownership of property.

Under Baldwin's various administrations, millions of Wemmicks set out for garden cities and ribbon developments, cultivating their tiny bits of garden over the sites of smithies, spinneys and dewy fields where once corncrakes sang. The irony was that the nearest that many could get to Baldwin's evocation of ancient England was through destroying the very thing that he had eulogised.

Baldwin personally embodied these contradictions. The family fortune was not based on the land or farming, but founded in the iron-making business, located in Wilden. He spoke peasant, but acted industrialist, reconciling those eternally competing English impulses: conservation and modernisation.

Nor was Baldwin a completely conventional man. The patriarch of the company, father Alfred, was a paternalistic Tory businessman, who had married remarkably, into a family of strong-willed sisters, daughters of a radical clergyman, the Reverend Macdonald. Alfred's wife, Stanley's mother Luisa, had as brothers-in-law the painter Edward Poynter, the pre-Raphaelite artist Edward Burne-Jones, and a nondescript bloke called Kipling, whose son, Rudyard (Stanley's cousin), was to become the poet of empire.

The Burne-Jones connection gave the Baldwins a big 'in' with the arty socialists of the late nineteenth century, such as William Morris. Together, as we've seen, they were commissioned by Alfred Baldwin, capitalist and exploiter, to create the stained glass for Wilden church.

In another characteristic of the English, Baldwin was no believer in conforming for its own sake. In the 1924 speech Baldwin praised the idea that the English were all individuals. 'Uniformity of type', he said, 'is a bad thing.' Certainly, the young Baldwin had made his individual mark when, as a schoolboy at Harrow, he sent his cousin, Ambrose Poynter, some pornographic literature in the post. The material was intercepted and Stanley was nearly expelled.

His other cousin, Rudyard, was a sterner Tory. A couple of years older, he would often come to stay in Worcestershire, and the two men were largely to agree politically throughout their adult lives. And when Stanley married, it wasn't to a freethinking woman like his Macdonald mama, but to a sporty, county gal, name of Cissie Ridsdale. Yet still his family was anything but strait-laced. The eldest son, Oliver, scarred by his experiences at the end of the First World War, first became a Freemason – which his uncle Rudyard could just about accept – then joined the far-left Social Democratic Federation, affiliated to the Labour Party, which had Rudyard fuming about his silliness.

What offended the poetic imperialist beyond redemption, however, was when Stanley told him in 1924 that Oliver had come out as gay, and announced that he was living in Oxfordshire with his lover, a bloke called Johnnie Boyle. Homosexuality of any kind was illegal then. Though the more decorous press of that time would not cover the story, what is fascinating is the sang-froid that Baldwin, leader of the nation, showed when dealing with this family crisis. He did nothing.

So my mother and her Baldwinesque Tory guardians did not fall out over her pregnancy or her – by their standards – weird marriage. The pre-60s model of stern and unforgiving families was a caricature, of the mercantile middle classes at any rate. It was amazing what contradictions they could accommodate when they had to.

Some of his own political contradictions Baldwin managed by compartmentalising different aspects of his life. His speech made in 1934 to mark the centenary of William Morris's birth, for instance, makes no reference whatsoever to the man's politics. There had been very little of Morris's aesthetics with which Stanley would have disagreed; Morris had stood for a peculiarly English kind of deeply conservative socialism. Both saw tinkling smithies as the height of civilisation.

In fact, Morris probably liked them more. Baldwin's words, as we've seen, were the disguise under which the massive changes between the war took place. He talked corncrakes, as roads shot out over the countryside, paternalism as the market took over, one nation as the gap between the rich and poor became more extreme than ever. Baldwin represented the selling of economic change. Yet this wouldn't have worked if it had been at odds with how the English actually were; if they hadn't, in those times, been backward-looking and calm.

In the 20s and 30s all kinds of bodies were active in defence of the heritage of England, partly as a reaction against the mechanised savagery of the First World War. One was the Council for the Preservation of Rural England. The archive of the CPRE for 1935 includes an exchange of letters between the Council and Oswald Mosley's British Union of Fascists. The CPRE had written to BUF to complain about the appearance of fascist graffiti on a bridge in Sussex. The fascists replied that their policy was against such acts of hooliganism. A further letter winged its way from the preservers to the right-wing revolutionaries who believed in the violent overthrow of the existing order. 'I now make an appeal to you,' wrote the author, 'on behalf of the CPRE, to do all in your power to prevent the disfigurement of bridges.'

And the fascists agreed. Of the many, many bridges I had passed under in the last six weeks, though they bore witness to the love affairs and passions of generations, not one displayed the lightning flash of the British Union of Fascists.

CHAPTER 27

Middlest England

After seventy miles I was back in the world of boats. From Stourport locks they poured out on to the bush-lined Severn: cruisers, small barges and narrowboats. But after the drownings in Bewdley I was somehow less confident. The poor Kidderminster man was still missing, my increased awareness of death on the river meant that every bobbing thing in the water for the next ten miles, I took to be his risen corpse. Even in Jerome K. Jerome's *Three Men in a Boat*, the pleasant quarrellings of the men and the dog are interrupted by the floating body of a young woman who has drowned herself.

To add to my anxiety I was then nearly sunk by a narrowboat; one crewed by five young blokes with no hair and lots of beer. There was nothing malicious about them, but they had clearly never heard of the speed limit on the river. They had gunned the boat's engine to flat out, and their wash was slapping hard against the edge, rocking moored craft and eating at the banks.

But for me they created a rolling swell of large waves and unsteady troughs, forcing me to paddle at right-angles into the wake and sending water into the cockpit. For only the third time since I'd set out I felt the canoe begin to go from under me. I shouted at them to slow down, and they waved their cans cheerily by way of reply. I suddenly felt very vulnerable. Going through the lock together – the lock-keepers on the Severn being relaxed about canoes – I explained my predicament calmly from four feet beneath them. They offered me a drink. Then they shot out of the lock as though a giant beer-stealing swan was after them. I barely made it.

Twelve miles on, and I left the boat in someone's garden at the top of Worcester racecourse, and marched the long mile towards the square tower of the cathedral. Office workers were strolling home early, some arm in arm.

I took a room in a converted glove factory, with large, airy windows and a view over the Worcester and Birmingham canal, showered and then crossed an incongruous four-lane highway into the town centre. This was a trendy and youthful town, where all the little boys seemed to be wearing Manchester United shirts, despite the distance between Worcester and Old Trafford. In half a generation the tribal and local loyalty of soccer appeared to have become brand loyalty, a statement of what you bought into, rather than what you were born into.

The same clearly went for churches. Hungry, I dipped inside a huge bar bistro carved out of the elegant seventeen-something church of St Nicholas. A long bar ran down one side, while – above – new, secular stained glass represented appropriate themes: Jesus being cast out by the moneylenders, the turning of water into Harvey Wallbangers, that sort of thing. An ornate carved pulpit was integrated into the stairs up to the cocktail level, a vast bouquet of large flowers sprouted spectacularly from the font. The food was Thai Fusion, the waitresses were very young and very pretty and I guessed that if you had to turn a beautiful church into anything, then this was as good as, say, an arts and crafts fair. No, better, actually. I liked the place, feeling certain a fair amount of Magnanimous and Providential business was done here over something wokked.

A long pedestrianised street led to Worcester's greatest glory, which is not its cathedral but its Guildhall. The city had been a royalist stronghold in the Civil Wars. The young Charles II lost a decisive battle here in 1651, and then began that escape so obsequiously described by Georgette Heyer; the flight involving an oak tree.

So when they came to build the Guildhall, in Queen Anne red brick, they added to the front, on either side of the doorway, golden figures of Carolus I – holding a cathedral in his hand, like something out of the Bayeux Tapestry – and the intrepid Carolus II and Anna Regina. There is no sign of poor old James II, whose Catholic tendencies had led to his being overthrown, or of William III who usurped his throne. But it must have been a magnificent place at which to be held up at the assizes for, say, coin-clipping, sentenced to hanging and from whence to be dispatched to the place of final imprisonment. The majesty of the law would have meant something here.

Beyond a boxy 60s mall, where a plaque to Edward Elgar reminded the world that houses had stood here in this place before the plate glass and concrete of the Elgar Shopping Centre, there was the cathedral itself, almost hidden by an enormous statue commemorating the fallen of the Boer War.

I'd done enough architecture, and was in a tomby mood, on the look-out for good burials. Neglecting the arches and vaults I scanned the walls and floors for what the dead could tell me about themselves.

Here, for instance, was brave Sir Henry Walton Ellis, killed at Waterloo. Luckier had been some old general of the East India Company, who had survived a roll-call of archaic and exotic campaigns. 'He had', said his marble scroll, 'fought in Affghanistan, Cabool and Punjaub, at Ramanggur, Sadoolapurr and Chillianwallah.' You could almost smell his moustache with the scent of cinnamon and cumin on it. Nearby was a monument to those who 'fell in three glorious victories on the banks of the Sutlej', a forgotten part of the Sikh wars of 1845–46.

Constancy was represented in the six kneeling Moores, carved in 1615: 'Here born, here bred, here buried.' From another part of the wall protruded the calm profile and Austenesque face of a Charlotte Digby, 'died at Malvern of a rapid consumption'. Quick death seemed to be a feature of Malvern. There was the memorial to Richard Selby of Portman Square, London, 'Who, whilft on a Tour of Pleafure with his Family, was feized with an inflammation of the Inteftines, which in five days terminated his life in Malvern.' Rapid consumption, death within a week from inflamed intestines – a bad place, Malvern. And what a way to leave a man to posterity. Did he exhale, as he lay on his deathbed, 'Tell them how I died. I want all the world to know about my inflamed intestines'? I don't think so.

There was the site near the centre where, in 1987, they

accidentally dug up the body of the Worcester Pilgrim, the corpse of a man with leather boots and the cockleshell badge of a pilgrim to Santiago de Compostela, who had died in the late 1400s. I felt some empathy with this traveller, and resolved that – should I too kick the bucket in Malvern – I would be interred along with my canoe.

By the altar was a marble effigy of King John, flanked by St Oswald and St Wulfstan. This John, created some twenty years after the body had made its journey here from Newark, possessed small features, pronounced nostrils, a very careful beard and was holding on tightly to his seal. Inside, the skeleton – intact when last they looked – wore the cowl of a penitent monk. Or so the legend goes.

As I ambled between two rows of wooden chairs set up for a concert or a reading, something caused me to look down. My feet were on a black flagstone set into the floor, recording the presence there of the ashes of 'Stanley, 1st Earl Baldwin of Bewdley'. So this was where he'd been put after he'd died, relatively unmourned, in 1947.

Behind the flying buttresses and the dead English people was the peace of the cathedral close. Choristers' voices combined and rose out from the choir school, and hovered over the close and the late afternoon riverside, as though part of the sound-track for a film.

But the sweetness and tranquillity seemed to be contradicted by the notices all around the close for Neighbourhood Watch. What need, when surely God was watching? The intention had to be different from the common-or-garden Neighbourhood Watch; more spiritual. All the cathedral clergy, the dean, warden, archdeacons and organist, would spend the evening keeping an eye open for villains. When a scoundrel up to no good was spotted, the entire close would come running out with food and valuables and shower them on the straying lamb. Who'd leave with food in his belly, money in his pockets and Christ in his heart. Like in *Les Misérables*.

I was thinking about Christian charity and responsibility, when, just where the cathedral backed on to a lawn which in turn led down to the riverside walk, I spotted a scruffy bloke lying under a bush, apparently dead. I'd spent the whole of the previous day worrying about bodies in the water, and now here (possibly) was one on dry land.

What, I wondered, should I do? If he had actually expired, then there wasn't much I could do, except call for a nun or a dean. But if he was, in fact, only sleeping, then, if I approached him, all I could expect for my trouble was a great, long 'Yaarghgraaarghyarggh!' Still, didn't I have a duty? I was agonising about this when something else caught my eye – a flower or a boat or something. And, just as Jane might have predicted, I forgot all about the dead man, he went clean out of my mind, something new entered, and I recalled him only as I was approaching Oxford a week later. In its own quiet way, this act of amnesia was probably the most shameful thing I did on the journey. And if the scruffy man isn't dead, and is reading this, I'm sorry.

The next morning a huge party of Americans was being processed through the breakfast room. Their badges declared these hale, sleek pensioners to be Don from Buffalo and Irene from Albany.

Outside in the foyer their mad intinerary was displayed in yellow and red. 'Grand Europe Tours,' it read. 'Tuesday. Good Morning – 7.15. Breakfast – 8.00. 9.00 – Warwick and Stratford. 6.15 – Dinner.' Thursday was even worse. There was still a Good Morning succeeded by Breakfast. Then there was simply 'Wales', followed by, 'Ferry to Ireland'. Wales! Between breakfast and tea! Six hours of Wales! Were they going to drive hell for leather from Worcester to Swansea, stopping for ten minutes at Cardiff castle, while their guides pointed excitedly at small, dark men with lamps on their heads?

Grand Aaronovitch Canoe Tours for the day read more sedately. Walk to boat. Change into silly canoe gear. Paddle for four hours through three locks. See Malvern Hills off to right. Arrive Upton-on-Severn. Change out of wet shorts. Dinner. Bed.

Things went according to plan. Paddling along behind the good ship *God's Will*, her grizzled captain calling the occasional invitation to salvation over the top of his 'Jesus Saves' lifebelt, I made excellent time. And I saw, scampering nearby, my first wild otter; its bum lifting exaggeratedly as it ran along the water's side, like a game brunette at a line dance. I'd missed a kingfisher at Newark, so this was my first (and last) big wildlife moment.

Sure enough, as the *Guide* had promised, there now was the dramatic strip of the Malverns, its highest point Worcestershire Beacon in the centre, running along the middle of the plain, as dominating, in its own way, as Ararat.

But I was having real problems with my hand. The pain that I'd felt in the evenings and early mornings was present throughout the day. Now the fingers and my entire wrist felt swollen and inflexible, despite the stretching exercises that I had been doing for the whole journey, the repetition of which had got me some very funny looks, especially in cathedrals. I had, so far, survived the various poisons lurking in the water, but it looked as though I was falling victim to that other great scourge of canoeists: tendonitis. If that flared up badly, I knew – with a guilty relief – that my paddling days would be over.

At three I arrived at the plush marina opposite the town of Upton-on-Severn, home of the Oliver Cromwell jazz festival (so named because the bewarted Lord Protector was, of course, something of a belter on the tenor sax, which he used to play in a band with blind Johnny Milton on the piano). It was obvious why the festival was held here: close to the river the town was just one big pub. Even the *God's Will* had tied up beside the bridge, while its holy navigator stopped for an evening's worth.

My berth was a few yards further down the high street. The White Lion had been an inn since around 1510, and a large cream plaster lion with a magnificent gold mane roared superbly over the porch. My room was directly over the great cat, and I could tickle his ears by leaning out of my window. Otherwise it was a small, oddly-shaped, panelled and beamed room, with a shower inset into an old wardrobe. If I wasn't careful I might find myself stepping, wet and clad in a towel, into Narnia.

The room was wonderful enough, but even better was discovering the role that the White Lion had played in that great English novel, Henry Fielding's *Tom Jones*, published in 1749. It was here that young Tom was seduced by Mrs Waters (who might have been his mother) in a chapter of extended metaphor never quite matched in English literature.

So I lay in bed that night, imagining the sounds of an eighteenth-century night-time inn, full of patterings, creakings, whisperings and hot breath; punctuated by the loud arrival of a coach or a chaise full of tired travellers, and then quiet again.

The *Tom Jones* connection is not, however, Upton's most trumpeted feature. The historic event of which Uptonians are most bizarrely proud, as I discovered the next day, is the great cholera outbreak of 1832. Down a side road I came across a plaque erected by the Upton Civic Society. 'The first victim of the cholera epidemic, costing over 50 lives, lived in the alley nearby,' it said.

In a town the size of Upton, fifty deaths was a holocaust. This pandemic had reached the coasts of England in 1831. From Bristol, it spread up the Severn to Tewkesbury. By July of the next year it had crossed the muddy threshold of a cottage in Upton's unpaved and undrained Lapstone Alley. There, Jane Allen, mother of a six-week-old baby, became ill. Within days she turned blue and desiccated, and died. Then others began to get sick too, first in ones, and then whole families.

At first the burials were held, as usual, in the local churchyard after proper funerals. But the number of deaths soon overwhelmed local organisation, and the vicar was asked to stop the tolling of the church bell as it was depressing everyone in earshot.

A cholera pit was opened in nearby Parson's Field, and the newly dead were bundled into their coffins, shoved on to a handcart, trundled across town and dumped into the pit. Three weeks after the outbreak began, as quickly as it had come, the cholera went again. And now the Civic Society gives detailed instructions to the passing tourist about how to find the town's famous cholera pit. Disappointingly, there is no T-shirt.

★   ★   ★

There have been six great journeyers across England whose accounts of their travels reach out to us across history. Five of them were John Leland, Daniel Defoe, H. V. Morton, J. B. Priestley and Bill Bryson. The sixth had spent some time in this part of Worcestershire, where I was now staying. At the end of September 1826, six years before Jane Allen died in Lapstone Alley, the Radical journalist and author William Cobbett crossed the Severn at Upton.

As he travelled, Cobbett was taking notes for one of the most famous books about England ever published, *Rural Rides*. At Ryall, just across the Severn, Cobbett recorded his liking for the countryside hereabouts. The fields by the river were, he wrote, 'The finest meadows of which it is possible to form an idea.' He also noted that the area was under-populated, and that many villages had difficulty providing sufficient souls to maintain the parish churches. He blamed capitalism and bad government. As a Radical, an opponent of exploitation and finance capital, Cobbett has long been a favourite of English left-wingers.

They've always managed, somehow, to ignore another facet of Cobbett's views. Running alongside his hatred of the new dispensation was his profound and constant anti-Semitism. While at Ryall, just across the way, Cobbett drew a bead on his target. 'The fact is,' he wrote, 'the Jew-system has swept all the little gentry, the small farmers and the domestic manufacturers away.'

The Jew-system! There were still precious few Jews in England at all, yet their 'system' was to blame. 'The working people suffer,' Cobbett complained, 'the trades people suffer, and, who is to escape, except the monopolizers, the Jews and the tax-eaters, when the Government chooses to raise the value of money, and lower the price of goods?'

Shades here of Priestley in Lincoln, wondering about the Jew who 'controlled' the hotel industry. Echoes too of the blood libel, of how the Jews killed little Christian boys.

★　★　★

Given Upton's preoccupation with cholera, there could, I thought, be only one place more interestingly unhealthy. All those memorials in Worcester to travellers who had got as far as Malvern and then died, made it a town well worth visiting. And there was a convenient bus to take me there.

Actually there was more than one bus. There were several bus stops, located at various points in the small town, but no one in Upton – not shop-keepers, mothers, passers-by – seemed to know from which stop which bus went and in what direction. Some appeared bemused and genuinely surprised that there were any buses at all. Obviously almost no one in Upton ever used a bus, or even knew anyone who did.

For the visitor this provided one of those dilemmas of travel. Where should you stand to have the optimum chance of stopping the correct bus? How could you avoid waiting at the wrong stop for an hour, just to find yourself gazing at the back of a speeding bus that had just picked up from a halt 150 yards away? In the end I backed a hunch and fortunately the hunch was right, and I took my place as one of two passengers travelling towards the Malvern hills.

Malvern is a mystical place. The fictional Piers Plowman had had a spiritual dream on the high hillside overlooking the plain and the Severn some time in the fourteenth century. 'In a summer season when the sun was mild,' he'd sat down by a stream, and an image of the celestial city had come to him. Now, from where Piers had gazed, you could get a good view all the way over to the shimmering junction of the M5 and the M50.

Perhaps because of these associations, Malvern was supposed, during the 80s, to have become the New Age capital of England, though there had been those more recent rumours of it being overtaken by Bishop's Castle. Still, incense must waft, I thought, over the Priory, and the sound of chanting rise above the traffic's noise.

No. It certainly wasn't the Goa of England. Beaded, naked hippies weren't floating down the main drag chewing magic mushrooms. There were no crystal-reading shops between Boots and Woolworths. As a last resort I examined the ads in shop windows for clues. One offered me the answer to the question, 'What is gnosis?' Another recommended, 'An evening with Bernie Prior.' Entitled 'From the Force of Living to a Life of Love', it went on: 'Bernie has just returned from a lone tour of Australia, New Zealand and Los Angeles, where he experienced a deeper realisation of Self.' But what might a deeper realisation of the Self of Bernie Prior mean? One suspected that it was much the same Self that he'd started out with; the kind of Self that no one else would want to help him find.

More to the point, though, did this Bernie Prior actually make any money realising his Self more deeply? I could do this, after all, following my tribulations. 'After two lone months in a canoe, David Aaronovitch has experienced a deeper realisation of Self.' I might call it, 'From the Force of Paddling to a Knowledge of All.'

Malvern's reputation for healing goes back two centuries, to when its mineral waters were first thought to be therapeutic. But it was the early Victorians Dr James Gully and Dr James Wilson who really put the place on the map with their famous hydrotherapies. In their awful establishment the patients would be wrapped in wet sheets, hosed down, forced to go on long walks and drink eighteen tumblers of water, all before breakfast. Then they could immerse their bums in water for up to an hour in the famous sitz baths, before the climactic douche, in which they would be subjected to 150 gallons of cold water dropped on them in three minutes. Many famous people preferred this treatment to leeches and bloodletting, probably quite sensibly.

One of them was Charles Darwin. Then, in March 1851, he brought his favourite daughter Anne to Malvern for the treatment, as she had been ill for some time. Her death a few weeks later nearly killed Darwin's Christian faith. She is buried under a cedar of Lebanon in the churchyard of Malvern Priory, with the epitaph, 'A good and loving child'.

A month after Anne's death, Charles Dickens' wife, Kate, was here taking the cure – probably for post-natal depression. It was in Malvern that the news reached her that her eight-month-old daughter, Dora, had died back in Kent. So I stood by Anne's stone, and thought once more of my own daughters, and blessed the fact that they and I were living in England at the end of the twentieth century.

The greatest Malvernian of all was England's most loved composer, Sir Edward Elgar. Reminders of Elgar litter the land between the Beacons and the river. He lives on, involuntarily, in the mall at Worcester and in the extraordinary Elgar Housing Association, which in 1994 bought the entire housing stock of Malvern Hills District Council. By the last year of the century there were 5,000 properties, all half-owned by the householder, and half rented from the Elgar; 15,000 people in all lived in Elgar homes, and the ubiquitous Elgar sponsored the junior football teams.

It's fitting, therefore, that Elgar was one of the first English people to give his house a naff name. I'd snorted when the bus took me through a picturesque village, in which one cottage was distinguished by those gold and black sticky letters, spelling out the dreadful name Brencliffe, where – we might guess – Brenda lives with Cliff. Old Elgar though, a kosher cultured Englishman if ever one lived, called one cottage of his 'Fork', and another, in Malvern Wells, he dubbed Craeg Lea, an anagram of his surname, his initials and those of his wife. You can't – in fairness – mock Brencliffe, and let Elgar get away with Craeg Lea, can you?

But the *Knife* was calling me while I tarried here in the shade of the churchyard. I hailed a cab, hurried back to Upton, passing then out of Worcestershire and into Gloucestershire. On to where the Avon meets the Severn, and where stands the town of Tewkesbury.

Here, I discovered, two historic acts of vandalism had been narrowly averted by local people, though four centuries separated the two events. In 1540 Tewkesbury Abbey, a gorgeous bit of old churchery, and burial place of the Despensers and that Duke of Clarence supposedly drowned in a butt of Malmsey by Richard III, was about to be pulled down during the Dissolution. As part of a former monastery it was declared redundant by Henry VIII's commissioners. The local townspeople had other ideas. For £453 – the estimated melt-down value of the bells and the lead on the roof – they bought the place and kept it as a church.

Likewise, in the early 60s, yet another council, transfixed by a science fiction notion of modernity – all sleek lines and fast transport – began to pull down the medieval buildings along one part of the High Street, and replacing them with yet another truly awful shopping centre. Worse might have been done had not a Preservation Society been set up and all such development stopped. Now, of course, the old untidy buildings of Tewkesbury are a major draw, attracting Americans and old ladies in floral print skirts from all over England.

In 1471, as every battle-nerd knows, the last great battle of the Wars of the Roses was fought just south of the abbey. There was a terrible slaughter, particularly in a water-meadow by the side of the Severn, afterwards known as Bloody Field.

Nerdy myself, I walked along a lane by the Bloody Field, past a BT man fast asleep in his van, and then turned up a footpath to a place called Margaret's Camp, a weedy knoll around which a large council estate had sprung up. There were no ghosts here on yet another boiling day, just a man taking his dog for a walk. The flats had views of trees and the abbey, though it was obvious that Tewkesbury was taking off to the south now, in a desperate attempt to join up with the sprawl of Gloucester.

I had nearly done with the Severn. There was just time to paddle past the spot where, a few weeks earlier, a John Lewis, sixty-four, of Minsterworth, had been tragically drowned. A coroner's court heard how Mr Lewis, a businessman, died after jumping into the river having accidentally set fire to himself in his garden. 'His partly burned ride-on lawn-mower, scorched clothing and two petrol cans had been found next to a bonfire he had been building,' said the *Telegraph*.

At first it was thought that he might have staged his own 'suicide' for obscure reasons of his own – a favourite re-invention myth in a crowded country – but a fortnight later his body had been found on the opposite bank of the Severn. Even so, local rumours had it that Mr Lewis's death was not all that it seemed. His business had been in trouble, there had been 'associates'. And, anyway, who'd be stupid enough to light a fire with a can of petrol while sitting on a lawn-mower?

Practically anybody in England, I thought. Including me.

CHAPTER 28

Farewell, Then, Oh Trusty Knife

It wasn't what I'd planned. On my last but one day I was going to come down the tide to the Richmond boathouse, waving triumphantly to Dick, Trevor and Wo Chung as I swept past. Heads would be shaken in admiration. Finally I'd be admitted fully into the confraternity of paddlers, and respect would be mine. Stories about the round England canoeist would continue to be told as long as boats floated on this part of the Thames.

Unfortunately, there was a problem. By Gloucester, I had become The Claw. Starting with the 'swivel' finger of my right hand, then the third, then the pinky and finally my index finger, I was finding it hard to unclench my fist. I became anxious that, if I didn't rest it, I might do some permanent damage to my writing hand, and have to go around begging for a living, holding out my claw for kind folk to drop euros into.

There was only one thing to be done. My poor boat had to be ditched. As in many close relationships, our fortunes had been the reverse of each other. I had grown stronger and lighter with each day, my arms and face had turned a pleasant shade of umber. The *Knife*, on the other hand, had not fared so well. Her washable seat was lost, her wheels were damaged, her hatches dented and her elasticated lines now drooped. Worst of all, when she was turned over, her once pristine white bottom was now a mass of scars and small holes, some inexpertly filled with Araldite. Sticky remnants of Scotch-tape wisped horribly from various places. Frankly, she wasn't the beauty that I'd taken up with.

It wasn't her; it was me. I don't mean to suggest that I was no longer fond of her, or that I now wished to paddle in another. We were fond enough, I suppose, having experienced so much together. She had been with me that terrible day on the Grand Union, wobbled at the end of my arm over the foaming Trent, had squeezed under the bridges of Yorkshire, and we had shot the Jackfield rapids together. They could never take that away from us.

If I walked beside the river, instead of paddling on top of it, what would I lose? The Richmond triumph, yes. Jane would suspect me of back-sliding, of course, but she'd cope. Plus I'd move a bit more slowly, perhaps round about a mile an hour less, cutting my maximum travel from 25 miles to 20. And I wouldn't be able to carry so much, so I'd have to go without the tent and sleeping bag.

What would I gain? There'd be no locks. No wondering where and how to embark and disembark, no elaborate urination rituals, no hour wasted each morning and evening folding everything into small parcels and feeding it into the hatches, no soaked groin, no nightly anxiety about whether the *Knife* was safe in her boatyard or garage, no need even to find a boatyard or garage. There'd be no worry about mad boaters, no problem about eating or drinking on the move, no threat from swans, no roach poles, no difficulty with taking a rest whenever I wanted one, no camping (since I'd have no tent), no back-ache.

It was better, I decided, for both of us if we parted now. We could still be friends after all. There was nothing to stop us going out for short trips on the Thames or elsewhere for years to come.

Jane drove out, picked up the *Knife* and the tent, handed over the silly alpenstock I'd asked for, told me that she had never thought that I'd last on the water, and left me at the top of the Thames.

Contemplating a journey without the *Knife*, the initial regret gave way alarmingly quickly to something that felt like elation. The question, could I manage on my own, was soon answered with an enthusiastic affirmative.

The Thames path now runs from the source to the Dome and beyond. And the nine days I spent on it were – with the exception of the days my children were born – the best days of my life. I had been right to seek a divorce. To begin with, from the banks of the river I could suddenly see what was on either side of me, instead of looking mostly at foliage. I met more people, stopped more often to look at villages and towns.

Also, as I walked, I contemplated and imagined. Rich skeins of thought unravelled in my head as my legs moved, as though pumped out by the motion, and uninhibited by the absence of danger.

Cloud was rare and it rained just once, a light shower, for about seven minutes. Otherwise my only enemy was the heat; a foe I fought pleasantly by stopping at many of the pubs that history has scattered along the banks of the Thames.

For the first three steaming days I stepped gaily across the water-meadows that lined the young river. There were few houses on the Thames banks between Cricklade and Oxford, presumably because the river floods here quite often, and it was possible to walk for several hours without seeing a soul on land or water. But, for some reason, this loneliness was much more tolerable from the vantage point of the path, especially since it was never more than three or four miles to the next pub.

Or perhaps it was because I had, somewhere along the way, lost my dread of being on my own. The evenings no longer seemed impossibly long or empty. My need to phone Sarah and the children was less, though I still called every night. And the physical exertion seemed also to have worked off my everyday irascibility. I was no longer looking to be slighted or offended, or to anticipate hooligans, attackers, officious servants of the law, homicidal drivers or pavement cyclists. As I walked I was becoming, for the first time in thirty years, calm. The sun shone, and so did Mr Sunny.

At Lechlade, a wealthy old wool town with a shabby boatyard and an elegant church, the navigable Thames begins, and from then on I was accompanied on my walk by boats, which began their journeys just above St John's lock, where a sculpture of Old Father Thames reclines by the gates.

Along this stretch the river looped absurdly, as though showing off, and I would sometimes hurry across the neck of particularly tight turns, simply so that I could magically appear in front of a boat that thought it had just passed me.

My favourites were two very contrasting craft. The first was an old narrowboat, the *Muskrat*. This was a lived-in vessel steered by a man with a vast beard and enormous stomach, who nevertheless managed a capable and nautical demeanour that put me in mind of a Captain Birdseye who'd eaten everyone else's fish fingers. In the bows his slightly more demure wife was irritated when I caught her hanging out her washing, including her substantial husband's voluminous boxer shorts.

The other boat was the *Duchess of Argyll*. There was no washing on the *Duchess*. Above a long, low hull of burnished wood rose a blue-and-white striped awning on gilded poles, through which thrust a delicate black smoke-stack. Baskets of bright flowers sat on the bows, and on the stern, next to the ensign. And kneeling by these flowers, in the pose of the Little Mermaid in Copenhagen, was a close-bobbed woman in shorts, who hailed me in the accents of the Home Counties. Her white-haired husband, meanwhile, tended a brass steam engine encased in glass in the centre of the awning, and occasionally leant on a round ship's wheel. Here, you could see, was a deal; he got to spend a lot of time messing around with elegant machinery, while she floated down the river being admired by everyone: it was the perfect match.

What the crews of the *Duchess* and the *Muskrat* couldn't quite see – but (aha!) I could – was the way the north bank was studded with octagonal concrete emplacements – one every 400 yards or so, their gun-slits pointing across the thin strip of water. In 1940 these were part of Stopline Red, an improbable line of defence designed to prevent the invading Germans from marching into the Midlands. The Thames – at this point a ribbon weaving through flat land – did not seem a robust barrier to the forces of the Blitzkrieg. Thank God, the Channel and Winston Churchill that they never got this far. We wouldn't have stood a chance.

A few miles beyond Lechlade, set slightly back from the Thames, is Kelmscott House. This Elizabethan mansion was, from 1871 till his death, the country residence of William Morris. The house, made of grey Oxford stone, grey gabled and mullioned, is, from the outside, every English-person's idea of a great place to live, right down to the ivy and the little balls on top of the walls. I couldn't find out what it was like inside since a notice proclaimed that the place was open for only half an hour very fourth Tuesday, a Tuesday I'd just missed.

This was a shame, since I'd wanted to wander the rooms where one of the great English ménages had taken place. Morris – all socialism and aesthetics – had appropriately married a Rapunzel-headed pre-Raphaelite beauty of great physical but minimal verbal presence, called Jane. He and silent Jane might have been all right, had Morris not also had the generous notion of sharing Kelmscott with his romantic poet friend, Dante Gabriel Rossetti. DGR was happy to pool the afternoon's sun in the walled garden, the view out over the medieval church and the bathroom. And he was happy to share something else. With Morris out of the house doing socialist or aesthetic things in London, Rossetti divided his time between walking the banks of the river abusing fishermen (apparently the opiate he took for toothache had a bizarre effect on his temper), and courting Janey Morris.

This angler-abuse and wife-pooling went on till 1874, but Morris – a good and almost saintly man – forgave them both. He was, in any case, more interested in arts, crafts, wallpaper, stopping Victorian church restorers from destroying the English heritage and supporting striking dockers.

Morris, had he been alive that hot day, would have launched one of his famous campaigns against the publican of the nearby Swan Hotel. On that sweaty lunchtime I slogged past the twelfth-century bridge at Radcot, bought a pint at the Swan, and took it into the tree-shaded garden bordering the river.

The scene could have been from any of the last three centuries, give or take a periwig and an ostler; Dante Gabriel's shade was at my elbow, whispering ruderies about men with long rods. Then, from the eaves of the old inn emerged a loud, disembodied metallic voice, as though God were speaking from a helicopter. 'Number Six please,' it thundered. 'Your food is outside by the barbecue.'

Looking up I spotted a red loudspeaker under the roof. It was like something from that 60s TV series, *The Prisoner*, where the population were given amplified improving thoughts to think while they golf-carted around. So Number Six, no longer a free man, but two plates of ham salad, obediently walked to the barbecue, where a smiling waitress met him.

I escaped from the alarming loudspeakers only to run into the scary cows. I am not normally afraid of cows, since they seem to have no idea that, collectively, they could do a human being a lot of damage. But instead of ganging up together against us small, aggressive, bald-bellied creatures − as in *Animal Farm* − they just scatter at the first yell, and consent to be slaughtered in their millions.

But just recently there had been worrying signs of a new strain of killer cattle to follow the famous epidemic of mad ones. The newspapers had reported that two men had already been killed that spring, not by bulls, but by cows. True, both cases of bovine homicide were committed against octogenarians, and there must have been a suspicion of slipping and accidental trampling, but it was concerning all the same.

Furthermore, in every field the Thames path passed through, the cattle seemed to cluster on the path, deliberately and silently assembling as soon as they saw me approach. There was something disconcertingly Hitchcockian about them. Was it possible that many of those bodies found floating in the Thames had been put there by cattle? No one had ever thought to ask whether this mark or that abrasion wasn't caused by the blow of a hoof or the prod of a crumpled horn.

Cows aside, if you like pretty, there was plenty of pretty. Clouds of butterflies rose from buddleia, picturesque footbridges crossed the water − some with watercolourists on them − silvery fish clustered in the shallows. Every now and then the path would skirt a beautifully manicured lock, with flowers and lawns and potted histories of that particular stretch of the Thames. And didn't I wish that I was passing through them in a canoe? No, I didn't. From time to time mellifluously named minor river − like the Windrush or the Evenlode − would flow peacefully into the growing flux.

I was not quite the only walker on the path. Twelve miles from Lechlade a spry elderly couple strode towards me, motoring impressively. I said hello, and the man replied by stopping and proclaiming, 'Nice day! I'm nearly seventy-seven!' This is, of course, an unfair opening sentence, much loved by pensioners. It means, 'You'll be lucky if you're even alive at this age, let alone dashing about like I am. Now pay me a compliment.'

So what could I say? For some strange synaptic reason, when my mouth connected with my brain, what it came out with was the Jewish blessing, '*Mazel tov!*'

So taken aback was I by this phrase emerging without warning from my head, that I made it worse by adding – as though by way of explanation – 'as they say in my part of the world'. I was staggered by myself. In my part of the world? Where was I from, already? Haifa? Most people in London do *not* say *Mazel tov*. It was a panicky act of ethnic piracy, and I was ashamed. I was over-compensating for Priestley and Cobbett.

My legs were not accustomed to this exercise, and it was sore-hipped and swollen-kneed that I limped through a bankside camper van display, exchanging greetings with friendly caravanners, and over the old bridge at Newbridge to the Rose Revived inn. Cromwell stayed here during his various peregrinations, and what was good enough for the sax-toting Lord Protector was good enough for me.

Remarkably, although the Rose was miles from any town, the inn and its large garden, fringed by weeping willows, was absolutely full. Small boys in (what else?) red Manchester United shirts flopped about the grass. On the tables groups of smart women, mysteriously materialised from offices in some far place, giggled and guffawed. Toddlers threw chips at their mothers, and dads looked on smiling. It was just blissful.

I spotted the *Duchess* again the next day, at a place called Bablock Hythe, where once the youthful Matthew Arnold celebrated nude in the 'stripling Thames'. Now a traileropolis extended along the bank, near which the unmistakable blue-and-white stripes of the boat rocked gently. I was limping a bit; and the bobbed woman, recognising me, kindly offered me a lift the eleven miles to Oxford. But there was somewhere I wanted to see a mile or so from the river, and I turned her down.

The somewhere was the tower at the village of Stanton Harcourt, where the journalist and poet Alexander Pope had lived while he was translating the *Iliad*. Pope was in this tower when a young local couple were tragically killed by lightning while out harvesting. His translation of Homer's classic may have been superseded by later linguists, but his couplet lamenting the deaths has not. He wrote:

> Here lye two poor lovers, who had the mishap
> Although very Chaste people, to die of the Clap.

I arrived at the tower that I had gone four miles out of my way for. I looked at it. It had a pointy top. I turned round and walked back to the river. That's how hot it was.

At Godstow, near Oxford, I saw the ruins of the abbey where Fair Rosamund Clifford had died. We were, by now, near the end of a late-twentieth-century globally-warmed July. On the bridge were kids and bare-torsoed teenagers, who swarmed all over the parapet, throwing each other into the water and jumping in on top of inflatables. Through the middle of this mayhem steamed the sedate shape of the *Duchess of Argyll*, and this time I agreed to be carried, wine glass in hand, to the city of spires.

She was Joan and he was Geoff, the design master at Eton. The boat – a gentleman's day launch – had been built in 1881, and was moored most of the time outside the riverside tied house near Windsor that came with Geoff's job. I didn't ask them if they were aware of a most recent Duchess of Argyll's interesting sexual reputation, or the modern opera about her, involving the only known example of musical fellatio. Instead, I was content to loll on the cushions near the stern and talk about canoeing on the Trent.

Ten minutes later we steamed in style by the village of Wolvercote, in whose churchyard Mrs and Professor Tolkien lie side by side. A year or so earlier the literary world had been horrified by a poll of Britons making *The Lord of the Rings* the greatest book of the century.

They shouldn't have been. Begun when Baldwin was Prime

Minister, *The Lord of the Rings* is as important a work of English mythology as any speech about corncrakes and plough-horses. The Shire, a place of rural loveliness and order, is clearly the England that I was passing though right now. In Frodo and his faithful servant Sam Gamgee, Tolkien created an idealised version of the English class system, with mutual obligations, but everyone knowing their place. At the apex of this system is a deity – Gandalf – who is himself as English as his hobbits and would probably have been an Oxford professor. Like Tolkien.

And what of the other races? England/The Shire reluctantly seeks to save the rest of the world, despite its small size and relative puniness. Its weapons are courage, fortitude, a sense of honour, sheer common sense and a capacity to improvise. The allies are the dwarves (who resemble the mining Welsh and Scots of the industrial era); elves (Dark Ages Celts); the men of Rohan (whose sudden emergence on the field of battle halfway through the action makes them Americans); and the proud, fractious men of Gondor (France, valiant but stubborn), who more or less have to be saved from themselves. The enemies from the East include Mordor's orcs (Russians and/or Germans to taste), and the various dark-skinned peoples of the South: Haradrim, corsairs and suchlike (Arabs, Turks, Africans, Indians and other rebellious colonial subjects).

Here again was Baldwin's country, with its curry mix of virtues and vices: big-heartedness and small-mindedness, brave and, above all, smug. Middle Earth, Middle England.

So now we were floating deliciously past the expanse of Port Meadow, given by William the Conqueror to the people of Oxford and speckled with cattle, horses, fishermen, ducks and lovers, all of whom looked at us and our boat with gratifying envy.

Unfortunately there were also urchins about. I don't know if they have urchins like ours on the continent, or whether – like railway enthusiasts and saucy grannies – they are native only to these shores, but since Dickens' day and before, there has always been a species of young English boy which has collected together with his peers for the express purpose of throwing or firing things at people: stones, snowballs, airgun pellets, mud, you name it.

Historically, urchins have shaven heads, ill-fitting (or no) swimming costumes, and hands full of ammunition, procured and stored God knows where. At best Just William, at worst criminal damage. I'd expected them long before now. Leeds, I'd heard, was full of urchins, dropping things from bridges on to canoeists. There was nary a one. Leicester was crawling with them, Burnley awash, the approaches to Manchester a shooting gallery for them, Bingley terrorised by them. But apart from the suicidal teenagers of Newark, I'd seen very few signs of delinquency.

Now, in the soft Home Counties, the urchins finally appeared. As we sybarites slid past Medley footbridge on our elegant craft, we came under a sudden and unexpected barrage of pebbles from seven or eight classic shaved urchins who had been waiting for just this moment. Their fire was constant, and only slightly accurate, but they were hurling gravel and stones as hard as they possibly could, and it was quite conceivable that they might break the glass over the engine or put someone's eye out. Their determination to try and do damage to strangers at minimum cost to themselves was remarkable.

But what really infuriated me was the adults close-by, who stood trying to pretend that nothing was actually happening. It is always a surprise to see just how frightened grown-ups have become of children. I yelled my most terrible yell, and the urchins yelled back and threw more stones.

Beyond the urchins, at Osney lock, I said a final goodbye to a fortunately undamaged Geoff and Joan and headed into the town of Oxford itself.

I knew the place quite well because I had studied here, briefly, in the mid-70s. For two terms in fact, but rebelliousness and a Swiss art historian had put a premature end to my Oxbridge career. I had been chucked out of exams for not being dressed correctly, fined by the authorities for fly-posting, missed matriculation and been found by an angry dean lying, naked in bed, while three very young and very beautiful girls sat close by.

The exam failure had been the natural conclusion to this saga of incompetence.

The truth is that I hadn't been able to cope with the place, its mad public-school customs and its discomforts. The bathroom on my staircase at Balliol was a wintry Purgatory, and in my first week, and without having any kind of sex with anyone, I discovered that I had contracted pubic lice. When for a second time I failed my German exams (I was studying history, so that tells you something), the college sent me down with great regret, and have been chasing me for contributions to their various funds ever since.

As a result I'd never been in Oxford during one of its fabled summers, when the *jeunesse dorée* pop champagne corks down by Folly Bridge and languid boys condescend to seduce floppy girls. Now here I was, a quarter century later, in streets teeming with people from the Far East and well-dressed youngsters attending various language schools and summer courses for the recklessly wealthy.

On the cab ranks every single driver had a turban, suggesting once again that taxi-driving in England is now a largely Asian profession. One building opposite my old college offered an entrance to 'The Oxford Experience', customers being waved in by a mannequin in gown and mortar board. If it were at all authentic, I thought, then they should emerge thirty minutes later with pneumonia and a curious itching sensation in the groin.

New restaurants were open on every corner, and I walked about looking at it all and recollecting till late. The cold, uncertain, difficult place I remembered, was now a hot, simple, crowded town. I went back to the Randolph Hotel, the venerable and expensive city centre hotel where I was staying and, exhausted, fell into a deep, deep sleep, from which a bomb blast could not have awakened me.

Something else did, however, because during the night I was thrown out of my dreams with a brutality that took my breath away. The most appalling, unbearable noise had gone off in my ear, as though some sadistic bedfellow had crept up on me and let off a klaxon by my head, or a hive of hornets had flown in through my nostrils. Before I was aware of where I was even, I found myself standing on the floor, horribly alert.

The green digits on the bedside clock said 1.30 a.m. I threw on enough clothes for decency, grabbed my notebook and wallet, and hurried out into the bright corridor. There I followed a grim-looking swarthy man in a suit jacket and pyjama trousers, who seemed to know where he was going. On the stairs a frail old Asian lady in a sari and shawl was being slowly led down, step by painful step, by her daughters. Going against the flow, alarmed hotel girls skipped up the stairs, faces white with purpose, searching for stragglers to bully.

No, they told the people on the stairs, this was not an exercise; real smoke had been detected; smoke as in fire. I permitted myself a mental image of the outside of the hotel in ten minutes' time, flames flickering out of upstairs windows, jets of water from the firemen's hoses, the thud of bodies hitting the pavement.

In the street the blue revolving lights of the fire engines and the dressed-to-extinguish swagger of the firefighters reduced the cowering guests to midgets. Along the way a gaggle of Hoorays – one of whose number had almost certainly, I thought, caused us all to be there – stood giggling and smoking; the boys in tie and tails, the girls in plunging ball-gowns.

The rest of us were distinctly under-dressed. There was a middle-aged woman in a great-coat and – as far as one could see – nothing else. A mum held tightly on to her small son, sleepy but excited in dinosaur pyjamas. Rich men pulled their dressing-gowns about them and scowled.

This was a rarely permitted moment of revelation; to see all these strangers in their night things, like hermit crabs drawn from their shells, fleshy and wriggly and less intimidating than the brassy customers one had shared lifts with the night before. For any traveller it is practically worth setting off the alarm in every hotel, just to see what comes out.

Within five minutes the hotel girls were back on the pavement, reassuring us impatiently and guests started to re-enter the hotel. 'A cigarette stubbed out on the carpet,' one receptionist told me, in tones mixing disapproval with relief.

In the lobby at nine the next morning, a group of well-fed older men with a nasty line in early guffaws were discussing the previous night's alarm. 'Well,' said one in a canary shirt, proprietorially, 'what would you expect at Colin's wedding? Hahaha!'

Three fit, gleaming young men, whom I'd last seen on the pavement the night before, smirked up to their uncles, and shared a joke about the waking of the hotel, and were duly indulged in the way that the upper middle classes have always indulged the youthful vandalism of their boys. Outside there was broken glass in the road, and the ghost of Evelyn Waugh strolled down St Aldate's.

CHAPTER 29

Wealth and Efficiency

The water-meadow interlude ended at Oxford. Just as in *Brideshead Revisited*, with Oxford over, purposeful England began, and the riverside was now increasingly divided up into wide strips of lawn that marched pompously down to the banks from impressive mansions above. Tacked on to the lawns were the boathouses.

The Thames path rolled a great U round the town of Abingdon, and threaded between estates with notices declaring that – in their kingdom at least – there was no entry, no mooring, no fishing and no swimming. You could, however, go and do tapestry weaving in their drives – or at least there were no signs to say you couldn't.

There wasn't much to Dorchester but the Abbey Church. Like Tewkesbury, it had been saved from destruction by a quick-minded offer of £140, this time on the part of a Richard Beauforest, who gave it over to the use of the people of the parish. Splendid though it was, I wouldn't have bothered mentioning yet another antiquity, if it hadn't been for the presence of the most wonderful sculpture that I'd seen so far on my travels. This one was the effigy on the tomb of a knight. But Dorchester's knight was not lying prone, feet slightly crossed, back flush to the coffin lid, hands in prayer on his abdomen, in a state of eternal repose. This warrior, covered from head to foot in fine mail, and then a flowing surcoat, was struggling against death. The left hip was slightly raised, the right leg lying well over the other, flexing to stand. And his hand was grasping his sword hilt, as though he had been caught in the moment of pulling out his weapon to fend off the attack of Death. He reminded me, this knight, of one of the figures from Pompeii, created when the volcanic ash covered those fleeing the eruption of Vesuvius. He had not been shriven or reconciled to death, but had departed, fighting. No one knows who he is, though some believe he may be Sir John de Holcombe, who died in 1270.

At Shillingford the super-rich Thames really started. Exclusive houses with names like River Acres sat amidst tennis courts, while old, hostile men in white shorts and white floppy hats mowed the long lawns seated atop large motor-mowers. From gardens where marquees were being erected, women with curly hair and dark glasses would stop in mid-instruction to their caterers and glance over their flint walls beaming suspicion and a sense that you were not wanted. This was their Neighbourhood, and they were Watching it.

The river itself was a bit more democratic; the Thames path full of careful cyclists and sunburnt walkers, the water adorned with boaters and young canoeists. At the locks, queues of boats waited to get through, their crews amiably comparing itineraries and engine sizes. I spotted the *Duchess* again, gliding past with new guests reclining on her seats.

I felt less kindly towards the new breed of boat that lorded it over the water down here. These were huge white ocean-going cruisers, whose dimensions were utterly inappropriate to the river. On the roofs of *Mimi* and the *Queen Popsicle* were draped the limp, brown bodies of girl sunbathers, spread-eagled, face-down and braless, next to copies of *Hello!* magazine. Twenty feet above the water, perched like cherries on the top of impossible meringues, sat their red-cheeked captains, High Kings of the Home Counties.

Wallingford was full of kids. Kids in rowing boats, kids in kayaks, kids in inner tyres, kids (like those of Godstow) diving from the bridge, kids running, shrieking along the lawn of a public recreation area on the other side of the river. Near to me a youngish woman took a photo of her little boy, gently removing his glasses, and I somehow knew that these two only had each other. There was a solidarity there, an idea of the two of them against the world.

Thirty-odd years ago these children could have been me. The first family holiday that I remember was taken here at Wallingford when I was five. I recalled hanging on to some railings, looking through them to the Thames, which seemed so enormous. And here I came across a stretch of rusty, warped railings, skirting a field by the river path. It could have been the place.

That was a warm summer, too, lying out in the tickling grass reading a comic, or stretched out awake at night, with the breeze rippling the canvas of our tent. But I can't picture my parents or my brother and sister at all. All I can be fairly sure about was that Dad wasn't enjoying himself.

Dad didn't like family holidays. In fact, looking back on it, I think he may have hated them. A driven man, he would have missed all the appurtenances of work: the meetings, events, rallies and pampleteering that were the stuff of Communist politics. He needed constant stimulation. He'd left school at fourteen, taught himself three languages, had a reader's ticket to the British Library before he was seventeen. By the age of forty he'd written three books: one on Kenya, which he'd never visited, and two on political economy. All his life my father, when in company, would look for the conversation, the hint of the conversation, that could bring him alive. Stupid people, especially those who did not need – by reason of education and privilege – to be stupid, hurt him. He would wince when they spoke.

He wasn't often home when we were young, arriving back after we'd been put to bed, and working most weekends for the cause. Often we'd be taken with him, my brother and I, and left to read the books about the Great War that lined dusty Party offices in central London and in Essex. And his small study at home was his sanctuary, to which he would retreat as often as he could get away with it. He never read to us, though he did take us to the children's concerts at the Royal Festival Hall, and was predictably disappointed when we failed to appreciate them properly.

It wasn't that he didn't care for his children. I suspect that, until I was twenty-five, I just wasn't interesting enough for him. For a while he certainly wasn't interesting enough for me. As soon as I was fifteen I refused to travel on any more family holidays. Dad might be forced to go, but I wouldn't.

A generation of men, like my father, were poorer dads than they needed to be, because no one suggested to them that they were missing anything. And certainly no one told them that we children were. My father only really became my friend when he no longer had to consider that I was his son, to whom he had obligations. After that we liked each other a lot.

Quite consciously it was a way of fathering that I didn't want to emulate. Quite unconsciously it was a mode I slipped into all the time; a mode, in fact, that I hoped the journey would jolt me out of. In Wallingford I reminded myself of this ambition. Well, not any more, I said to myself, as I took an alleyway by an old flint-coursed church, crossed a tree-shaded brook over which leant the timbers of a Tudor cottage, and – finding the river again – headed south. I'd do better by my kids.

They did pretty well for theirs round here. Materially, at any rate. Even the schools in this part of the world had lots of money. Every prep and private school I passed carried, by its driveway, under its coat-of-arms, an announcement that this or that builder was, even now, adding a new classroom block, a science wing or a sports complex. To these schools would go the grandchildren of Jenny and Quinlan, whose Ruby Wedding party covered the lawns and filled the river view arbours of the Beetle and Wedge. While cultured pleasant people talked into the early evening, sounds of accordion and the clacking of Morris dancing floated over from the village of Moulsford.

My legs were stronger now, but it was with badly blistered feet that I came down next day to the Goring gap, that passage through the chalklands that marks the fording of the river by the Stone Age thoroughfares of the Icknield Way and the Ridgeway. Sorer and hairier feet than mine had passed this way in the last three thousand years. Mine took me up a large wooded hill and along a mysterious path that dropped me half a mile from the river.

When I emerged, at an operating toll-booth, I was opposite Pangbourne, where my companion from Bingley lived, where the three men in a boat got out, and where Kenneth Grahame, author of *Wind in the Willows*, had lived his last few years. Several large houses along the river bank were, naturally, nominated as his model for Toad Hall, though most went for Mapledurham House, a mile or so further down.

And it was opposite Mapledurham House that Reading now began. True, it didn't say it was Reading, it said it was Purley Park but, take it from me, it was Reading; expanding, burgeoning and bulging.

What Reading had became famous for in the last year of the millennium was the fact that unemployment there had, to all intents and purposes, dropped to zero. Burnley might be in the doldrums, but everybody wanted to come here to work and a huge problem was looming – where were the homes to come from to house all these people? Reports slid across ministers' desks talking of a million new homes to be built in the South-East, half of them on land never bricked over before.

So a howl had gone up from those already living in the green bits of the South-East: no more! No room, no room! The awful prospect of yet more new developments eating into the Green Belt was dangled in front of the nation. Did we want to become one huge dormitory suburb, stretching from Brighton to Milton Keynes?

We'd been here before. As the Second World War began, George Orwell described who would inherit England afterwards. In *The Lion and the Unicorn* (1941) he wrote:

> The place to look for the germs of the future England is in light industry-areas and along the arterial roads . . . In those vast new wildernesses of glass and brick the sharp distinctions of the older kind of town, with its slums and mansions, or of the country with its manor-houses and squalid cottages, no longer exists . . . It is a rather restless, cultureless life, centring round tinned food, Picture Post, the radio and the internal combustion engine . . . To that civilisation belong the people who are most at home in and most definitely *of* the modern world, the technicians and the higher-paid skilled workers, the airmen and their mechanics, the radio experts, the film producers, popular journalists and industrial chemists.

It took longer than Orwell had anticipated, but – changing radio into TV and Internet – his prophecy has now come true.

These inheritors, however, do not desire to live in glass and brick wildernesses. They want, as Stanley Baldwin said, their bit of garden, their Wemmick's fortress. They want Purley Park.

Thoughtfully, for my purposes, the Thames path now diverted away from the river bank and described a long dog's leg into the heart of suburban darkness, into that hermaphroditic hell that snobby writers hate so much. Neither city nor country, what could it be but banal and boring?

It was quiet, I'll give you that; the adults must have been at work, the children off at the swimming pool or bowling alley. There were no skyscrapers to amaze the eye, or meadows full of leaping lambs to rest it. In this development, in which houses hung like grapes from the short stalks of driveways, clinging to the undulating vine of the road, each semi or small detached house was slightly different from its neighbour. This one was half-timbered, that one Rhode Island clapboard. The Hogue, Sharghita, and Ardshiel lay sheltered by large, old trees that must have pre-dated the houses – perhaps they had been part of an original, lost Purley Park, where a mega-Sandbourne had once stood, the home of earls.

In some driveways matching cars (His and Hers, both silver, or both black, or both red) reclined outside double garages. So perhaps the missing families were really there, at quiet leisure in the invisible back gardens.

It's one thing to say, as many do, that we cannot afford for everybody to live like this in the South, spreading out over a garden, a small house and a bit of front lawn, and that – if we allow them to try – there will be no more tranquil places left. This may be true. But it's another thing altogether to disparage those who want to own houses in England's Purley Parks. Time and again these places struck me as fair places to live and bring up your children, and that our problem was that too few people lived like this, not too many.

Back by the Thames there was now a sign: 'Welcome to Reading. Twinned with Düsseldorf.' By the sign small boys fished. The river was much wider now, and over on the other bank, by some houses, I could see the *Duchess* again.

I hailed Geoff, doing something strenuous by the glass case, but he seemed too busy to look up. Three crumbly narrowboats, lashed together, now passed precariously up-stream, Over them swarmed a band of New Agers with red dreadlocks and white spliffs. The contrast was rather wonderful, and I felt, happily, that I could make friends as easily on the dinner launch as I could on the New Age boats.

In this sunny mood I came to the long riverside park just north of Reading. On the far bank were large Newport beach houses with cupolas, gazebos, ha-has, and boathouses. On my side was the detritus, human and otherwise, of a pop festival. There was nothing else it could be. The last lingering folk sat among mounds of rubbish, some desultorily tapping bongos, others doing slow-motion tai chi with pained expressions on their faces. The narrowboat *Baba Yaga* was offering tea and, puzzlingly, something called cofie at 15p a cup.

I asked a post-festive young woman what the occasion of all this rubbish was. She told me that it had been the WOMAD festival of world music, which had celebrated the need for East and West to get together in saving the environment and stopping the despoliation of the planet. 'But it ended this morning,' she lamented, 'and I've been waiting five hours to get my car out of the carpark, because the traffic queue now stretches right the way across Reading.'

Barratt's and the Magnanimous and Providential were up to it again by Reading bridge. Riverside Villas, 'a luxury development with stunning views of the Thames', was rising beside the tow-path. The executives coming to live with the views would have to be vigilant, though. A few yards down from Riverside Villas I nearly bumped into a criminal. Stepping from the stern of a moored cruiser in front of me, a boy of nineteen or so, slightly unsteady on his feet, wearing track-suit trousers and carrying a lager can, shuffled down the towpath and then into a street of newly-built houses. He was definitely not the owner of the boat, nor did he seem familiar with it. My guess was that he was a bit pissed, and – walking by the river in search of mischief – had found an untended cruiser. He'd probably been about to smash a window and get in when I'd come along with my pointed alpenstock and look of robust rectitude, and put a temporary end to his burgling.

Soon I was back in the land of long lawns and private grounds. At Sonning lock a low gate had a plaque on it to tell the world that Blue Coat School was yonder, and that this was the Denys Amess Memorial Gate, 'In memory of a much loved master who drowned, 1953.' Another plaque in a country full of plaques, and stories that are hinted at, but never explained.

In the churchyard of St Andrew, nearly abutting the river, was a memorial to a less cynical age. 'Stuart Carnegie Knox. 1860–1939', read a black inscription on a white background. 'He loved sailors and served them.' You couldn't put up a stone like that now; even the Church wouldn't allow it.

All this inscribing and memorialising was making me feel regretful that we hadn't anywhere erected a stone or named a park bench for my dad. At first, after his death, it felt absurd to do something so obviously for the benefit of the living. He never made any stipulation about it, largely because he didn't really believe that he'd ever die. But now, passing Amess's gate and the sailor-loving stone, I wanted something that some future traveller, passing by like me, could stumble upon and wonder about.

Just as, a half-day later, I followed the pretty path, in my old and slightly smelly trainers, into the village of Cookham, where I found myself recalling another aspect of my father's life.

CHAPTER 30

Hilda

In front of a brass bedstead stands a youngish woman in an ochre-coloured broad-brimmed hat and a light blue knitted dress. She's wearing a necklace of different-sized stones, yellows and reds. On a raised surface off to her right is an open artist's box of paints and brushes. But it's her face that captures your attention. The light from an unseen window catches the right side, the line of difference running from the middle of her strong chin, up to the groove above her determined but sensitive mouth, before – just below the deep-set eye – it is lost in the shade from the hat. The eyes, which are dark-rimmed, look at the viewer with a clear intelligence and spirit. Yet the face is that of someone who has just nearly been crying. Or maybe of someone who has some crying to do.

The picture, a self-portrait of a woman called Hilda Carline, was painted in 1923, the year that my mother was born. It hangs in the Tate Gallery and, since I first saw it, I can't get it out of my mind. If you've never heard of Hilda Carline, perhaps you know of her husband, the artist Stanley Spencer, who came from, and went back to, the Thames-side village of Cookham, which I entered in the last, warm week of that July.

When I first planned to canoe down the Thames it was Stanley who I thought I'd be interested in; an artist who became one of the three or four most famous British painters of the twentieth century. Described as 'a painter the English can understand', his pictures – though highly stylised – were usually located in a recognisably English place (mostly Cookham itself) and the characters in them wore the everyday clothes of the first half of the century.

A small man with glasses and an odd straight-cut fringe, Spencer was also famous for some fairly extraordinary nudes, including immensely unflattering, graphic ones of himself with his second wife, Patricia; and I quite liked those. It's always reassuring to see people in the nude who look even worse than you do.

And then, two months before setting out, I came across the Hilda Carline self-portrait and fell in love with it and with her. Even so, it wasn't till I arrived in Cookham, and walked around the small Spencer museum in the old Wesleyan Chapel, that I began to realise how extraordinary her story was, and how badly this talented woman had been treated.

Hilda, the fourth of five children and the only girl, was born in 1889 in Oxford, into a family of artists. At school she won prizes for her drawing and painting, but her father invested in some risky enterprises, the family lost a lot of its money, and there was no support for her to enter the famous Slade School of Fine Art, where her brother and most of the well-known artists of the period went.

Hilda, then, stayed with the family till just before the Great War, when her brothers took a flat in Hampstead in London, and she and they attended a local school of painting. They drew a bit, daubed a bit and generally hung out. Then she worked for a spell in Suffolk with the Women's Land Army, helping the war effort by replacing called-up agricultural workers. Only when the war was over, aged thirty, did she get to study part-time at the Slade. She was pretty good.

In December 1919 (the month my father was born, and now I'll shut up), her brother Richard invited a friend from the Slade back to the Carline house for dinner. He fell in love with Hilda, he later said, as she served him his soup. This was Stanley Spencer, and conceiving a lifelong passion over the potage was very much in character. First he flattered Hilda by asking if he could buy a small painting of hers, and then, gradually, he wooed her.

Spencer's wooing was not sophisticated. At twenty-eight he was probably a virgin, and Hilda was his first great love; his desire for her perhaps enhanced by the fact that his brother, Gilbert, was also interested. Stanley began turning up quite often, accompanying the Carline clan on painting holidays, including one in 1922 to Bosnia. Where, in Sarajevo, as Hilda painted a watercolour of the old town, he proposed to her.

I try to imagine Hilda then, before she was married. She was clever, sensitive, not stubborn but with integrity, very talented – but not, perhaps, yet the finished article – striking but not beautiful. And almost certainly lacking that unquestioning belief in herself that, had she been a man, she would very likely have possessed. While Stanley was not exactly love's young dream, he was unusually passionate, intelligent and, of course, already a remarkable artist.

What was in it for him? Before the war, when he served with the ambulances in Greece, he'd hardly been outside Cookham. He was provincial, lacking in social connections and drifting emotionally. Hilda offered security, sympathy and sex (which was to play a dominating part in his life), and she was an artist herself, capable of understanding the strange necessities of an artist's life.

All these virtues didn't stop him messing Hilda about. In the next couple of years he broke it off and then re-proposed six or seven times. It's possible that he couldn't make up his mind about her. In 1923, the year that Hilda painted that fabulous self-portrait, she had in one of her letters praised a still-life that he didn't care for. He wrote back to her: 'It is rather comical that I hate myself and love my ideas, whereas with you I hate your ideas and love you.' Is that comical? It seems ominous to me.

Finally, in February 1925, they were married, and began to share a studio in Hampstead, where they would be husband and wife artists, painting in uxorious equality. There were a few problems realising this vision, however. The first was that Hilda was soon pregnant, and didn't feel like painting sometimes. The second was that Stanley's great masterpiece, 'The Resurrection, Cookham', a vast and splendid picture of the dead clambering out of their graves, dressed in their usual clothes (Hilda appears three times), took up most of the space in the studio.

After their first daughter, Shirin, was born in November, Hilda did not do any serious painting for four years. The home-maker and mother, she and Shirin followed Stanley where his commissions took him. Under the pressure of being the person who held everything together, there seemed to be no room for her art.

Soon she and Stanley fell into the common pattern of male–female relationships. The very things that he had liked about her to begin with, were now becoming the occasion of his anger. He criticised her for always being tired, for being disorganised, for being moody. It was made clear to Hilda that he had clearer ideas about how to bring up children, even how to put on a nappy.

And at the same time he complained about her wasting her talent. He genuinely wanted her to paint, nagged at her to do it, and then – unwittingly, I suppose – did everything he could to make it mentally impossible for her to create. In making his demands so clearly, he did, overtly, what many men of his generation and later generations did, and have done, without reflecting on it. He made his version of the woman and then he unmade her. And all the while, he blamed her.

Hilda was hurt and bemused by his attitude but, being a feminist and having a proper sense of herself, could not simply bend to them. By 1928 she wrote that she felt 'hopeless and crushed'. 'Why don't you', she asked her husband, 'look into other people's minds and even size up what they may be feeling or what their impulse is, or their need is?'

But Stanley loved Hilda, and she knew it, and they had good spells. In 1929 she was painting again. Even so, Stanley couldn't help elbowing his way in. When Hilda decided to paint Elsie, their super-efficient maid, Stanley could see that it was going to be a great picture. So what did he do? He stuck his easel behind Hilda's and painted Elsie himself. As he wrote to Hilda (they wrote to each other compulsively, like some people now use email): 'With everything you do and think I have to feel in myself a *possibility of doing the same myself.*'

A year later, and the Spencers had a second daughter, Unity, and by 1931 Stanley was agitating to go and settle permanently back in his home village of Cookham, with its water-meadows, familiar cottages, the church and churchyard, and even the swans which, typically, Stanley seems to have liked.

Hilda did not particularly want to be buried in this backwater, so close to all Stanley's associations and so far from her own. But she went. They bought Lindworth, a big house set back from the hundred-yard main drag that Cookhamites call the High Street. Looking at it now, it is still an impressive house.

Spencer was now in his early forties and restless. Being an artist, his biographers have described his impulses at this time as 'a bid for sexual freedom' – anyone else would have got shorter shrift. Simply put, Stanley wanted more sex with more people.

In 1929, on one of the Spencer family's occasional trips to Cookham, they had bumped into a striking-looking woman in the tea shop. Patricia Preece was refined, sophisticated, and had expensive tastes in clothes that the shabby painter admired (though, in the pictures that he was subsequently to paint of her, she was rarely wearing any). She was an artist, too, a good one apparently, praised by no less a figure than Augustus John. Finally, and giving her an almost religious quality, she was a returned native of his beloved Cookham, living in the one thatched house in the village, Moor Thatch Cottage, with another paintress, Dorothy Hepworth. In short, Patricia had most of Hilda's virtues, and then some. Stanley was smitten.

I walked on to Moor Thatch Cottage. It is, by modern standards, a large house, detached and set in a lovely garden, with views over the Common to the Thames. But what was going on under the thatch seventy years earlier was much more interesting than the sounds of running water and the buzzing of the bees among the honeysuckles. For a start, Patricia and Dorothy, with her page-boy haircut, were not just cottage-buddies, they were a Sapphic item – albeit a secret one. And it was Dorothy, not Patricia, who painted the admired pictures; but she was so shy of meeting people and travelling around that it was agreed between them that Patricia would sign the canvases and that the world should believe they were hers.

Spencer had no idea that this was the situation. By the time he and Hilda were living in Cookham he had already conceived a passion. 'Her high heels and straight walk used to give me a sexual itch,' he wrote to Hilda later. He now wanted Patricia but he feared to lose Hilda. So, like most men, he began to work on ingenious schemes for enjoying both of them – to their advantage (naturally), as well as his own. 'I often think,' he told a friend, 'that irritableness that men so often experience in themselves in their homes is because they are wanting a change of wife.'

The attractiveness of Patricia Preece is, for me and many other observers, a mysterious and elusive thing. Stanley described her as having a 'peculiar excruciating exquisiteness'. But the only thing I saw, looking at the pictures that he painted of her and photographs of the time, was the peculiarity. She had a round face with slightly pinched, sharp features marooned in the middle, surrounded by nondescript blondish hair. Usually braless, her large, pendulous bosoms sat just above her waist. Most of his portraits and nude studies also suggest a sallowness that these days we would associate with hepatitis, rather than sexiness. And yet, he later admitted, 'I felt a sort of religious fervour towards her.'

Patricia noticed Stanley's interest, and encouraged him. Hilda later said that she would deliberately come to the door half- or three-quarters dressed, so as to 'vamp him up'. But why? Why should a lesbian want to have an affair with a 5 foot 2 inch man of forty-four, break up his marriage and make herself notorious? The truth was that Dorothy and Patricia were broke. In 1930 Dorothy's dad, who had paid her a monthly allowance, had died, bankrupted in the crash of 1929. Somehow, with the help of Dorothy's mother and the sale of 'Preeces', they had managed to survive and to keep Moor Thatch Cottage, but their position was precarious.

And then along came Mr Stanley Spencer, who by now was successful and clearly had a bob or two, and whose hormones went chaotic every time he laid eyes on Patricia. Who, it seems certain, at some point decided that she could manipulate the situation to hers and Dorothy's advantage.

Late in 1932 Hilda, who was aware of her husband's growing fascination for this strange Preece woman, left Cookham for a while to go and nurse her brother George, who was dying in Yorkshire. During this absence something started between Patricia and Stanley. When Hilda returned, her third brother now dead, she could tell that her marriage was in deep trouble.

She soldiered on through 1933, spending more time in Hampstead, but nevertheless completing a portrait herself of the woman who was destroying her marriage. In it Patricia looks away from the artist, her lips slightly pursed, her hands almost fumbling with her necklace; she is the picture of calculation mixed with guilt.

By the end of that year or the beginning of the next, Hilda had left permanently. She still hoped that Stanley's madness would pass one day and that they would be able to live together again. Not least because, given her financial situation, she had had to farm Shirin out on the mother of one of her dead brothers' wives.

In 1934 she wrote: 'Sometimes I almost hoped to go out of my mind, as that I thought would break up my train of thought, and stop all recollections and puzzles or hopeless hopes and so on.' The next year she revealed to Stanley, 'Physically and mentally I am going under.'

Meanwhile he was congratulating himself on his decisiveness. Before Patricia came on the scene, he told a friend, 'I was afraid of the business of losing Hilda as I had not then found anyone sufficiently strong to make me able to break away.'

Though Stanley was able to work through the emotional upset of their separation, and to carry on earning, he first reduced the maintenance he was paying to Hilda, and then stopped it altogether. The increasingly frantic letters that she wrote to Stanley concerning money were now being intercepted by Patricia (who had become his business manager), and Stanley rarely saw them. Besides, he had a lot of expenses. In the same period that Hilda was begging for her maintenance, he spent over £2,000 on jewellery for Patricia.

Eventually, realising that Stanley was not likely to drop Patricia, Hilda sued for divorce. In May 1937 the decree nisi was about to be granted, and Stanley and Patricia were to be married. Patricia wrote to Hilda begging her to co-operate with the timing of the decree, so that she and Stanley could enjoy a surprise honeymoon in Cornwall. She further suggested that Hilda use this honeymoon to collect those of her things that remained in Lindworth.

When Hilda got to Lindworth, after Stanley's wedding in

Cookham, she found to her astonishment that he was still there, finishing a landscape. Patricia and Dorothy had meanwhile gone on ahead to Cornwall.

How had this strange circumstance come about?

For some time now, Stanley had been confiding in Patricia that the ideal arrangement for him would be a *ménage à trois*, in which Hilda would be the *troisième*. Patricia encouraged him in this idea, not least because, at worst, it meant that Hilda could do all the sex stuff that Patricia almost certainly disliked. So Hilda arrived at Lindworth, the torch she carried for her former husband never quite extinguished, and was welcomed with an open bed. Yes, Stanley assured her, Patricia was fine about all this. Overwhelmed – 'beguiled' – by the place and the company, she consented. The ex-husband and wife spent a last night together, and the next morning headed in separate directions: one for London and the other for the West Country.

Stanley's Cornish revelation to Patricia that he had indeed slept with Hilda seems to have been just the excuse she was looking for. There was a huge row, and when Patricia – refusing him consummation of their union – went to sleep in Dorothy's room, Stanley stormed out of the cottage and found somewhere else to lay his head. Back in Cookham, Patricia Spencer, as she now was, went back to live in Moor Thatch Cottage, 125 yards (past the war memorial) down the road.

To have any sense of the tragic peculiarity of that time, you have to look at two Spencer pictures from 1937. The first, 'The Artist and His Second Wife', shows Patricia Preece, nude, legs splayed. Behind her squats the equally nude artist, looking down at her – or, rather, looking down at his genitals. In the background is a lit stove, in the foreground a leg of mutton. The frigidity of this picture, the fleshy hatred in it, has led it to be dubbed the 'Leg of Mutton' nude.

The second painting is 'Hilda, Unity and Dolls'. In this stark, moving picture, Hilda, looking strained and tired, stares over the head of her second daughter. The child herself gazes directly at the artist, one eyebrow slightly raised, as if to say, 'What an idiot you are, Daddy.'

By now even he knew it. At some point he'd made over the deeds to Lindworth – the house that he and Hilda had shared – to Patricia. In 1938 she decided to let it in order to earn some income from it, and had Stanley evicted. Now his maintenance payments stopped because he genuinely had no money. He left Cookham, and went to live in Hampstead, not far from Hilda.

They never did get back together. With the outbreak of war, Hilda's mental equilibrium was lost. She woke up one night with delusions that someone was about to murder her and her family, and spent nine months in Banstead Mental Hospital in Epsom. Stanley visited every Sunday afternoon. When she emerged she was no longer as strong as she had been. Nevertheless, they wrote to each other all the time, as they always had – some of his letters reaching over 100 pages in length. And in the years immediately after the war, Stanley began to think about returning. He was even planning a divorce from Patricia on the grounds of non-consummation.

Then, in 1947, Hilda was diagnosed as having breast cancer. She had a mastectomy, but the operation was not completely successful. In 1950 she became very ill and was taken to the Royal Free Hospital, where Stanley stayed by her bedside. One afternoon, when he went out for a moment to the café down the road, she died. She was sixty-one.

Now Stanley could absolutely make her exactly as he wanted her. She became the ideal companion and lover, the artist's alter ego. Many of his paintings from 1950 onwards are remarkable for their depiction of her. One, 'Hilda Welcomed', painted in 1953, is unbearably poignant. It is, once again, the time of the resurrection. A man and two small girls fall on a middle-aged woman in a patterned jumper and floral print skirt, and take her in their arms, the man kissing her desperately.

Stanley Spencer was knighted in 1959 and died later the same year. And Patricia Preece, the Other Woman to end all Other Women, became Lady Spencer. Forty years later the first exhibitions of Hilda Carline's works were held in Britain, but I can still find no plaque, no memorial to her anywhere

I stood in the old Wesleyan chapel and wondered what kind of artist Hilda might have been, had things been different.

So now I'll tell you another story – shorter this time and closer to home – because our history is full of Hildas.

After my parents were married, Lavender essentially lived for my dad. She worked part-time and brought up the kids. But he was the focus. She would pack us off to bed as early as she could to be sure of having his undivided attention when he came home.

The Communist Party paid an absurd pittance to its full-time staff, and we would have lived in complete poverty had it not been for help from her guardian, Uncle Bob. He gave her the house that we lived in, and the stocks and shares which, ironically, brought in a small income. But it was hard going.

She got no help from her own father, Wyndham, who visited once when I was a few months old, and left, complaining, according to family legend, that I was ugly and that my dad was 'a hairy Jewish gorilla'. I wasn't to see my grandfather again until I was over twenty, and then only once – for tea at the In and Outs (the Army and Navy Club) – before he died.

In the late 60s times were even harder, as Dad packed in full-time politics and went to Oxford to study for a Doctorate of Philosophy – his first formal qualification. He spent the weekdays in Oxford, returning at the weekends, when he always had a mass of work to do. I was in my early teens, a thorough-going little bastard – a junior Storm – and I cannot recall how Mum coped with all this. But she did. He got his degree and came back to look for work in academia.

My father had always been a ladies' man. I don't mean by this that he was a Casanova, seeking out dalliances wherever he could find them; but he was a man of enormous charm, who would turn this charm, like a powerful searchlight, on the youngest and prettiest woman in the room. It was just something he did. As a result he was sought after; lots of women wanted to get him into bed, and few men can resist a woman intent upon his seduction.

So Dad had a number of minor affairs, some of which my mother got to hear about. They made her miserable, since she knew how hard it was, as a mother in middle age, to compete with a younger, less encumbered woman. But none of these flings was terminal.

Until Annie. Annie was the young mother of three sons, one of whom became my youngest brother's best buddy. Though twenty years my mother's junior, Annie soon became a constant visitor to the house. By now, although in her fifties, Lavender had herself completed a three-year course to become an occupational therapist, and was rapidly appointed as head OT at a major hospital. This was a huge achievement, and Annie's help with the kids had been invaluable.

One summer in my early twenties, I came back from hitch-hiking around Europe to find everything utterly destroyed and my home as uninhabitable as a bomb-site. Mum had discovered that Annie and my dad had been having an affair for months, using the children as a cover for their assignations.

Dad's first reaction to being caught out was contrition and regret. That was soon followed by the Spenceresque sugges-tion of a ménage. When that was laughed out, he said he couldn't agree not to see Annie any more. Mum threw him out.

Her agony at the end of her marriage was so awful that there are moments that I have completely repressed, so much do I not want to recall them. She was suicidal, she tried to run Annie down one day, she covered Dad's new flat in spray paint when he forgot her birthday. She used everyone around her in the battle against the betrayer, especially my eleven-year-old youngest brother, whose friendship had opened the gates to the Trojan Horse. Just as she had been betrayed and deserted as a child by her father, so had she been again, and she just couldn't take it. The anger and irreconcilable bitterness lasted twenty years. Writing it now, I can hardly believe it.

Annie left her three kids and her husband and moved in with Dad. She became a talented teacher and primary school head-mistress, but always seemed to suffer an intense jealousy of his intellectual friends and anyone who might threaten their relationship.

After they had been together for a number of years, my siblings and I lost our resentment of her, though my mother never could. In any case, I'd never sought to judge my father, believing that he was moved by feelings that he could not control.

In the week before his death, standing by his bedside in a north London hospital, gradually realising what the doctors were telling us, Annie and I were quite close. She, after all, held the key to his last twenty years, and there was a lot that we could tell each other. We hugged like Americans out on the Victorian veranda of the hospital on a glorious afternoon at the end of May.

A week later we met at the funeral, she and my mother treating one another respectfully. And then she cut us off completely. She wouldn't answer the door, pick up the phone, reply to messages or to letters. By chance I met one of her sons in the street and – through him – begged her to get in touch. She didn't. She was distraught, of course, but even so, she had fucked us over a second time.

Walking out of Cookham I thought about what Stanley and my dad had done. By the river bank I came to a conclusion which was not the one that I had expected. It was this: that no one has the right to cause as much hurt and agony to someone else as they did to the women who trusted them. My dad should have dumped Annie and stayed with my mother, no matter how strongly, at that moment, he felt he was in love. What the hell use is love without compassion? Do we owe everything to ourselves?

Fortunately, feminism has begun to alter the rules. The greatest change between the time when Hilda Carline was born and today has been the liberation of women. All over millennial England you see them, these bright, confident young women; scary but brilliant. One day my daughters will join them, and I'm hopeful that they won't end up married to men like Stanley Spencer. Or like my dad. Or even like me. 'I hate your ideas but I love you,' some arrogant beau might say. And she'll tell him that it's her ideas that matter, and that he can jump in the fucking river.

CHAPTER 31

Power

In *A Man For All Seasons*, the ruling classes of Tudor England all live along the banks of the Thames, and rush between each other's houses by boat. Sir Thomas More, face full of piety, is sculled by honest boatmen to Hampton Court to see Cardinal Wolsey. King Henry VIII arrives from Richmond at the More residence in Chelsea by royal skiff, muddies his golden hose and lets out a great, mad guffaw. Treacherous Richard Rich sneaks off in a muddy coracle for a rendezvous with sinister Thomas Cromwell. In the 1500s, earls, chancellors, monarchs and cardinals were up and down the river like high street traffic wardens on market day. The next stretch of the Thames was then, as it still is, England's river of power.

I was due to spend that night in a modest 100-room Italianate villa set in wooded grounds high above the Thames. Cliveden House, built originally by a Duke of Buckingham (but not *the* Duke of Buckingham, the one in *The Three Musketeers*), was bought and altered by the super-rich Astor clan from America in the 1890s. While they were there the nation's elite came for weekends, to discuss matters of state while sitting on the terrace or taking a turn in the Russian Valley. The National Trust acquired first the grounds, and then the house, which today is let to a hotel company.

Now I trudged down the endless gravel drive, in the footsteps of Shaw and O'Casey, Chamberlain, Lord Halifax and Christine Keeler, past the weird brick and gilt Toytown clock tower, and into the portico of Cliveden itself. A discreet desk by the door was manned by a large, ruddy young man in a reddish coat and shirt of dazzling white. He looked at me, in my sweaty shorts, Aertex T-shirt and trainers, taking in the rucksack and regarding the alpenstock warily.

'Hello,' I said, with enormous pleasure, 'I am staying the night. My name is Aaronovitch.'

He recovered too quickly. 'Of course, Mr Aaronovitch. May I take your luggage? And the, um, stick? If you would like to take a seat in the lounge I will send a *porte-cochère* to show you to your room.'

I had no idea what he was talking about, but I handed him my rucksack and went obediently into the lounge anyway. Here the bright light of the summer's day fell through the large windows, only to be eaten up by the decorated wooden panelling running from floor to ceiling.

I sat on a sofa the size of an aircraft carrier, afloat in a mahogany sea. Suits of armour flanked the doors to other rooms, an ornate St George and the Dragon fought over the enormous fireplace. Models of Thames slipper boats mouldered in glass cases on the tables, and in the centre of the room was a flower display larger than the dinosaur skeleton at the Natural History Museum.

The *porte-cochère* arrived to show me to my room. He turned out to be a porter, but not looking like your standard hotel bag-carrier. This one was dressed in the apron, shirt and bow–tie of an Edwardian porter, perhaps from Biarritz or Cannes. About twenty, he was also absurdly handsome and husky, his hair curly and black, his arms muscular. When he spoke it was with a French accent.

My room was the Gladstone Room. It wasn't huge, but everything was there, a lot of it in brown leather. The french windows gave on to a ground–floor balcony next to the pool. Outside a small assortment of young and middle-aged women, displaying all the physical advantages that money could buy, were sunning themselves by the azure rectangle. Their menfolk were obviously occupied elsewhere.

For an hour in the heat of the late afternoon I explored the hidden gardens and grottoes of Cliveden, wondering whether Christine Keeler had ever felt anything for John Profumo, no matter how bald and unlike a *porte-cochère* he looked. Probably not.

In the men's sauna there were many fluffy white towels and a few old Profumo types. I spent an hour getting hot and then cold again, before skipping past the now-empty pool and into my room. There I discovered that the hotel's management had thoughtfully provided a video about Cliveden, narrated by Jenny Agutter, an actress most famous for her role in the film *The Railway Children*.

This was an older, prettier, Jenny in soft focus, pretending to be a plummy woman who had come to Cliveden with her husband. He was tall and be-suited with white teeth and his name was Charles. Charles was a businessman who was here to do the business for his business. So, while he made full use of the conference facilities for his go-ahead enterprise, Jenny revealed that she filled her businessless day by enjoying every facial and seaweed wrap known to humanity. Then she and Charles – his business concluded for the morning – had lunch together.

'After lunch,' revealed Jenny, 'Charles said he had more business to attend to.' Off goes Charles in his suit, and Jenny returns to thalassotherapy and reading copies of *Hello!* magazine by the pool. In the early evening, Charles, his business attended to for the day, returns from some far-flung corner of the mansion, and they enjoy a candle-lit dinner overlooking the terrace.

'Then,' gushes Jenny, 'we came back to the bedroom and we fucked like tigers for an hour.' No, of course she didn't say that.

But what did the guests get up to here? On the escritoire was a red leather visitors' book. I looked inside for names and stories. Nancy Astor, Queen Bee of Cliveden between the wars, had once complained that the reputation of the place had been hugely exaggerated.

A whisper at Cliveden causes Legations to tremble and Embassies to rock [she mocked]. What Elstree–Hollywood nonsense it all is! I wish those people who believed in the legend of the Cliveden Set could come to Cliveden and see the Visitors' Book. They would find to their surprise that names of obscure social workers who are in need of rest and refreshment occur more frequently than the better-known names of politicians & statesmen.

The first social worker's name that I noticed in the book – partly because of the size of the letters – was one shared with an up and coming young actress. Remarkably, it seemed that she had spent the weekend there with another obscure person from the social services, whose name also was possessed by a thespian; in this case a slightly less well-known male. I have changed the names.

'I love Errol Flynn – Doris', said the page-high looping letters.

'I love Doris Day – Errol', replied the man's hardly more discreet though more angular hand-writing. This inscription, one imagined, followed a Jenny-and-Charles romantic dinner, and a night of earnest discussion about the state of social work in England.

Most of the other messages were the standard American 'We came here for Waldo's wedding, and thought it the most beautiful place in Scotland' stuff. One captain of industry, however, had stayed at the remarkable house, set in the incredible grounds, and had left only the observation that, 'The bacon was tough.'

I wouldn't know. There was fruit at Cliveden and the opportunity not to have an English breakfast was too good to miss. The old man next to me called the waiter over and, instead of requesting melon or kippers, asked for a weather forecast. Within a couple of minutes a senior *porte-cochère* was on hand to advise the outlook for the next three days, according to the Meteorological Office. He would probably have thrown in a tip for the 4.30 at Haydock Park if asked.

Reluctantly, I shouldered my pack and took up my stick. Even more reluctantly, I paid the bill and set off down the mile-long walk through the trees of Cliveden, southwards and towards the river.

Now I found myself walking down a road towards the village of Taplow, and past Taplow Court, the great house of the Desborough family now used as the British HQ of the Soka Gakkai Buddhist sect. I knew one thing only about this group: that they were currently involved in a libel trial in Japan, after accusing the leader of a rival sect of having taken nude photos of a Seattle prostitute. Soka Gakkai eventually won, and were enjoying their victory in their stately home, secretive and intriguing behind its walls, like the sinister hideaway of villain in a 60s comedy thriller.

I decided to bypass Taplow village and took a side lane to the river's edge. I had gone half a mile when I found the lane was blocked by men in hard-hats, evidently embarked on some immense excavation. I retraced my steps to the beginning of a footpath over rough land that might take me to where I wanted to go. But would it? It was entirely possible that I would end up walking another mile to find myself blocked again.

Luckily, as I was pondering, an old woman came up behind me.

'If you're wonderin' whether this path takes you down to the Thames, the answer is yes,' she told me with a smile, adding, 'I saw you ahead of me takin' the wrong road, but I couldn't catch you up.'

I thanked her. She was about sixty-five, her hair a helmet of white, the effort of walking causing her bosom to heave alarmingly under her shapeless blouse. She was hefty, but the dog that she was exercising was absurdly small. It occurred to me that this was a dangerous combination, and I hoped that either her eyesight was very good, or that the animal wasn't in the habit of sleeping in the armchairs.

The woman's voice was pure Roedean.

'Yes, they've blocked it all orf, y'see. Cuttin' a channel. All those Rolf Harris type people have been buildin' their villas and whatnot too close to the river down at Maidenhead. They were warned about floodin', but they never take any notice, do they? So now, every winter old Father Thames gives their garages a good soakin', and they've bleated and the result is what you see before you.'

What I saw before me was a large trench, some of it already dug, with water in it, and some of it just marked out with tape across the bottom of the scrubby common on which we stood. In a year's time or so, it would be another branch of the Thames.

'It's all changing, y'see,' she added. 'D'y'know, the county Conservative Association was havin' a do down at Remenham.

William Hague was there with his beautiful wife (bit thin if you ask me, but pretty, I'll give her that), and it was an evenin' event – ball, that sort of thing. So there we are, all sploshed-up, the works – despite the heat – and there was this man in a rust-coloured shirt, no black tie, no tie of any sort. And he doesn't hide himself away, but he marches straight up to Hague and begins a conversation! Well, he was from one of those houses in Maidenhead, and that says a lot.'

Maidenhead itself was now on the opposite bank, the mansions of ex-Beatles and TV personalities scattered about the outskirts of town like cushions in a harem. Two Maori war canoes – garishly painted figureheads front and rear and young rowers pulling to the beat of a drum – whizzed past me at a tremendous lick.

So I was lulled into a liking for our traditional ruling classes as, appropriately, I passed the village of Bray, whose vicar famously trimmed to whichever king was in power, and headed towards Dorney Reach. Then this short-lived sympathy evaporated.

About half-way between Maidenhead and Windsor, beyond the point where the M4 hurtles above the river, is Thames Field, or Dorney Field. If you look at the maps of the Thames, this meadow – half a mile south of the pretty village of Dorney – is probably the largest open riverside area between Oxford and Tilbury. That at least was what the Ordnance Survey showed.

Not any more. For forty minutes, as I walked along the path with the Thames on my right, the vista to my left reminded me of those story-book illustrations of the building of the Pyramids. A vast gash had been dug through the middle of the field, the excavated earth in golden brown heaps beside the impossibly long hole. Part of this was already full of shimmering blue water. Around the mounds and beside the trench buzzed a couple of dozen diggers and dump-trucks, their yellow bodies wobbling in the diesel haze.

What was being built was a lake, to be called Dorney Lake. But this was not to be just any old ducks-'n'-pedalos lake, it was to become Eton College's Rowing Lake (with attached park and arboretum). This man-made expanse of water would eventually be 2000 metres long – over a mile and a quarter. It would be still, with 'consistent water conditions unaffected by flow (tide, eddies, run-off)', and with no bends or obstructions or rivery-type irritations. There would be eight lanes, a minimum depth of 11 feet and a return channel, and water of the highest quality.

Beside this massive folly would sit a four-million-pound boat-house, 'featuring retractable glazing to assist ventilation'. Very important when you have a whole lot of young athletes working on:

25 weight stations
6 multi-gym equipment stations
8 cardiovascular training equipment stations
25 Concept ergometers with PM2 plus computer interface

So at least all the little ergs would get plenty of exercise. Or rather, 600 or so out of the 1200 ergs attending the College. And, to be fair, Eton is making the lake available for other serious rowers from around the country. But somehow the College had found £15 million to fund just one sport, and was building its private Xanadu on a huge area of open riverside, at a time when state schools were appealing to parents to stump up money just for books, and there was a hot debate about any building on green-belt land.

What irritated me beyond measure was that, ever willing to use whatever advantages they could, the whole Eton enterprise was officially registered as a charity. Here was a school whose entire reason for being was to confer a very particular status on its pupils; to allow them to inherit the place in the British establishment that their fathers already enjoyed. It had money coming out of its walls. And it was enjoying the same tax advantages as Oxfam or Help the Aged. It was completely mad, an absurd foolishness.

Angry for the first time in weeks, I left Dorney, evidence of Eton and its ancient privileges now all around. Two miles down, at the edge of an unkempt field, a seat and a plaque by the river announced that this was Athens, the swimming place bequeathed to Eton in 1917 by a chap whose son had died in a flying accident. Orwell, among others, had swum here. The plaque also said something obscure about how fifth-form Nants of the Middle Hundred were allowed to dive at Athens, but that if they were undresssed and ladies passed by, they should immediately get into the water. I didn't know what Nants were (were they older or younger than ergs?), but I liked the idea of them being unexpectedly joined by half a dozen lusty *portes-cochères* from Cliveden, rudely anxious to show the squealing boys the difference between barbel and chub.

The word Nant was like the gear the boys wear. It was the summer holidays now, and I would see no Eton lads in topper and tails, but people only put on stuff like that for one reason. Originally it was the costume worn in 1820 for the funeral of George II, and the school had had 180 years to change it. The Hasidic Jews of Stamford Hill in London wear the winter clothes of 1850s Poland – even in the height of summer. Oxford students attending exams are forced to put on a gown and a mortar board (so that, as I once heard the historian Hugh Trevor-Roper explain, 'townsfolk' don't intrude). Judges have wigs dating from the days of William and Mary. It's a conscious sign of separateness, a deliberate claiming of status, a statement of superiority.

Then, in the next breath I nearly succumbed once more to the charms of that other world, as I rounded a bend and saw before me a long green field, some houses, a pub, a bridge, a thousand pleasure boats and, rising high above the lot of them like a vision out of Mervyn Peake, the many towers and walls of Windsor Castle – the palace that gave its name to the Saxe-Gotha-Coburgs.

Windsor Castle is one mile away from Legoland, where children clamber around plastic landscapes full of little lorries, dinky trains, moving boats, tiny bands playing audible music, and ten thousand teeny eeny weeny people, frozen in their particular roles. There's even a Windsor Castle in Legoland, and, perhaps, among the miniature crowds, there is a chunky version of a backpacker with an alpenstock stood outside the walls, full of childlike pleasure at the quaintness of it all.

The monarchy often seems like a Danish children's fantasy. Even the planes coming into Heathrow use Windsor as a landmark, and roar overhead disrespectfully, turning into their final approaches. In the days of Good Queen Bess, when the flame-wigged Elizabeth walked daily on the battlements, it is difficult to imagine such liberties being taken so close to the royal residence. Now the institution exists only in so far as it is seen by the public.

Moving through the Edwardian throng, my sleeve was tugged. It was Joan from the *Duchess of Argyll*, wheeling a bicycle. The day after I had left them, she told me, the beautiful boat had developed some terrible fault deep inside the glass-cased engine, and – when I spotted it just outside Reading – had stopped, not yet to restart. Geoff was still with his launch, like a loving husband at the bedside of a sick wife.

I had forgotten that Geoff taught at Eton, and because he and Joan had been good to me I felt guilty about my thoughts concerning Dorney Lake and the Pharaonic rowing course.

Immediately I imagined myself in an embarrassing discussion with the two of them, in which, like Nancy Astor, they told me at length about the wonderful charitable works of the College, and the fabulous social mix of the scholars, and how the whole thing was misunderstood by those who were envious and stereotyped in their thinking. But in this particular internal debate, the class warrior within me still won. I was glad that Eton provided work for Geoff and a house for Joan. Nevertheless, the existence of Eton itself in its present form was just not fair, not conducive to fairness.

We said farewell for the last time, Joan and I, and I trudged out of Windsor, forced by the royal appropriation of the Thames towpath on the south bank ('for security reasons', say the guidebooks, though it was done in the 1830s) to walk along a road skirting the commuter village of Datchet. There American-style houses sported British flags, and very large cars lay sunning themselves outside garages, like chromium lizards emerged from their rock homes.

Once more I was in the footsteps of John. In June 1215, one Monday morning, the embattled king and his retinue, including the Archbishop of Canterbury and an envoy from the Pope, rode down from Windsor and arrived at the great waterside meadow of Runnymede. There awaiting them were the barons of England and their men: Bigod of Suffolk, de Vere of Oxford, de Bohun of Hereford, de Quincy of Winchester and Serlo the mercer who was Mayor of London.

John got off his horse, the terms of the agreement between him and the rebellious barons were read out, and the king agreed them. Four days later the document was witnessed, signed and, literally, sealed, with the Great Seal of John, depicting him seated with sceptre and sword.

At two in the afternoon of an Alice in Wonderland day, I entered the meadow at Runnymede where this Magna Carta was drawn up. Stanley Baldwin's cousin, Rudyard Kipling, had once asked:

> At Runnymede, at Runnymede,
> What say the reeds at Runnymede?

But I couldn't see any reeds at Runnymede, let alone hear them having a conversation. On this dusty afternoon the principal sound was the constant drone of the traffic passing along the road that slices directly through the meadow. Not content with their aural monopoly, the cars had colonised the river bank too, parked in lines, only kept from encroaching on the Thames path itself by a line of wooden bollards. Once again I was struck by the sight of middle-aged English people, turned towards the busy road, setting up folding chairs by the boots of their cars, rather than walking two yards further and sitting by the gurgling river.

To add to the incongruity, a paddle steamer was plying up and down the river, lending a touch of the Mississippi to the glorified carpark that we have made of our greatest historic place.

But I soon saw that there was something appropriate about this. The monuments to Magna Carta round here are all American. On a piece of US territory set back from the road is a memorial to John F. Kennedy. More accessible is a little classical shrine, designed in the style of Washington DC Ionic, built by American lawyers. Well, paid for by American lawyers. A couple of lanky trans-Atlantic teenagers on half-hearted pilgrimage were lounging over the floor of this pillared templet when I got there, clearly underwhelmed by the significance of it all. Perhaps later, when they too were corporate lawyers on Wall Street, they would return and pay proper homage to the birthplace of freedom.

Inset into the floor, and visible between brown limbs and Tommy Hilfiger long shorts, were the periodic rededications to the cause. 'June 15th 1971. On this day the American Bar Association again came here and pledged adherence to the principles of the great charter.' Educated Americans know that we English have proved too complacent about freedom to be entirely trusted with it, and so they feel they need to revisit Runnymede, and make sure we haven't enclosed it, or given it to the Ministry of Defence or something.

What we should do is close the road, ban all cars from the meadow, shut the American temple (I mean, how would Americans react to us buying part of the field of Gettysburg from which to trumpet our role as one of the first anti-slavery nations?) and re-create the meadow where the Charter was created. Then you could walk here and almost see those lines from Kipling:

> And still when Mob or Monarch lays
> Too rude a hand on English ways,
> The whisper wakes, the shudder plays,
> Across the reeds at Runnymede,
> And Thames, that knows the moods of kings,
> And crowds and priests and suchlike things,
> Rolls deep and dreadful as he brings
> Their warning down from Runnymede!

Kings and priests perhaps, but not hoteliers. Half a mile on, next to the Thames path and under the lea of the M25, I found my berth for the night, a smart red brick and glass hotel. A room here cost £120, just under a third of the Cliveden price for a service not a tenth as good. A place of many bars and cream armchairs, the flags of a score of nations flying over its flat, landscaped drive, it could just as easily have been a local HQ for the Magnanimous and Providential, as it extended its hold over the insurance and mortgaging market of the South-East.

Dozens of young executive types thronged the riverside bar, or wandered the lounge in tennis gear or carrying swimming costumes, looking as though they were there for corporate training from the Mag & Prov's finest human resource motivators.

I was given a plastic keycard by a stunning and disinterested receptionist, and then left to find my room myself. Climbing a flight of stairs, turning a corner and then padding along an endless thick-carpeted corridor where no sound could be heard, I eventually arrived at No. 1011. Immediately on entering I saw that the policy here was the standard one applied in most large English hotels: put the passing customer in the worst possible room, and then move him if he complains. So my room, while possessing all the equipment of the rest of the hotel, had a window that did not give on to the river, or onto the driveway, but whose light came from a source beyond the brick wall facing me. I could not be bothered to complain.

Clearly, the obviously passive psychology of anyone who was prepared to stay in this room had suggested itself to whoever had cleaned it. An old, dirty wet cloth had been left on the toilet seat; the little squishy tubs of bath essence were empty; dirty glasses stood by the bedside. Nevertheless a folded card on the pillow proudly told me (and I am not joking) that, 'Your room has been serviced by Lingham'. Sourly I added a line. 'Next time,' I wrote, 'do it by hand.'

Outside, as evening came on, I sat close to some companionable Americans, doubtless pilgrims to Runnymede, and consumed inferior cocktails served by informal, friendly lads with ponytails. I went to bed and dreamed once more of growing a pony-tail myself.

I had passed outside the ring of the M25 – the English beltway – on the outward journey at King's Langley, on Richard's boat in the drizzle. Now, this morning, more than seven weeks and 900 miles later, I walked under the bridge carrying the infamous motorway, and re-entered the atmosphere of the metropolis.

Most of England is a suburb of one kind or another. Or the son of a suburb. Virtually everything that we now think of as inner-city was once a suburb, and some are now so far from fields and corncrakes that they no longer attract the title. Others, much newer, like to imagine that they are rural, though their dwellers all commute to work in cities, the farms have become riding-schools, and everyone drives a BMW.

But what lined the banks of the Thames here were now suburbs that celebrated their suburbanness. A succession of small villas and developments with lawns separated from the river by a road, or giving directly on to the water, marched on for mile after perfectly agreeable mile. These were the houses derided by the county set and metropolitan elite alike as neither country fish nor urban fowl; the sorts of façades behind which were lived lives of 'quiet desperation' as Pink Floyd, paraphrasing Henry Thoreau, sang about the English suburbs.

One by one I ambled past them, peering over their hedges at their washing. Egham, Staines, Laleham, Chertsey, Shepperton with its foot-passenger ferry of which I was the only customer, Walton, Sunbury, East Molesey with its reservoirs.

But in the summer light they seemed sensible places to be, with their modest conservatories and sweet-smelling honeysuckle. In 1966 the comic writer and former MP, A. P. Herbert, who had a lifelong love affair with the Thames, wrote of this strip: 'There is little real beauty, perhaps, but there is prettiness everywhere, and, not unimportant, contentment.'

I was nearly home.

CHAPTER 32

My Father's City

Much though I was looking forward to seeing Sarah and the girls, and although I envisaged our happy times together now that I was a reformed character, still, as the end of my journey approached, I felt its loss. I really did. In my two months I had been very lonely indeed. For long stretches I questioned the value of doing the trip at all. As my arms tired and my back ached on some interminable and unpopulated stretch of anonymous canal, or as I calculated the empty hours between supper and sleep, I had cursed myself and my blithe optimism for having invented a voyage of encounter and self-discovery.

And then it had gradually happened. I had smoked for a long time, and given up on many occasions – the last time successfully. And there was a moment, about ten weeks after the last fag, when I realised that I hadn't thought about smoking for nearly a fortnight. The obsession, the craving, had both gone and I could contemplate a full life again. After six weeks of physical travelling, my internal journey had begun to work.

Not least I had come to a settlement in my mind about what had happened between my mum and dad, and had a better idea about how their histories had shaped mine. It wasn't a matter of blame or recrimination, just a case of establishing how it was and dealing with it. I was walking back, aware of a greater distance between myself and some of those emotions that I had sometimes felt crowded out by.

I had experienced a great deal of England far more intimately than I ever had before. Not all of it, of course. I hadn't stood outside pubs on Saturday nights looking for drunken fights, or sought out down-trodden prostitutes to discuss the spermy perversions of their clients. You can get all that on television. But what I had seen, I liked. It seemed to me that the century-old image of Middle England as the home of genteel racism, of quiet lace curtain intolerance, of under-educated complacency, of sub-imperial superiority, is no longer true.

A revolution is going on in this country, and probably has been for a generation. Derek and Lesley, whom I had met near Nottingham, were evidence of it, early school-leavers themselves, bringing up two graduates who brought home with them boys and girls of different colours, and experiences of other ways of living.

Middle England is a land of saucy grannies, voyaging landladies, of the ubiquitous Magnanimous and Providential sponsoring everything that moves, of Barratt's estates with well-tended gardens, of Willow Cottage, childhood museums, 50s' nostalgia, opticians, aromatherapists, steam railways, scented candles, shopping malls, computers, coffee cake, stress phalli, Man Utd supporters, rock festivals, soap opera behaviour, of young men driving too fast and waterside views. We are a nation of Cliff and Buddhists, of urchins and dead deer, of private property and new universities, of Maori war canoes and tattooed anglers, Bernie Prior and ponytailed men, dog-poo campaigns and pewter herons. Of Middle Earth, middle management and *Middlemarch*. A country, for all the public pessimism, surprisingly unafraid about its future.

But we keep our past at hand. Not far from home, and from now the land and its inhabitants became familiar from my childhood expeditions and summer day-trips. Past elaborate and fascinating houseboats – some swish with white paint and wrought-iron railings, others dilapidated and filthy – through a pretty park, I came in sight of the bridge at Hampton, and, above it, the twisting Tudor chimneys of Hampton Court. Inside its ornate gates tourists packed the gardens and the maze, or paid a staggering nine quid a head to look inside the house which Cardinal Wolsey built and Henry VIII took over.

Almost more than anywhere else in England, this is where the national myth of Englishness as a non-European – as a counter-European – identity was born. When Henry VIII was thwarted by the Pope in his desire to divorce the sonless Catherine, he and his creature, Thomas Cromwell, sold an unpopular divorce to a sceptical people by appealing to an infant nationalism.

Cromwell organised plays, poems, tracts, pamphlets and treatises. They worked (along with a judicious use of thumb-screws and hanging), and set the scene for Anglicanism, Queen Elizabeth, the besting of the Armada and the Enterprise of England. Our image of ourselves as a doughty, awkward, independent, superstition-free and priestless people originates partly in the dynastic needs of the Tudors. The origins of modern England are to be found in Leeds in those armoured cod-pieces of Henry VIII's.

At Hampton Court a pleasure boat was drawing up to the jetty, and I felt the need to enter London proper on the water, to see things from the river. I had wanted to do it in the *Knife*, but a seat in the sun, beer in one hand, seemed almost as attractive. At the landing stage beneath the gilt gates of the Court, I boarded the large vessel, but the twenty lines of plastic chairs on the foredeck were so spaced that only amputee dwarves could have felt entirely comfortable sitting in them. Pack 'em in, make 'em pay, the London tourist-fleecer's motto.

As soon as the rope had been raised to the ticket-holders there had followed a scramble for the best seats. Two young women with mobile phones, good tans and scary sunglasses took over a square of about ten chairs, hoisted their feet and belongings on to them, and silently defended them against all comers through judicious deployment of coats, cans, indifference and, if none of that worked, glares of ineffable hostility. They were only eventually bested by a pair of wonderfully determined and obtuse Swedish pensioners.

So we sailed, the girls, the Swedes and I, through the lock at Teddington where the Edwardians had thronged on just such warm Wednesdays as this one, past the 60s' party venue of Eel Pie Island and right over the site of my capsize three months earlier.

At Richmond I ducked beneath the gunwales, lest a scanning Dick with a telescope might be standing on the clubhouse veranda and, seeing me, report my craven failure to Wo Chung. It would hardly be convincing to shout 'tendonitis!' while making gripping gestures with my right hand. They might misunderstand. To a genuine canoeist my dumping of the *Knife* would seem an intolerable treachery. They would be bound to take her side over mine.

Now the Thames widened and became tidal; an imperial river for an imperial city. England temporarily disappeared from the banks, to be replaced by the United Kingdom or, more grandly still, Great Britain – the Britain that had for so long subsumed England, and was now surrendering it back.

The wash from the boat's big engines raised seismic ridges of water from the bows, threatening any small boat which might (as I once might) have been foolish enough to try its luck in these waters. We powered at 15 knots or more, towards the heart of the capital whose now-inverted association with the Levant and the East was given emphasis by the appearance, on the right, of the Harrods Warehouse, owned by Mohammed al Fayed, and, on the left, by Fulham Football Club, whose chairman was the same desperate Egyptian. Like the British in his country, Mr Fayed could rule, but he couldn't belong.

At Chelsea stands the statue of Sir Thomas More, and Vauxhall bridge sports statues representing Pottery, Engineering, Architecture and Agriculture that cannot be seen by anyone not on a boat. 'In this reach, long ago,' wrote A. P. Herbert, shortly before his death, 'a porpoise passed under my stern.'

As we came alongside the Houses of Parliament, it was all so familiar to me. I knew and had walked every inch of the river on both sides since I was a child. There was nothing about it, I felt, that I didn't know.

Not so. Between Westminster and Charing Cross bridges, the river was half-blocked. Somebody had carefully laid an enormous metal wheel on its side over the water, the spokes and rim held on piers.

As the alien structure slipped past on the starboard side, it became obvious that, one day soon, this wheel would be laboriously pulled upright at the water's edge, where it would tower over its surroundings. The little boy in me was so excited that, once more, I broke the English contact taboo. 'Look!' I called to my fellow passengers. And (almost losing my catapult), 'Cor!' The foreigners on deck were evidently impressed; a northern couple asked me what it was; the young women – London English to the core – shot me a pitying glance.

One Christmas my father gave me a book of photographs of working-class life called *To Build Jerusalem*. On page 87 is a picture of a narrow street littered with bricks, the remains of a barricade of wood and barrels, and a policeman leading a dark-haired young man with glasses towards the camera, his arm held uncomfortably behind his back. Under this photograph my dad has written, 'Dad's birthplace. 70, Cable Street.' The picture was taken on that day in 1936, when Jews and Gentiles got together and successfully prevented Oswald Mosley's fascists from parading down Cable Street. Inside the front cover is a dedication in small, quirky handwriting: 'For David, Christmas 1980. Lithuanian or cockney, these are our roots. Dad.'

I had disembarked at Westminster, unpeeling my wet shirt from the back of my plastic chair, and was now standing at the top of the Monument. The dome and pinnacles of St Paul's Cathedral were behind me now. Looking eastwards, the brown pile of the Tower sat unimpressively next to Tower Bridge's weird lines – the two gawky uprights, the slightly curving, low-slung road-way, the deep quarter circles of the support cables. To the north, running parallel to the river, deep grey with glints of sun-reflecting glass from nearby high-rises, lay Cable Street itself and the old East End. Down the river towards me had come the ship carrying my unseen grandfather and mad grandmother (though perhaps she wasn't mad then), who thought that they were arriving in New York.

They'd made it about a mile inland, to the place where everybody spoke and looked as they did. Moishe (Morris, who died when I was three months old and bequeathed me his middle name) went into tailoring, making new buttonholes in old coats for nearly no money. Gittel (Kate), according to my father, ran her tiny two-room household imperiously, dismissing my father's older brother Joe's new wife as a 'whore'. Though my dad's first wife, whom I have never met, told my mother recently in a letter from Israel that Gittel was a most hospitable woman, and Moishe was 'a saint'.

I can still see Grandma. At eighty-five Gittel wore a smock and a headscarf, her skin yellow and etched with grooves the depth of the Limehouse canal. She gave us matzohs and sixpences, while babbling toothlessly in a guttural language that, only much later, I realised was Yiddish. We children did not enjoy these outings. My father obviously hated going to see her in that large room in Dalston, and probably hated her too. She was illiterate, superstitious, delusional and stood for a life that he wanted no part of. Only later was he in any way reconciled with his past as a poor Jew.

A few years ago, in the week that my first daughter was born, my uncle Joe died. Together my dad and I drove up to Ilford, where Joe's family (my cousins, none of whom I had ever met) lived in a taxi-driver's semi. We had gone to sit shivah. In the knick-knacked lounge sat a group of relations and friends, walkers in John Lewis's, quantity surveyors, Jews who had changed their surnames to Arnold and Foster, and called their kids Gary and Marilyn.

My Dad put on a kopel – a skullcap – an item that I had never seen him wear before, and draped a prayer shawl over his shoulders. Then, to my astonishment, he picked up the Book and, as the oldest surviving relative, chanted the words of the prayer in Hebrew, the others adding the Amens. I had never before heard him use a word of Hebrew (he had told us that he remembered no Yiddish), and I calculated that it must have been over fifty years since he had last heard the prayer for the dead. I was spellbound by this other possible life that could so easily have been mine.

It didn't seem quite so inappropriate then, when Dad died, to ask the son of his best friend – a man who had rediscovered his Jewish roots in his twenties – to sing the Jewish lament at the funeral. His voice was unbelievably loud and sweet. The ancient sound rolled around the congregation and battered at the roof and doors, connecting that moment in a crematorium in Finchley, with ten million others going back three thousand years.

Identity is an accident. We talk about it as though it's preordained, as though there was something genetic about Englishness or Frenchness, as though we shared more chromosomes with a chimp than with a South American. In a parallel England in another universe, the version of me that was born when my mother stayed in Worcestershire and married a vet, fishes for chub in the river, and tuts in annoyance as the canoe flashes past. In another Lithuania, the possibility of another version of me – the DNA of one that might have known how to say Kaddish – lies scattered in the forests.

An accident, but an important accident. That's what he meant by roots. The city I had been looking at had once been the city of my father's boyhood; of tailors and docks, of Irish and Lascar sailors. From St Katharine's Dock, through Tobacco Dock, London Dock, West India Dock, Milwall Dock, to the Victoria and Albert Dock, the place had been dominated by an international trade in things and people. Today's mixed England was anticipated in its ports and markets.

The docks themselves had been destroyed, once by the Germans in 1940 and a second time by economic change in the 1970s. From the ruins of those disasters, a completely new riverside had been conjured into existence now, its most visible, boastful symbol from the top of the Monument being the huge silver obelisk of the Canary Wharf tower.

I descended the 311 steps, turned right, and headed for Docklands.

Beyond the crowds outside the Tower, clamouring for a glimpse of the Crown Jewels, I entered St Katharine's Dock. Now the warehouses were apartments for youngsters in the City, and the wharves were walkways. Instead of an iron ship being noisily relieved of its cargo by bolshy stevedores, there was a black-and-yellow hulled replica of a seventeenth-century pirate ship, complete with a stripy shirted buccaneer with eye-patch and cutlass, offering a Caribbean experience for £5.

Next door, on the waterside, were a dozen tables with umbrellas, seating latte-drinking customers of Madison's Coffee-house, whose round, glassy, two-storey kiosk lay just beyond. I went in and pondered on the menu of a hundred coffee combinations, and dozens of cakes. There are a million sandwiches out there in the big city – and most of them were here.

Not so long ago, near this spot, there was probably a small café (without an accent), where the choice of beverages was between instant coffee and metallic tea, and of sandwiches between sausage and bacon. Don and Else were long gone, and now all around was cornucopia. As in America, there is now nothing you can't get in England. Except fatty bacon in a white bread and marge sandwich.

But in England progress means going boldly backwards as often as boldly going forward.

I rejoined the Thames path at Wapping, and stared across the river at the bizarre sight of the Globe, the reconstruction after four centuries of an Elizabethan wattle and daub theatre, nestling between Southwark Cathedral and the slab-and-chimney of the refurbished, re-topped and tailed Bankside power station, shortly to become the second Tate art gallery. Between it and me was growing another bridge over the Thames – still just scaffolding and piles – the first new crossing for half a century.

This is all part of the great shift of the city's centre of gravity from west back to the more historic east. For mile after mile the old buildings had been knocked down or, just as often, converted from industrial use, into flats and houses for new Londoners – mostly the single and well-off. Sales boards were all around. One, whose dimensions must have been 16 feet by 6, advertised that a wall by the path contained what would soon become 'Globe View', built (of course) by Barratt's. Two 'Computer Generated Impressions' of the completed block were accompanied by a text whose structure and use of capitals read like a playbill of Dickens' time: 'Superb Apartments Many with Stunning River Views Centred Around a Magnificent Atrium.' I could almost hear the voice of Vincent Crummles booming across the water from shore to shore.

In a small park, around which elegant old harbour houses

looked anxiously at encroaching developments, I met an old man and a very old man, sitting near where, as boys, they had swum in the dirty Thames. Then the riverside had been a land of slums, docks and Hawksmoor churches, now it was utterly transformed, as altered as any city could have been by revolution or war.

"'E drives me down every Saturday from 'ackney,' said the very old man, his arthritic fingers resting on his walking stick. 'And we spend a couple of hours sitting 'ere.' Then he slipped into a pronunciation out of the *Pickwick Papers*. 'It's wery nice today, wery bright.' He continued, 'It used to be all ships. You walking all round 'ere, are yer? You ought to go down Stepney library. Bloke there, 'e knows the 'istory of the 'ole place. 'E'll tell yer. It was buzzing then. Look at it. Not much going on now.'

And there wasn't. It was a Saturday, and row after row of balconied warehouses stood deserted by their weekending singletons. There was no child's voice or high-pitched calling, no reverberating footsteps or slap of ball against brick. Half a mile from here the streets would be heaving with Bengali men in white caps, women in olive robes and their children. It was unimaginable that, within living memory, naked boys had sunned themselves on the rubble and mud beaches of the Thames at low tide, not ten yards from where we were talking.

Further on, the old Shadwell basin was now a large square of water surrounded on three sides by modern brick townhouses with arched entrances and red-painted iron balconies. Behind their patio gardens the elevated Docklands Light Railway operated its little continental trains, their blue-and-red-striped carriages negotiating high concrete loops, as though put there for the visual pleasure of passing tourists, rather than the transport needs of a mighty city.

Now, across the line of sight, cranes danced with each other, while bulldozers coupled in the dirt below. New building was everywhere, forcing the path away from the river, as the gaps between ten-year-old developments were quickly filled by apartments for the millennium.

At the top of the Isle of Dogs – the last place on the north bank of the river still to have children – was the self-contained city-state of Canary Wharf, created as though by one of those computer games of metropolis construction. Most of the building was done here in an age – our age – that had become worried about innovation, and most of it was commissioned by corporations that were anxious to do what they knew would be successful; in other words, what had already been done. The result was an almost Victorian uniformity of house and flat, the world as perceived by Barratt's and the Magnanimous and Providential.

From the tip of the Isle of Dogs the old Greenwich foot tunnel took me to the venerable pleasures of the *Cutty Sark* and the Maritime Museum. Then the path cut past some old almshouses, and threaded between the sites of the last dirty industries still actually on the Thames. High waves slapped at rusty pipes and coolant tanks, and – for the first time in a month – small, cold spits of rain attacked my skin.

Beyond the railings and the nameless industries of the recent past, across a wide road and past a stranded 50s' semi with an old car outside, I arrived at last outside the Dome. It looked small from the outside, its unique shallowness diminishing it to anyone standing nearby and making it the first major public work (save, perhaps, for the Nazca lines in South America) designed to be seen from the air.

Around this shell, men in hard hats scurried about, and there was no glimpse possible, through the tangle of fences and the wall of portakabins, of the tawdry delights with which rumour had populated the Dome's innards. Its notoriety belonged to a later season. Here, at the very end of the journey, was one cathedral, one stately building on my route that I could not enter. Which was as it should be. The past had been all around me, the present visible though in need of interpretation. I couldn't know England's future.

And since I couldn't go in, I realised I had come to the end of my journey. At the Dome's new bus station, I boarded a red single-decker on a line that had never existed before, and bought a ticket for home.

When I arrived back the front garden was full of lobelia, the back garden full of children. Sarah gave me a quick peck on the cheek, and said, 'Well that's it, then.' And it was.

Epilogue

'You've got to go,' Jane said. 'They're expecting you.'

They were the Canoe Camping Club of Great Britain, whom Jane had at one stage solicited for help, and whose advice on pitching a tent on the towpath ('Just do it, it'll probably be OK') had been interesting, if not very useful. The quid pro quo for this assistance was a loose agreement that I should address their AGM in the early autumn. By September, needless to say, I had forgotten all about it.

Then Jane got phone calls, so I got phone calls from her. Something had to give.

To get an idea of just where on the scale between 'hugely entertaining' and 'a bit embarrassing' such an appearance would sit, I rummaged around in the mound of maps, correspondence, guidebooks and mouldering canoe-wear left over from my expedition. All I could find was a ten-page newsletter on green paper, including some fairly antique stories of blissful childhood weekends spent under canvas by the sides of rivers, and a series of announcements about get-togethers on various watercourses in central England.

There was nothing that gave me a clue about the age, social background, sexual inclinations or political attitudes of the club. Except that I guessed them not to be wealthy. Eventually I located a leading member in her kitchen making roast lamb for her husband, and told her to expect me as the guest speaker at the forthcoming great occasion. Good, she told me, without any particular excitement, they would see me on Saturday night at seven. The club-house was in the centre of a caravan site near Chertsey bridge. And we left it at that.

It was dark by the time I got to Chertsey, having found my way there along small Thames-side roads by instinct rather than map-reading. In the Stygian campsite, where no lights shone from the windows of the trailers, and no one trudged to and fro from the toilet block, I was hailed from the gloom by a pleasant and vague man and escorted to a hall in the centre.

Inside the freezing room were two dozen or so assorted canoe enthusiasts. Well, maybe not so assorted. Of those assembled two were under thirty, and the majority would never see fifty again. One woman was vaguely smartly turned out, but the others evidently expected to be back in their canoes by midnight, and had dressed accordingly.

There was no athleticism here. Indeed, the two most prominent activists (she was making the tea and he was handing it around), were both very ample individuals, far bulkier than I, and both nearly sixty. I could hardly imagine either of them fitting into a tent, let alone into a kayak. The idea of them travelling together was mind-boggling and heart-warming at the same time.

The twenty of them gathered round in plastic bucket seats, as Mr Big introduced me more or less accurately.

From behind my trestle table I spoke of rivers and canals, of wet times and dry times. And as I talked they began to nod, to look at each other and smile, occasionally to laugh.

They had been where I had been, and knew the lore of locks and the perils of swans. Their canoes had been shaken by the wash of drunken narrowboaters, they too had ducked under swingbridges, laboured along impassable towpaths, had endured the taunts of wags.

These, for the moment, were my people, connected by an odd affinity, the discovered shared enjoyment of getting in small, unpowered, unstable boats and paddling from one field to another. They made no great claims for the hobby on the grounds of health or national importance. They just liked doing it enough to want to get together once a year and discuss doing it more.

I looked round the room: at the man with the scrubby beard and navy-blue cagoule who had himself, once, canoed from Watford to Tring and ported the murderous twenty-six locks; at the smart lady with long grey hair and a hat whom I couldn't quite mentally place in a canoe at all; at Mr and Mrs Big who would have required a plastic battleship.

England is a land, for all that people might try to organise it, of the contingent, the incongruous and the accidental, where the mildewed novel about Anne of Cleves may be read in a room dating back to James II, where the flags of Wales and Norway adorn the modernistic plaza at Milton Keynes, where a cold hall in a caravan site in October can unite twenty-three citizens in discussing how much they enjoy putting together two uncomfortable hobbies.

Let's leave them there, the happy folk of England. Because I can imagine some readers complaining that, in the summer of 1999, I saw my country as I wanted to see it, only by the best, warmest light. But where is the violence, the darkness, the xenophobia, the winter?

There's some truth there. My story started on the River Great Ouse thirty odd years ago. It almost ends there. In the wee hours of 11 June 1999, as I lay in the spare room of Patricia's empty house and dreamed of my father, an eighteen-year-old called Jonathan Coles was leaving a nightclub in Milton Keynes.

It was 2 a.m. and a kebab stall was plying its greasy trade. Around it had gathered a group of young men, some white, some black. According to evidence presented to a court nine months later, Jonathan was asked for a cigarette and refused. Perhaps his manner was brusque, or perhaps his attackers were looking for an excuse. Whatever, he and two of his friends were then chased by a number of other young men to an area of waste ground and beaten up. Jonathan himself, now missing his glasses, was forced to give them his bank card and the code number. Then they left him.

So this was an unpleasant assault and robbery after throwing-out time at a nightclub. But Jonathan, shaken, unable to see very much and needing to get to a girlfriend's house, then flagged down a passing car to try and get a lift. Like something out of one of those relentlessly horrible movies, of the four men in the car, three were the very guys who had beaten him up. Now they had him again.

~ Epilogue ~

First they drove him to National Westminster cashpoint, and discovered that all he had was £1.03p, then they took him on to the girl's house and, finally, to Tyringham bridge over the River Great Ouse – equidistant between the spot where the Grand Union had carried me over the river two days earlier, and where I had capsized in 1966.

Here, 25 feet over the river, he was lifted on to the parapet, and his fingers prised from their grip on the bridge. Almost blind, unable to swim, Jonathan was drowning even as his attackers drove off.

All four of the men in the car came from the pantiled estates of Milton Keynes. Two were white, two were black. One of them was unemployed, another had once been convicted for joy-riding, but that was the full extent of their statistical relationship with the under-class. There was a shop-assistant at a supermarket, a waiter at a chain-restaurant and a dustman. Now there are four convicts, two of them serving life imprisonment.

Maybe they didn't mean to kill him, believing, like the drowned men of Bewdley, that the water was too shallow, too harmless, too everyday actually to cause death. But in the same week another boy, very like Jonathan, was similarly robbed and thrown from a bridge, this time over the Thames at Blackfriars. He too died.

Yet murder is still rare, and most people live their entire English lives without once being assaulted. Far more of them are likely, at some point in the next year, to have hands laid upon them by an aromatherapist than a mugger.

One or two of you will want to know, so I have to admit that, by the time I arrived in Chertsey, I had already put back on half of the weight lost while not eating sausages. Most of the rest gradually re-coated me in the following months. But I still keep the fitness sessions going, so the muscles beneath the flab are harder and more sinewy than ever, and I recovered the full use of my hand.

After a good start, I put back on some of the anger too. At first I felt wonderfully calm at home. The reflection had been useful, not least in determining that there were patterns from my own childhood that I was surely not fated to repeat if I didn't want to. I stood outside myself more, winning those important moments between event and reaction. I decided to dedicate a bench on Hampstead Heath to my father, and to see more of my mother. Above all, I would invest more in my children while I could.

There is as yet no bench, and I call Mum no more than I did. I am still too like my dad, with my energies devoted to work and achievement. And yet something has changed, a quiet person occasionally slips into my clothes and whispers, 'Be good!'

Meanwhile, in one corner of the garden, in a sheltered spot by the side gate, between the dustbins and the wisteria, a familiar shape takes its ease. And on summer's days infant hands tug at its painter and clear, high voices call their papa to tell them once more the story of how, in the last year of the millennium, he set out on his great journey in this slim, silent friend.